Angel with a Gun

Joe DeCicco

Second Edition Published: October 28,2012
ISBN-13:978-0-9897227-04
ISBN-10:0-9897227-0-8

Printed in the United States of America
Charleston, South Carolina
for

J
N
J Associates Publishing Co
Hampstead, North Carolina

First Edition published 2006 by Tenko Books

Angel with a Gun

First in a series of novels featuring
NYPD cop Mike Romano

Acknowledgements

I wish to personally thank my wife, Judy, and Bill Fawcett. Both are true friends. It is their confidence that made this story possible. Another thank you should go to Mark Roberts for his editorial expertise. Also, a big, heartfelt thank you, to the literally hundreds of men and women who were on the Job with me. Without their input, this work would lack its flavor and substance.

Joe DeCicco

Joe DeCicco

"TO PROTECT. . .AND TO SERVE."

Over the past twenty years, this slogan has been adopted by many of the major police departments across the nation. It denotes the best attributes of the men and women of the "Thin Blue Line;" their courage and their compassion. Every year, police officers are slain in the line of duty in increasing numbers. Their surviving brothers stand shoulder- to-shoulder in the face of ultra-liberal judges who, finding no blame in these miscreants, with increasing frequency, release the most heinous, violent criminals on the flimsiest excuses, popularly called "Technicalities." And, if a case actually goes to trial, they suffer blatant abuse from attorneys who constantly bleat to juries about how "It's not our clients' fault." The victimization of criminals, the criminalizing of their victims, and the demonizing of the police, has brought our system of jurisprudence to its knees.

One need only examine the recent Melendez and O.J. Simpson cases. Or the New York State case of the female drug dealer/mule from Michigan, who was freed at arraignment by Federal Judge Baer who ruled that the police search of the trunk of her car, was a violation of her 4th and 5th Amendment rights. The woman had possession of $55 thousand in cocaine and heroin and confessed to drug trafficking, and the incident occur-red while the officers were on a drug deal stakeout, and after observing four men place heavy bags in that trunk, one at a time, and the fourth man fled the scene when approached by police. Complaint and outrage ranged from the Mayor of New York City to the President, who had appointed Baer to the bench. Finally, and reluctantly, Judge Baer reversed his decision in this matter and reinstituted the evidence. Only the brave perseverance of our local law enforcement can prevent our court system from being rendered moribund. Small wonder, then, that more and more of our policemen and women see our society in the divisive terms of US and THEM.

Angel With a Gun

In a society that sometimes seems gone mad, with the inmates running the asylum, it is a wonder than anyone would voluntarily stand up to protect the law abiding from the animals among us. Yet, thankfully, they do. It is to these brave men and women that this book is dedicated.

Although the following is a work of fiction, it is based on the real life and career of one of New York's Finest.

CHAPTER ONE

August laid a stultifying blanket over New York City. The damp night air had an almost tangible quality, like peering through a gossamer curtain. Everything beyond the distance of three feet became hazy to the human eye. Gradually the muffled drone of a police cruiser, slowly making its rounds, became barely audible to the sole occupant of the street.

Gradually, the muffled drone of a police cruiser slowly making its rounds became barely audible to the sole occupant of the street. It was new; the best pursuit model General Motors made in 1972. The 1973 models were due out soon and no doubt the Department had saved a few dollars by buying up the last of 1972s. The interior had lost its new car smell a few days before when a drunken perpetrator lost his lunch, literally, in the back seat. Still, the outside had yet to gather the dents and scratches that were the side effect of hard use and the facts that its occupants occasionally had far greater concerns than the condition of their assigned vehicle; like pursing criminals, preventing what few crimes they could, and staying alive in the muggy, restless summer.

At the wheel of the RMP (Radio Motor Patrol) sat a young cop, obviously newly appointed because his eyes went everywhere; his head constantly moved in an attempt to miss nothing. In his mind New York Police Officers were truly Guardians of the City; like the soldiers of Old Rome. Next to him, in the front passenger seat, sat an old veteran with twenty eight years on patrol, who lazily took in the street as his partner drove. The older man appeared to be the opposite of his young partner, eyes fixed straight ahead.

Through the corner of his right eye, the old centurion spotted the figure of a man slowly walking on the sidewalk. Alert now, he automatically recorded what he saw on his mental scratchpad: male, white, six foot, 175 pounds, about twenty- seven years old, olive skin. Thick jet black curls on

1

his head.   The man's hair glistened with moisture in the humid summer air. He turned to his partner and spoke gently.

He turned to his partner and spoke gently. "No threat here, the man's walking his dog. He's a regular."

That "regular" was Michael Romano, a local resident, whose body had grown tacky with salty sweat. As he turned to look at the passing patrol car, Romano's shirt clung to his back. His clothing had become increasingly annoying to him.   Each time the dog pulled on the leash, his shirt grew taut across Mike's back increasing his desire to rip it off.   It felt like wearing plastic wrap.

Despite the fact Mike's Jackson Heights, Queens, apartment lay within one mile of La Guardia Airport and Flushing Bay with its normally cooling breezes, nothing stirred. The cops had gone past. Only the tapping of the dog's toenails on the cement sidewalk broke the renewed silence of the still night.   Mike listened to that sound and watched shadows change as he passed street lights. To his right stood a row of two story attached homes with their porch lights on. These too cast shadows, but a softer variety.   The resulting intermingling shadows constantly changed across the sidewalk and against the sides of parked cars. To Mike they appeared to be dancing to silent music as he walked. Across the street, to Romano's left loomed six story apartment houses.

"Rabbit hutches," Mike spoke his distaste aloud.   The dog eyed him over one shoulder and walked on.

Mike continued, now mechanically striding behind his furry charge, deep in thought. He had a wife, a new car and best of all, Anne his little girl, yet he was not satisfied with his life. This neighborhood is okay for now, but it's sliding down the scale of desirability just like all neighborhoods in the City eventually do. There must be something he could do to get his family into a better environment.

While the curly haired Italian plodded along behind his dog, Mike tugged at his shirt as he continued his mental odyssey back to the early evening in his four room apartment.

Anne, his three year old daughter, had squealed in delight every time he fell backward when she hit him, mimicking actions of TV characters. The thought made him smile.

His mind drifted through his apartment. To the right of the entrance doorway was the kitchen. Long and narrow with enough room on the far end, near the front window, for a small kitchen set.

Down the long hallway adjacent to the living room was first the master bedroom, two closets on the opposite wall. Anne's room and the bathroom were at the rear of the apartment. The child's room shared a wall with the marital bedroom. Apartment 4E faced the front of the building and 34th Avenue. The entire apartment had been painted white except Anne's room. It was pink.

Not too bad, Mike mused, as he remembered the apartment he grew up in; two small bedrooms. One occupied by his parents, the other shared with his younger brother. The living room was nothing to speak of and the kitchen and bathroom were the size of postage stamps. At an early age he vowed to do better for his family if he ever married. After graduating High School, he attended two years of college. During his freshman year he met his wife-to-be, Betty. After a short courtship, they married. The birth of his daughter and the subsequent need for additional income had ended his college education.

Mike absentmindedly brought his pet around to the front courtyard of the apartment house on 34th Avenue. While he looked up at the soiled tan bricks, and wondered at the age of the six story building, the wail of police sirens pierced the stillness as they approached from down the block. Even the dog froze as two black-and-whites sped past, their rooftop domes flashing like arcade lights.

Mike and the dog watched with interest as the cars turned into 90th Street adjacent to his block. Mike jerked the dog's leash, causing her to yelp. Together they ran around the corner. After a few steps the dog pulled him along. She had no idea why they ran, but for her, it was fun.

Red and white beacons from the roof lights cast their own shadows to mix with those that Mike had noticed earlier. He stopped to lean against a parked auto. The run around the corner, combined with the dense moist air, had made Mike light headed. He waxed poetic; *the shadows had danced; now they have music.* Mike chuckled at how silly that sounded. Good thing nobody could hear that, they'd put him away.

Romano looked around the neighborhood. From the row houses he saw people coming out onto their porches. From the apartment buildings, heads poked out of windows. The lights and sirens had aroused the neighborhood.

Brakes squealed and a third car slid to a stop next to the first two against the curb mid-block in front of the apartment houses. The odor of exhaust fumes, burning tires and brakes permeated the air. As car doors opened, from each police cruiser erupted a team of two officers. All six cops ran into the apartment house that fronted the street. The red bricked building was one of four in a complex that boasted open, screened, external landings between floors.

The hairs on the back of Romano's neck bristled. This is not just a bullshit police run. *What the hell happened?*, wondered Mike. He watched the officers' progress as they passed each screened landing, running to the roof and out of sight. The sound of muted voices drifted down toward Mike. After pacing the sidewalk for several minutes he attempted to find out what was going on. Mike called out to several other persons who left their houses, attracted by the commotion, and had gathered near him.

"Do you know what's going on? Did anyone make the call? Is anyone hurt? I was out here and didn't hear anything."

He received no reply. Mike grew agitated.

4

Instinctively, he knew that whatever brought the cops to that building had to be serious, extremely serious.   Despite the warm night, a cold chill gripped Mike as he strained his eyes to view the top of the building that the cops had entered.   He began to become worried about his family.   Maybe the sirens scared Anne.   Maybe Betty's wondering what happened to him.   Bullshit.   He'd been unnerved by the unknown and he need the comfort of his family.   He gave the dog's leash a quick tug and returned to his apartment.

When he opened the entrance door, Mike heard his 25 year old wife, Betty, humming softly in the shower.   Abigail, the dog, now released from her leash, trotted down the long hallway to Anne's bedroom and settled into her corner next to the sleeping child's bed.   The kitchen was directly to the right of the entrance doorway. After hearing the dog settle down, Mike entered the kitchen, opened the broom closet that doubled as a grocery cupboard, and pulled out a bottle of scotch.   From a cabinet over the sink he took out an eight ounce tumbler and poured a healthy amount of the amber liquid into the glass then added several ice cubes.

Romano left the kitchen and headed towards the bedroom.   Abruptly, the bathroom door opened.   Out walked Betty.   Mike stared at the five-foot-five, 127 pound woman before him. It brought forth a big grin.   She wore only goose bumps.   She dragged a towel behind her, in a little girl gesture.   Erect nipples capped her glistening, ample breasts. The blonde mane on her head, matted down with dampness, only slightly spoiling the picture. The triangular tuft of her femininity sparkled.

Betty had not heard her husband enter the apartment. She had been lost some-where in her own thoughts. She blinked at Mike, poised in the hallway.

"Oh my God, you startled me. What's wrong? You look upset." Her breasts bounced, arousing him for a delightful second.

Mike took a quick swallow of his Scotch. "Something happened around the corner a few minutes ago. I don't know what it was, but I have an uncomfortable feeling; it's not good." As he spoke, he seemed to forget the naked vision before him.

"Is that what the sirens were for? Did you see anything?" asked Betty, as she ever so slowly twisted her curvaceous body in an effort to bring the smile back to his face.

"No, but it had to be important," Mike replied and continued on, to describe what he saw.

Slowly wrapping the bath towel around herself, Betty said, "Pour me a drink Michael and we'll talk about it." She could see the look of genuine concern in his eyes.

One of the things that Betty loved about her husband was his willingness to help people. She first saw her husband assisting an elderly woman. The senior citizen had been struggling to get her shopping cart up several steps that led up to the entrance of an apartment house. Michael had been sitting at a traffic light in his car and apparently saw her dilemma. He pulled his car to the curb, got out and lifted her cart up the steps and into the building. Betty, walking past, was impressed at his kindness and walked over to tell him so.

They had an instant attraction to each other and began to date. Mike explained to her that as a child he had been told that policemen helped people. He became fascinated by cops and the mystique surrounding them. As an adult he had cultivated friends on the force and spent many hours at the local station house and an equal amount of time drinking with them in the local "cop bar". Betty had casually stated that she too had been introduced to police officers as helpful good guys at an early age but never explained further.

Joe DeCicco

While sitting upright on their bed, Mike began, "You know, tonight made me think again about joining the Police Department." As he spoke, Mike got up and walked to the window. He leaned out and looked to the left, toward 90th Street.

"What are you looking for Mike?" Betty asked. As he turned into the room, Betty tugged at the top of the towel.

She wanted to ease his tension. She raised one knee. The towel silently dropped to the bed. Mike noticed and smiled. His heart skipped a beat. *She's beautiful.*

He continued, "I want to do something to make it better for you and the kid. I want to guarantee that if society goes down the toilet; my family would have their own protector." He liked that. He was on a roll.

Betty smiled and arched her back. *My own Saint Michael, that's my guy.*

"Besides after twenty years there's always a pension. It's half pay!"

Her reply came short and tart. "If you live to collect it." She thought; *Hey Mike, yumm, yumm, a late night snack!*

Mike seemed oblivious to her efforts. "There's no such guarantee in the private business world. Sure my job pays well, but there's no pension at all, and guys do drop dead of heart attacks all the time from stress," he continued.

Mike had been employed in the private sector as draftsman and designer for a manufacturing company for the past seven years. He had seen men let out only one short year from pension eligibility. Sighing, he returned to the bed and sat down facing his wife.

Betty had reached saturation. "Let's see if you have the strength to become one of society's protectors," she said, reaching over to remove his sweat-drenched, musky shirt.

Once she had it off, she blew across his chest chilling his body. Her tongue slid across his abdomen. "Mmm, salt, I love salt." She stated reaching for his belt buckle.

7

Mike's skin tingled. He lunged and grabbed her hard enough to make her giggle with delight. "I'll show you strength".

Their lovemaking possessed a vigor that night, unlike any in a long time, almost primordial.

Michael had the following day off from work. Leaving Betty and Anne at her mother's house, he visited the local station house, the One-Ten (110) Precinct. He had developed a friendship with a Sergeant, John Cutbert.

Mike spoke to the desk officer, "Sarge, is John Cutbert in?"

The old desk officer replied, "He's downstairs in his office, young fella. Go right ahead." Mike was well known there and needed no escort.

In keeping with police traditional jargon, Mike replied, "Thank you, Boss." and then headed directly downstairs.

Romano went straight to Cutbert's "office". He found the door closed.   Being anxious to find out if John knew anything about the previous night's incident, he tapped twice then opened it.

The "office" was a room used by the patrol sergeants, doubling as a lounge/locker room.   Covering the floor was industrial flooring tile, the color of dried blood. In the far left corner was a television set and dangerously close to it a coffee pot. In front of the set sagged an ancient recliner with a small refrigerator acting as an end table. Two walls were lined with olive green lockers.

A bulletin board on the wall opposite the doorway was littered with wanted posters and Department bulletins.   The pictures on the fliers were not what one would expect. In the center one did not find the faces of hard looking criminals and social mendicants.   They were all covered over by photos of naked women. The people depicted on those posters were

Joe DeCicco

certainly wanted; by every male police officer in the One-Ten.

Sitting in the center of the room was a square table covered with dark green linoleum. John and three other men, all sergeants, filled chairs there. On the table rested an equal number of piles of five dollar bills. John looked up as the other men attempted to cover the money.

"He's okay, don't worry. Mike's a good personal friend." They relaxed a little after Cutbert's statement.

John, a big man, stood six-foot-four, and carried 350 pounds, with a barrel chest that extended down to his belt line. In his younger years he had been all muscle. Despite the addition of some extra fat around his middle, Cutbert could hold his own against any three men in a physical fight. Romano knew what they were doing. The sergeants were cutting up the weeks take or "pad" in police vernacular. The money represented "gifts," a euphemism, for graft, or gratuities, from the owners of local businesses within the confines of the precinct. Favors; for ignoring construction permits, double-parking not enforced, and the like.

"What brings you here, Mike? Last time I saw you was in the Abbey," asked John, referring to the bar frequented by most of the cops in the command.

Mike, despite his excitement at possibly quelling his agitated curiosity about the previous night's incident calmly answered, "Last night there was a run around the corner from my house, John. It was out of the ordinary. Do you know if anything happened that I should know about?"

Before he responded to his friend's question, John motioned for each of the other sergeants to pick up their shares of the counted money. Slowly he picked up the pile in front of himself, folded the money and pocketed it. On John's face, and in his gray eyes, Mike thought he saw a slightly guilty look. It was quickly covered up with the expression of a man disgusted with what he was about to say.

9

Angel with a Gun

John almost shouted, "Yeah, late into the four-to-twelve tour some little four-year-old girl was found on a roof. She had been physically molested and raped!"

Upon hearing his friend's words, Mike's body temperature rose. It caused beads of sweat to form on his forehead. Mike imagined what it must have been like for her, there on the rooftop confronted by a tall, smelly, adult male. His cheeks probably pock-marked with the remnants of teenage acne, on his face a lecherous smile.

John, looked at his friend, saw the sweat form on Mike's forehead, the glazed look in his eyes as though he had drifted off in his own distressed world. "Mike," he called out, "come on back boy. Shit like that happens. The damn incident went down in one of the sectors that I'm responsible for. But you live there, you already know that."

Mike shook his head as if the action chased away his thoughts and responded, "Yeah, John, it's okay. That poor little kid must have gone through some bad experience. Do you think she'll ever forget it?"

John's face clouded with regret and uncertainty. "Don't know Mike, I'm no psychiatrist. You can read the detectives' report if you want. Because it happened in my area I have a copy." John got up out of the chair and walked to a locker. He opened the door and took several papers from the top shelf. He held them out to his friend.

Mike took the offering and began reading.

"Detective Unusual Report, Borough of Queens
Subject: Molestation and Rape of Child."

He could go no further, reached for the nearest chair and sat down heavily. What followed was a description of the incident and the little girl's statements. Mike's mind raced as he read. The sick son of a bitch claimed that he was going to teach her the difference between boys and girls. He should be killed. My God, it could happen to any kid. Mike could feel the fear in the young child. He could easily visualize his own child, Anne. Her tawny head full of ringlet curls. Her clothing covered with little pictures representing her favorite cartoon characters.

Then he read about the assault itself. Bile burned its way up into Mike's throat. He could smell the musty, humid tar that he imagined mingled with the nighttime odors. His nose twinged. For a few minutes, Michael became that little girl.

Mike fumed internally as he dropped the reports on the table. *Damn it. I was out there. Maybe I could have done something to help the little kid. Maybe I could have beat the living crap out of the perverted bastard. Maybe I could have thrown him off the roof. How the hell can I tell Betty?*

"John, I was out there at that time. Did they get him? How's the kid?"

Someone, perhaps John, had blacked out the child's name on the reports. Mike picked up the papers again and began to wave them as he continued, "What's her name? Who is she?" He was becoming agitated now. He wanted to do something. Anything.

"It's a bitch of a thing. She's real young. And, no they didn't get him Mike. The detectives have the case now. The little girl lived in the building and the DT's (detectives) think it must have been a family member or someone the kid knew. They canvassed, you know, knocked on every door in the building without any results. Stay in touch. I know you live right there and I'll keep you informed. You know that I can't tell you her name. Confidentiality."

Extremely disturbed by his friends answer, Mike came halfway out of his chair. He could feel the pounding in his temples. "The bastard got away? John, do you have an application for the job. I gotta do something. Anne is never gonna get attacked and see the ugly side of life. Not if I can help it. No way."

Angel with a Gun

"Sit down Mike and have a taste with us. You look a little upset, you look pale for God's sake." observed Cutbert as he slid his chair backward to the fridge. John put a chilled bottle of scotch on the table and five small plastic cups.

Nobody in the room knew how close to home the report struck for Mike. They would never know.

One of the other men said, "Kid, you can't save the world. This is just another job like any other one. Sure sometimes you can help people, but don't forget to help yourself too".

Mike looked at the speaker with disbelief. The man actually said the words. He and the other men in the room took money. The man must be stupid. Nobody admitted to it. It just wasn't done. Romano made a mental note to chastise and caution his friend about the practice when they were alone somewhere.

Mike knew that if he was a cop, he would never become cynical and opportunistic like these men. He, Michael Romano, would work to prevent little girls from being hurt. Not sit around splitting up questionable money. He liked his sergeant friend, but not the part of him that took money. He felt that if given the chance, he would even find out who hurt the girl last night if nobody else ever did. The child rapist would someday face Justice. Mike's heart was pounding like the engine of a freight train at the thought of catching up with the rapist. It would almost be like going back in time and righting the wrong that had been perpetrated against his wife Betty long before he ever met her.

Mike's blood temperature rose as he remembered the look of apology on Betty's face when she told him of her first experience with cops. As if the rape had been her fault. She was only six years old when the guy grabbed her. How could it have been her fault? He was never caught either. He would someday get this guy. For the little girl he never met and for his Betty. He downed a mouthful of scotch hoping that the burning of the liquor would shift his concentration. It did.

While he sipped the whiskey Mike's mind drifted. It was quite some time since Mike had last attended church. Even so he could recall the stained glass windows of his local parish, the murmured Latin of the priest as he said Mass. Vividly, he remembered one particular window depicting a winged angel, dressed in armor, standing on a large snake representing Satan. The angel was plunging a sword into the body of The Beast.

When he asked the parish priest for an explanation of the window panel, Mike was told the angel was Saint Michael, the Archangel, God's soldier, the avenging, enforcement arm of the Almighty. As an afterthought, perhaps commenting on the future of the young parishioners before him, the clergyman added that Saint Michael was also the Patron Saint of Policemen.

Remembering that conversation, Mike reached a momentous conclusion. Michael the Archangel is the Patron Saint of policemen everywhere. That's it. His name was Michael, that's who he'd become; an avenging angel. What he had told Betty last night was now firm. He would join the Force. Shortly thereafter, Mike made his excuses and returned home.

On the following day, Michael stopped at the Thomas Street offices of the Department of Personnel New York City Police Department.

"Excuse me," he said to the clerk behind the counter. "I would like an application for the exam to enter the Police Department."

"No problem," he was told. The clerk reached into a tray. "Here you are. You may take that home to fill it out."

Mike's eagerness made his smile a bit lop-sided. "Thanks, I'll do it here."

When he had completed it and turned it in, the clerk gave the top sheet a cursory glance and looked up at Mike.

"You're fortunate, Romano. There's an exam scheduled within the next three months. Within three weeks you'll be notified by mail if you have been accepted. Also, when and where to report."

Three weeks and a day later, a thin, Government Issue envelope waited for Mike when he returned home from work. It surprised Mike that his fingers trembled when he went to open the missive. He unfolded the sheet inside and swiftly scanned it. His heart began to race. He could not believe what he was reading. He hurried to the kitchen.

"Sweetheart! Hey, Sweetheart," he yelled at his wife like an excited kid. "Guess what I just got?"

Betty Romano turned from the bowl where she was mixing a meatloaf. It was Mike's favorite, made with ground chuck and Italian sausage. "I'm sure I haven't the slightest." A small smile played on her lips. She had seen the envelope and read the return address. "Is it good news?"

"Good! It's the best. I've been accepted to take the exam for the Police Department. Oh, Baby, this is almost as good as our wedding day."

"Almost as good?" asked Betty archly.

Mike stumbled over his words. "Well, yes, exactly as good. Only in a different way, of course. This is my career we're talkin' here. My future."

Over the years since they had married, Betty had learned exactly how to curb Mike's frequent bursts of boyish enthusiasm. "You have yet to pass the exam, and then the Academy. Then it will be your future. Our future, really."

Reined in slightly, Mike still bubbled. He nodded toward the bowl. "You want to put that in the fridge and we'll go out and celebrate.

"Mike, it's the middle of the month. Do we have the money?"

Mike shrugged.   "Hell with that.   We'll use the plastic."

Betty crossed the space between them and gave him a peck on the cheek.   Then she planted a long, juicy, passionate kiss on his lips.   "Honey, you sure know how to get around a girl.   I'd love to go out."

Several weeks after receiving his exam notification, Mike enjoyed a beer in the Abbey with the small circle of cops with whom he was friendly.   The men had been discussing a rumor that had wide circulation.

Ed Danner, an older uniform cop, narrated the content to Mike.   "The story goes that the child molester from that 90th Street incident has been identified.   Though the man's identity is known, he's never been arrested.   The prick has never even seen the inside of a police station.   My rabbi (patron, in police jargon) claims that reports were altered because he had a very high connection inside the Job."

It struck Mike hard.   John and his Sergeant's club was one thing.   Minor corruption was one thing.   So long as he was not involved when he was on the Force he could live with that. He saw not arresting rapists as another matter.   Someday he would be brought to justice.   And Mike hoped to be the one to do it.   Then it occurred to him.   This could be nothing but bar talk.   Gotta check with John Cutbert.

All too soon, Mike would find that the rumor proved true.

CHAPTER TWO

In November of 1972, Michael took the Civil Service Exam to become a New York City Police Officer. When the list positions were formulated Mike found himself in the top fifth percentile.

Betty glowed with pride for her husband. "My smart Mikey. You should have finished college."

Mike did not like reminders of that particular failure. He frowned slightly as he replied. "If I had, they'd probably say that I was over-qualified for the job."

While awaiting appointment to the Academy, Mike had shared his obsession with Betty about finding and apprehending the child rapist. Sure, she was proud of Mike and his exam score, she was equally worried about his safety. She knew it was dangerous on the streets for a cop.

"It's also dangerous to buck the system," she reminded Mike. Then she dropped the subject. Betty knew that once Mike set a goal, he was as tenacious as a bull dog until he achieved it.

Several months later, in April, he was among the first to be hired.

Police recruit Michael Romano approached The New York City Police Academy; a seven story glazed white brick building on East 20th Street in the Borough of Manhattan. His stomach felt like thousands of large, overweight butterflies fluttered around inside.

Mike looked up at the facade with a critical eye. The entrance to the building looked like a cheap hotel, not like the school for the greatest police department in the world. Inside, to the left of the entrance Mike saw the gymnasium. The

16

thought of physical training heightened his excitement. Should he find and capture the rapist that launched his new career, he would be ready to do whatever he had to. Mike knew that he would soon be at his physical peak. The second floor housed the Police Museum along with some classrooms and offices.

Mike spent his first lunch hour in the collection. While inside the museum, Mike picked up a brochure explaining some of the physical attributes of the building. He read aloud, "Floors three through six, with the exception of the fifth floor, contain the bulk of the building's classrooms. On the fifth floor is the Law Library and administrative offices. The Police Laboratory, with a complete Chemistry lab and Ballistics lab uses the entire seventh floor.   In the basement is an Olympic-sized swimming pool showers and a well outfitted weight room."

The next paragraph had been set in bold, black letters.   "The building also contains two elevators that the ROOKIES ARE FORBIDDEN TO USE. THEY MUST ALWAYS USE THE STAIRWAYS."

That afternoon, after locating the only pay phone available to rookies, he reached Betty on the third ring. "Sweetheart, it is everything I expected. And a whole lot more. I know I made the right decision."

Not entirely as convinced, Betty responded in a small voice. "I hope you are right, Mike. Uh--go knock 'em dead."

Mike thought Betty could have chosen a better turn of phrase as he got off the phone quickly to allow another probationary officer to use it. Then, back to the auditorium for further orientation and the swearing in.

When Mike heard "Raise your right hands and repeat after me. . . ." he thought his chest would burst. Only on the day he got married had he felt that way. He remembered the nervous excitement of starting a new life adventure. The swearing in ceremony awoke much of the same emotions.

After the ceremony, Mike took note of the dais. Several ranking officers sat there in metal folding chairs. Some of them spoke to the recruits. Mike took special notice of one man in particular.

He sat second from the end to Mike's right. Something about the man-made Mike uneasy. Then it occurred to him, these guys are all cops, bosses. Why didn't he like that big redhead? He seems all right. Maybe it's those big protruding ears.

On the following day, Mike, along with all the other recruits, reported to the Equipment Bureau to receive his grey rookie uniforms. He was ecstatic. So much so that not even the harassing tactics of the instructors could spoil his day. They loomed over the line outside the issue room and brayed at the bewildered young officers in their charge.

"All right, pecker-heads, move it along. This ain't a Delancey Street block party. No socializin', ya hear? Keep up--keep up, damn it."

"No, you dumb-dumb. Not three shirts and four trousers. Four of each. Can't you count?"

"No talking in line!" brayed another. You got only two things to say. 'Yes, sir.' and 'No, sir.' Got that right?"

Mike surmised, and rightly so, that this was intended to condition them for more of the same, and much worse, handed out to them by the good citizens in the course of their duties. Already, their US and THEM syndrome received its first fine tuning.

Arriving home after purchasing his "Grays" Mike bounded into the apartment and without saying even hello to his wife retreated into their bedroom. Betty heard the rustling of packages and stiff clothing.

In what seemed like only seconds later to Betty, he came out.

"Hi, Honey. What do you think? Not bad huh?" He self-consciously modeled the uniform, albeit with his face aglow with pride. On his head was a dark blue, "flying saucer" police hat.

Betty smiled and asked, "Mike, how come the hat isn't grey too?"

"Don't know Bet. That's what they gave us. Maybe it's because we don't have badges and there's one on the hat." Mike paused, suddenly self-conscious. Do I look professional?"

Betty replied, "Mikey, you look terrific. Probably the best looking rookie in the whole class."

Anne, who had been playing in her room, heard he father's voice. She rushed to the living room and now stood next to him seeking his attention. He picked her up, walked over to his wife and hugged them both. During that dramatic moment Betty announced the impending birth of their second child.

"Honey, that's fantastic," Mike enthused. He kissed his wife and tossed Anne into the air. She squealed with delight as he caught her. "When? How soon?"

Betty's eyes glowed with her good news. "The doctor says six months, give or take a week."

Mike meant it when he told her, "I'll count the days."

Later that night Mike explained what training he would be receiving.

Mike began, "We work forty hours a week. Imagine, Betty, going to school is work. We get paid full rookie salary to attend classes. Six months out of the Academy, my salary exceeds that of my last job."

His emotions lingered on the earlier announcement, "My God, Bet, maybe well have a son this time. All this and a new job too." He gently kissed her cheek as though she would break if he was rough.

Acknowledging his side comment Betty replied, "Yeah, we'll have a boy, Michael. One just like you." Not to take the enthusiasm out of his narration, she brought the conversation back to him, "Of course Mike, you're a sworn police officer employed by the City. Naturally they have to pay you." Betty put her arms around her husband and thought fondly; sometimes Michael Romano, you act like a small child. There's so much little boy inside of you. You have the strong emotions of a child. That's one of the reasons she loved him so.

Mike hugged her again, held her at arm's length and continued, "We spend eight hours a day there. For four hours we attend classes, basic law with a focus on the New York State Penal Law and the New York Criminal Procedure Law. Included with this will be some basic Psychology and Sociology courses. On a more local level, the Vehicle and Traffic Laws are covered with a touch of New York City Health and Administrative Codes."

Mike was really going now. He continued, "The other four hours we spend in physical training. Most of the classes will be in the Gym. Twice a week we'll have staggered two hour sessions, in the pool. It's a little play time and it's required that all police officers know how to affect water rescues."

Betty took particular note of the type of language used by her husband. He had started to change already. He sounded like a lawyer. Using phrases like "effect water rescues." She found was proud of her husband. *He's growing up, becoming an even better man that he was. If the change is so quick and he learns everything they throw at him, then she could worry less. Maybe he'll be more cautious about going after the child rapist.* Because, damn him, she knew he'd keep trying.

Joe DeCicco

On his third day in the Department, actual training began. In the classroom, the laws concerning Rape and Child Molesting were what interested Michael the most. Penal Law section 130.00, the Sex Offenses and PL 260.00, Offenses Relating to Children and Incompetents, respectively. Michael soon knew them inside and out. During one of those classes he was called upon to tell fellow classmates why he joined the Department.

An imperious sergeant conducted the class. He peered down a long, Roman nose and spoke directly to Mike. "Recruit Romano, we would find it interesting to learn why it is that you decided to become one of New York's Finest?"

Mike rose in place. "There couldn't be a better place to tell about it, sir. It has to do with a goal I set myself. I want to find a rapist. Not just any rapist, sir. A very special one." He described the situation, then concluded; "I study hard, because I want to get that S.O.B. I can't forget that hot summer night and what happened that motivated me to join the Department, sir."

Most of his classmates listened politely and, behind his back, called his statements rookie enthusiasm. Sometimes Michael would even catch the ear of a friendly instructor. They would listen without any comments of consequence. Completely absorbed in his studies, time sped by for Mike. Scholastically Mike soon saw that he ranked near the top of his class.

Mike knew that anything he could assimilate from his training would keep him alive and give him an edge over the people he might encounter during a long career ahead of him. John Cutbert had explained to Mike that a cop must make decisions in an instant. That decision had better be correct. Rarely did a cop have time for second thoughts. Mike was determined to always do his best. One of the training requirements dictated that recruits wear their "Grays" when traveling to and from The Academy. It was designed to get the new men used to being looked at as being different. They were different, they were now police officers. Mike found it exhilarating. His new vocation rapidly became an avocation. He wore his grey rookie uniform proudly.

During his training in the Academy, Michael attempted to excel in the Phys Ed classes. Attendance at all classes was mandatory. The rules permitted no excuses. Only a slip from a police doctor could excuse a recruit. Notes from one's mother didn't cut it. He knew that he should be in top physical condition upon graduation.

Daily exercise workouts began each day, before the actual training for physical confrontations, such as subduing and handcuffing prisoners. Warm-ups the instructors called them. Mike would never forget that first day. The PE instructor stood in front of their formation in gray sweat pants, and a T-shirt with NYPD Academy stenciled on the front.

"All right, Ladies. Assume the position. On your backs. Twenty five sit-ups, on my count. One. . .and two. . .and three. . .and four. . .and four. . .and five. . ."

It went on like that, with the instructor repeating numbers several times so that the total count came closer to thirty-five. Mike was surprised to find it an easy exercise. The sit-ups were followed by the same amount of push-ups, followed by squat thrusts. In the beginning, Michael and most of the other rookies panted like steam locomotives long before the last exercise. After the first two weeks, Mike hardly raised a sweat. That condition proved short lived. *The instructors are really sadists; they have to have all been Drill Instructors in the Marines. They're trying to kill us.* Mike embellished on that image as the number and speed of the exercises increased almost daily.

Included in the training received during "Swim class" was one particular exercise that required an officer to tread water for fifteen minutes. Most of the new recruits muttered, "No problem."

Their cadre creates a problem. It came in the form of a

five pound rubber brick to be held by each individual during that emulation of a cork. That wasn't easy. The instructor explained to all that the brick exercise was to give his students an idea of what it was like to hold up a drowning victim while awaiting assistance. Of course, the brick didn't panic and attempt to climb on top of the rescuer. The instructor had a solution to that, too. The students took turns acting like drowning victims.

Grinning, their trainer gave them their instructions. "To make it more like the real thing, I want you who are the rescuees to act as though you were panic stricken. Really put on a show, okay?" At times it got too real.

During one of the exercises, Mike had to pull a "drowning" victim from the water. One of his classmates went into the pool. The instructor had the man treading water for about five minutes after putting him through a vigorous exercise regimen.

The man in the pool tired eventually. He actually sank momentarily and when he surfaced, he coughed and spat, then asked, "Please sir, let me out."

"No," replied the instructor. "Romano, count aloud to fifty and go get him."

"Yes sir," replied Mike. He began counting, fast. He had reached twenty-five.

"Too fast Romano. Start again. Then get him out."

By the time Mike reached fifty, the guy in the pool looked scared to hell. Mike jumped in and swan to him. He swallowed gallons of water as the "drowning victim" attempted to climb onto his body.

"Let go, damn it. Cool it, Dave," Romano barked. They both went down.

Mike swallowed what he believed to be half the smelly, chlorine water before he got "the victim" to the edge of the pool. Eager hands of classmates plucked them both from the water.

Angel with a Gun

As the physical training continued, Mike became proud of his new body and jokingly displayed it to his wife Betty as often as possible. One evening he came out of the shower, a towel wrapped around his middle, checked to see that Anne slept soundly, then proceeded to find Betty.

He walked into the kitchen where Betty ran her hand-held mixer in a bowl of cookie dough.   Mike stood tall, tightened his muscles and inhaled. His chest expanded, his abdomen imploded and his towel fell.

Betty's reaction came instantly. "Michael, you're a sick man but you're mine and beautiful, too."

It worked perfectly.   Exactly as he had planned it.   It did every time after that.

They made love often during his days at the Academy. Betty often thought; *This is like having a new man, it feels almost sinful. But it's okay. The man's my husband.*

Eventually the exercises, physical training and studying became routine. Even one hundred sit-ups no longer offered a challenge.   In later years, nothing stood out in Michael's mind from his days in the Academy except a female rookie affectionately dubbed, "Fran the Can."

Derriere is defined in most dictionaries as, "Backside, seat, rump, buttocks, hindquarters, rear," etcetera.

Mike and the other male rookies in his class, Company 73-28, preferred to define derriere as "Fran the Can's Ass". She had, in their opinion, without a doubt the finest posterior in the world. Truly "New York's Finest."

Michael was fortunate enough to be positioned behind Fran during most work-outs and for every run.   He completed each five mile turn around the oval track with a huge grin.   At last, the PE instructor challenged him on it. "What could possibly have you smiling after a five miler in this heat?"

"Sir," Mike responded with a straight face. "I have a great source of internal inspiration."

Later he was overheard telling the other recruits, "Fran is an inspiration. I never get tired during a run. Listen, I love my wife, I don't want to boff Fran. Not really. If I wasn't married, I sure would try."

His friends replied "Sure, Mike, tell us another one." Accompanied with a heaven-ward cast and googly rolling of their eyes. "You never try to take her out for a drink after work?" they persisted. "Who the hell are you kidding?"

"Listen, I'm no saint, just faithful to my wife. Sure I like looking at Fran. You guys all get tired. Right? That's because you think about the pain. Me I think about watching that perfect butt in front of me to hold my concentration. She blocks the pain during any training. After all the calisthenics they have us do, we gotta run. Right? People get tired and drop out. I don't. During the run, I never even think of letting anyone get between me and that backside. It keeps me going."

Firearms training left many of the rookies in a sea of confusion. Not so, Mike Romano. He had a fine hunting rifle, a 300 Wetherby Magnum, given him by his father, when the senior Romano became too old to tramp the fields. He also had a shotgun. He was more than proficient with both. His obvious skill came to the attention of his instructors.

"Romano, we want you to assist me in the classroom with these people," Sergeant "Horse" Nelson told him one morning while the rookies fumbled through the -- to them -- intricacies of loading and unloading their .38 service revolvers. The weapons were "red barreled," the firing pins removed and the rounds spent shells.

Modesty aside, Mike knew better than to protest. One did as one was told at the Academy. "Yes, sir. Where do I start, sir?"

His features in a scowl, Nelson pointed to one hapless rookie. "Over there. McGuire seems to have ten thumbs when it comes to loading a revolver."

Mike readily complied. He knew that the request was out of the ordinary, but who was he to argue. Several sessions later, in the basement firing range, Sgt. Nelson exhibited even further trust of Romano. He approached the cadet with a serious expression.

"Romano, I want you to stick with McGuire. You'll be his coach."

"Yes, sir. But, uh---this is our first live fire exercise, isn't it, sir?"

"Right, Romano. Do you know what to do?"

"Yes, sir, my Dad and I did it together when he taught me to use a rifle."

Nelson looked hard at him. "When was that, Romano?"

"When I was twelve, sir."

"Then I doubt if you've forgotten how. Take your place."

Mike joined McGuire. "I'm gonna be your coach, Tom."

"How's that work, Mike?"

Mike thought a moment, recalled what his father had done. "I watch you, take you through each step and correct anything you do wrong."

"Oh--ah--okay." Tom McGuire grinned boyishly. "I guess you can start by telling me how to keep these bullets from rolling off the ledge."

Mike produced a smile to ease his correction. "Only the tip of it is called a bullet. This part here. All of it is a cartridge. Or, as they call it here, a round. It's simple, Tom. You take only take one out of the box at a time. Put it

26

in the chamber and then get another, until the cylinder is fully loaded."

Tom looked confused. "But they said we would fire five rounds. Will it work with only five in it?"

"Trust me, it will." Mike patted the uncertain recruit on one shoulder. "Go on, load it."

When that had been completed, Mike took his position. He put his ear protectors in place and made sure his shooting glasses fitted properly. "Okay. When the command is given, raise your piece to shoulder level, arm straight, wrist locked. Line up the rear notch sight with the top of the blade front sight. Sit that on the center of the black. Keep both eyes open. Cock your hammer and take in a deep breath, let out half, hold it. When the command comes, fire."

"Attention on the line. You should all be loaded. Ready right? Ready left? All ready, on the firing line. Raise your pieces and take aim. Do not cock your weapons. All firing will be double-action. Some of you may have been misinformed. Steady your aim." A buzzer sounded. "Fire."

A ragged volley crackled along the line. McGuire's bullet popped a black hole in the white above and to the right of the silhouette target. Mike sighed. "You've got to hold it steady, Tom. A slow, steady, gentle squeeze. Like you're squeezing the nipple of your girlfriend's titty."

"She don't like that. Says it hurts."

That gave Mike some insight. "That's probably because you squeeze too hard. Like you did now. You jerked the trigger. That makes the muzzle rise off target and you get a miss. If there had been a citizen standing behind the target, he'd be dead now."

Mike Romano continued to coach Tom McGuire through the remaining four rounds. He offered corrections and encouragement. Only two of the five rounds went in the black. Then it became his turn. He took Tom's place and spoke to him in a low voice.

"Okay, Tom. Now you stand there and watch me. See how I do it."

Mike put three in the ten and two in the nine just outside the line. *I should have done better,* he told himself. Sergeant. Nelson approached. "Good shooting, Romano. You've got the knack, I can see."

"Thank you, sir. Tom's--er--Recruit McGuire is doing better."

"Stick with it, Romano."

By the end of the third day's training, Tom McGuire could put three in the nine space and two in the seven. Unfortunately, the trio in the higher score did not as yet group. One would invariably be on the opposite side of the ten space. Mike began to despair that Tom would qualify. Then a sudden, unexpected bang, followed by a loud clang and shout of alarm changed Mike's mind.

"What the hell?" McGuire blurted.

Mike stepped out of the booth to see a thoroughly chagrinned Thad Stevens gaping back at his shooting station. His face glowed red with embarrassment as he shakily held his service revolver in both hands as though he did not recognize it. Mike came back to Tom's side.

"Someone put a round through the roof of the firing line. I've got a ten says he gets to repeat the course."

In the end, every one made it through and received their marksman badge. Mike Romano felt proud of the Expert Pistol badge presented to him.

After the completion of firearms training, the brass issued the recruits their shields. Finally, six months after entering the Academy, Graduation Day finally loomed on the horizon. Betty watched Mike spit-shine his black uniform shoes until they became mirrors. "Is it going to be like this every day?"

Mike looked up and nodded. "Yep. At least until I make detective. They get to wear loafers."

Careful to avoid smudges from the polish, Betty hugged her. "It's a funny thing, Honey. I remember my Daddy. His shoe polish always smelled so good. I think I'm going to like this."

Mike could not resist a small tease. "Yeah, until I turn it over to you to do."

Betty responded in kind. "Mike! That's tantamount to slavery."

Grinning, Mike sat his shoes aside, hugged his wife to him and toppled the both of them over on the bed. Nimble fingers began to pluck and soon loose clothing lay scattered on the floor. "Um--ummm, nice. Yes, Mikey, oh, yes. There, do it there. Like that. Yes--yesssss!"

Early the next morning, Mike Romano hurried off to the academy as he had done for all the weeks past. On the following day, the formal ceremony, with family present, would be held in an armory somewhere on Lexington Avenue in the upper Fifties. Now the Rookies gathered for a far more important occasion. For the last time, the cadre assembled the new Police Officers in the Academy gymnasium, to await their precinct assignments.

Mike could hardly wait to receive his assignment and leave the place.

Now that the training had ended, he viewed the gym as if for the first time. He could now see the small chips in the yellow oak flooring where he spent so many hours. The stale air mingled with the smell of chlorine from the pool below. He could smell the sweat of hundreds of toiling bodies. He felt closed in. A nervous glance at his watch told him it was time to go.

About to be graduated, Police Officer Michael Romano turned to see a familiar old face. John Cutbert managed to be

29

present when the assignments were given out. Mike was happy to have his friend share the moment. "My God, John, it's taking forever to get to my name."

With a crackle of static, the loudspeaker came to life again, "Michael Romano, Three-Two Precinct." Mike was the only member of his graduating class so far assigned to that command. His adrenalin level rose to new heights, equal only to when he learned that the identity of the little girl's rapist was known and not arrested because, "he had a hook in the Department".

Then the import of his assignment struck him. They are killing cops there on a regular basis. Why send him there? He studied and did well. He should get a choice assignment. He felt resentment at that, being married now and with two children. His son Donald, was only two weeks old. They should send single guys there. His family needed him.

In the next moment, John Cutbert stepped forward. "Congratulations Mike, you're going to a busy house. You'll love it." Cutbert pumped Mike's right hand and slapped his back at the same time.

His friend's enthusiasm made the new duty easier to accept. "Thanks John. It's strange. I feel like I'm watching my crabby mother-in-law go over a cliff in my brand new car, you know. Happy to see her go, but sad over the loss of the automobile.

"Don't worry. You'll learn the job there. You'll do fine. Someday you'll probably receive an award for something. Let's go celebrate with a taste."

After some rational thought, Mike decided to make the best of it. If he survived, he'd be some tough cop. A real Archangel.

"Sure, John. Soon as I change to civvies."

Joe DeCicco

Their Graduation Ceremony went exactly as Mike expected. Present were almost five hundred ramrod straight rookies, all spit and polish, in blue uniforms for the first time, with white gloves and all. Betty attended. Mike strained his eyes and found her in the gallery. Betty thought Mike to be the most handsome man in the world in his new dress uniform. The sharp creases on his pants and shiny shield on his chest. She smiled and gave a small wave.

"Officer Michael Romano."

When his name was called to step up and receive his diploma, rolled in tubular fashion and tied with a crimson string, Mike felt ten feet tall. As he stepped up on the platform erected for the day, his heart skipped. The first man he noticed was the big redheaded boss from the Police Academy. The man leered at him with a sardonic smile on his fat face. Mike remembered his instinctive dislike of the man. He wondered why and suddenly thought; *it's stupid, but maybe that guy is the child rapist's connection.* Mike forced himself to ignore his own reaction.

"Congratulations, Romano," the burly man with the big ears said as he handed Mike his diploma.

"Thank you, sir."

Then they shook hands and the ritual congratulations were repeated with the Police Commissioner. A few short steps, in a state of numbness, and Mike started off the dais.

What he didn't know was that the redheaded boss from the Police Academy had heard of Police Officer Romano's boasts to "catch the child rapist."

As a result, he had arranged to have Romano assigned to the Three-Two in an effort to channel his attention in another, more productive, direction. As Michael descended to the floor, the redhead thought behind veiled eyes; *this potentially troublesome rookie might even have a short career in such an environment.*

Once again seated, Mike turned toward his wife and held up the scroll in his hand. He also had a big, sappy, lop-

31

sided smile plastered on his ruggedly handsome face. After the ceremony, Mike and Betty celebrated with a night on the town. The kids stayed at the home of their maternal grandparents. For the occasion, Mike had selected a favorite restaurant, Cabarini's on 34th Street, in Little Italy.   At dinner they discussed his assignment to the Three-Two.

Over a pre-dinner scotch and soda for Mike and a white wine for Betty, Mike's wife revealed that she had already assumed the life of a policeman's wife. "Mike, its common knowledge that anti-establishment, racist groups were assassinating cops there."

"Where did you get that idea, Sweetheart?" Mike attempted to defuse the issue.

"I talked with some of the other wives at your graduation."

Mike nodded soberly and held his peace while Betty went on. "And there are almost daily reports in the Post and the Daily News. Honey, I'm scared for you all over again."

Mike forced a smile he did not feel and an expression of confidence. He reached across the table and gently patted Betty's hand, covering her engagement ring and wedding band. "I'll be fine, Sweetheart." At least he hoped his self-confidence and training would get him through.

Betty remained unconvinced. "But, Mike, those gangs---and that's really what they are,---they hate the police. They're doing it because. . ."   She lowered her eyes and her chin drooped with it. "Because most police are white."

Mike did not have a prejudiced bone in his body, nor did his darling wife, so her words actually shocked him. What he found worse was that he agreed with what she had said. He forced himself to take a sip of his drink before replying. "We have to accept the wisdom of the big brass in this.   And besides, I'm Italian, right? I look just like a lot of those street punks. Now, let's order and forget about all that for a while."

Once home again, Mike and Betty continued their celebration.

CHAPTER THREE

Pulling onto the 200 block of West 135th Street, Mike saw the building for the first time. My God, he thought. Old is the only way to describe this place. "Hell, it's ancient," he said aloud.

Squat and substantial, the 32nd Precinct station house was, and still is, located at 250 West 135th Street in the Borough of Manhattan between 7th (Martin Luther King Boulevard) and 8th Avenues; the very heart of Harlem. The Uptown Harlem that the songs and music of the Thirties have immortalized. The building could have come right out of an old movie.

Built at the turn of the century, its skin of red brick had darkened with age. The street level facade, including the corners and the roof trim, had been done in grey granite. All of the trimmings; window frames, door frames, drain pipes, fire escapes had been painted dark green. Across from the structure clustered other aged buildings, all three or four stories high. When he scanned the block, Mike observed, several broken windows in occupied dwellings, buildings with damaged front doors and entrance stairs that needed work. Shocked at what he saw, he summed up his first impressions. *These buildings look terrible, what kind of people live here? They all need repairs.*

Mike found a parking space and pulled in. It was the first time he had ever stopped in an inner city area. Sure, he had driven through on many occasions, but he never got outside his car; never actually walked around. He felt as if every eye on the block had focused only on him. Lounging, blank-faced people filled almost every doorway. *Who were they? What were they doing here?* The questions sprang immediately to the mind of Mike Romano, New Cop on the

Block.

Mike shook his head as if to expel his fears and approached the building. To cover his nervousness, he concentrated on what he saw. About six feet above the third and last step to the building entrance, the traditional Police Department green globes sprouted from the granite facing. One hung on each side of the entrance doorway of this edifice to Law and Order.

With a confident yank, Mike pulled open the outer oak paneled station house doors. Walking past them Mike could see the "lobby" through the inner glass windowed doors. Continuing inside Romano saw a wrought-iron rail, slightly to the right of the entrance way. It hadn't moved from its anchors in almost a century. The floors were faded terrazzo, worn slightly near the doorway. About twenty feet beyond Mike saw solid double doors labeled, Muster Room. He stopped momentarily and thought to himself; *that's where the roll calls are held.*

Still feeling the rookie, the newly assigned officer slowly walked around the railing and presented himself to the desk Sergeant. Mike snapped to attention with, "Probationary Patrolman Michael Romano reporting for duty, Sir."

From behind the huge oak desk, darkened with the years, came a gravel throated, "Thank you officer. Please wait in the muster room."

When he turned to walk away, Mike saw serpent-like heads that protruded through the plastered walls. They were old pipes for the gas lights that had once illuminated the place. Mike would later find that throughout the station house remnants of other pipes appeared in unexpected places. Some had been painted to match the walls. Others had become so tarnished as to be difficult to tell exactly what their purpose had been. The entire interior of the building had been painted a pale sickly green of an over-ripe avocado that must have been secretly required of all municipal buildings.

Angel with a Gun

Mike thought that it might be to discourage the public from remaining inside without purpose.

Self-consciously, the rookie turned again toward the high oak desk and thought, the damn thing is right out of an old gangster movie from the Thirties. Two of those serpent-like appendages stuck themselves out of the wall on each side of the Desk Officer's chair. It appeared to him that the valves remained intact. He would later find a flame burning from them during some of the Midnight tours. Mike assumed that they were lit nostalgically. He never learned why the gas lines remained live. Mike's mind raced. This place is unbelievable, it's only seconds since he reported to the desk sergeant and he'd seen so much. What about days from now?

Inside the muster room Mike continued his observations. In front of the left corner of the room rested a marble platform with two red leather upholstered chairs. The sagging seat cushions had worn to a weak shade of pink from the numerous posteriors that they held over the years. The 32nd Precinct was, at that time, the only and the last command to have the luxury of an in-house bootblack. In front of the chairs were cast iron foot rests. After a few years in the command Mike would learn the Jessup, the bootblack, also took numbers right there in his corner of the muster room.

On the far wall hung a rack of small pigeon holes used to dispense mail and notices for the members of the command. Each little coop bore a single letter for a label. Slumped in a chair under the rack, in his usual habitat, reclined the station house mascot, a local drunk. Fast asleep, Mike observed. He chuckled to himself. *Hope he's not DOA. It's probably the only safe spot in this whole command to sleep it off.*

Next to the "mail boxes" a corridor led to the solid steel door guarding the entrance to the holding cells. Still alone in the room, Mike entered the area. At once, he saw the cells. Solid old cages, six of them, constructed of 3/4 inch steel bars. These, too, had been painted that sickly, municipal green. The entire ceiling used to be white. In that area it had peeled, and stained to a faded yellow color. Mike had to jump sideways as a large section of the flaking paint dropped down on him. *Pheew, this entire cell area smells like a wet mop.*

When he exited the cell entrance Mike moved to his left. On the wall he saw a large cork bulletin board littered with various notices. What caught Mike's eye were the "Hot Sheet" (car alarms) and a smattering of wanted posters. Those posters had pictures of criminals, not nudes like the ones Mike had seen in John Cutbert's office. The reminder of purpose encouraged Michael. He liked it. He couldn't wait to stand roll call one morning and hear the sergeant say, "Don't forget to check 'The Sheet' for recent plate numbers."

Mike realized that he was still alone after several minutes. He walked back to the desk officer. "Excuse me, sir," stated Mike. "If there's going to be a few more minutes before anyone's ready for me, may I walk around for awhile?"

"Fine, Romano. You're about half an hour early." He cracked a warm, genuine smile. "You're also one of us now, my boy. Feel free to look around."

Accustomed by six months arduous training, under the command to have to ask permission for everything except to breathe, Mike replied lightly, "Thanks Sarge," and continued to explore.

On the second floor he found the Squad Room that housed the Detectives, the arrest processing room and some clerical offices. It also contained a small locker room for the bosses, (Sergeants and above) and another for the female cops. There were no female superior offices at the time. The third floor housed the male police officer's lockers.

Romano kept thinking that the place looked like a Hollywood set. His heart began to pound with excitement. To his surprise, he found himself happy to be there. His reluctance upon hearing his assignment announced the day before had faded away. He judged the place to have real charm and mystique. In a burst of honest self-examination, Mike suspected that he was an incurable romantic.

By the time Mike had completed his cursory inspection of the precinct house, some other new men had filtered in. They all shared an air of expectation that Mike knew within himself. His academy class had been too big for Mike to know everyone, so now he introduced himself to the other rookies and the old, familiar struggle began to remember names. Larson, O'Banyon, Doyle, Hopper--no, Hooper, the names slid through his mind like sand and water through his boyhood fingers at Coney Island. Would he ever remember them? Later still, some of the regulars began to drift into the Roll Call room.

After being introduced to some of them and more of the new men, an orientation session began. Mike looked around and saw cops of every size and shape. In the last row Mike saw a white haired rookie. The man was short. Mike wondered if he met the minimum height requirement or if he used "juice" to pass the physical. To his right was a man whose hat came down over his ears. *That guy looks like he's wearing his Dad's uniform and is "playing cop,"* thought Mike. Near the muster room door stood some more of the veteran cops. One or two of them looked as though they slept in their uniforms.

Comparing himself to the other men in the room, he decided that he looked pretty good.

As the desk sergeant came in and ordered all the men to sit down, he felt an adrenalin rush. Now he knew where he belonged. This is what he was made for.

In his gravel voice, sergeant began with some history of the area. "For the sake of you new-comers, listen up, already. The buildings in this neighborhood used to be clean apartment houses and elegant brownstones. You may not believe it now, but Harlem was once a haven for the rich. Over the course of years the buildings fell into disrepair with the exception of two blocks."

Mike found these facts only mildly interesting. He wanted to get out and patrol. He itched to get started.

"Now listen up you people," the sergeant continued. "On West 137th and West 138th Streets, there are to this day, some of the finest Turn of the Century brownstones found in The City. Sandwiched between them at the rear of these homes, are the old carriage houses where the rich kept their horses and their fancy buggies. They are serviced by a common driveway. Now they are garages for automobiles. Those two blocks are a designated landmark area."

Mike stirred restlessly. *Why tell us about those houses?*

Mike soon found out when the sergeant went on. "Living there are prominent wealthy people. Don't let the fact that you're working in a "shit house" give you a lazy attitude. All the people of this command are entitled to your best service, especially, those people. They are politically connected and can either hurt or, in some rare cases, help you."

Holy shit, thought Romano, *politics everywhere*.

Satisfied he had left the proper impression, the sergeant continued, "For the most part, the residents of the Three-Two are black, blue collar working class, with a smattering of professionals and more than their share of criminals."

That remark made Mike remember something that had been driven home during the sociology classes he attended. The fact is that there is more crime in an area where the residents are packed together. Studies showed that if people have to compete for the basics; shelter, food and room to breathe, they will be short tempered. Stealing and violence became an avenue to get what they want. Move those same people into an area where they are not forced to live up each other's butts and they will conform to the expected behavior of society. People were certainly packed together here in the Three-Two.

Angel with a Gun

Michael liked people. He resolved to make the best of it and always remember that all people are basically the same. They all can hurt, laugh, cry and should be treated with respect whenever possible. He remembered the day he met Betty. He had stopped to help that old lady. It took only minutes from his life and he had been rewarded more than a thousand fold. The Roll Call sergeant continued with statistics on crime in the precinct and issued summons books along with maps of the command. Included with the material were the foot post roster and a listing of corruption prone locations.

"Due to the violent and corrupt nature of the command, take note that the Three-Two is authorized to go out of Borough to secure a decent meal." The sergeant put particular emphasis on what he said next. "Officers leaving the command and crossing into the Bronx --out of Borough-- to get their meals had better notify the radio dispatcher and obtain an okay. Otherwise you could be listed as absent from your patrol area."

Ten minutes before mid-tour, the men received locker assignments. Then the sergeant made an announcement. "You new men are to take your meal hour in the station house for your first day and spend the remainder of the tour setting up your lockers."

Mike obtained a sandwich from the little shop next door. One of his favorites, a hero made of Genoa salami, capagolla (red peppered Italian ham) ham, and provolone cheese, to Mike's surprise he found it to be excellent. The lettuce was crisp, the onion tangy and the tomato tasted like . . .
...tomato. He ate quickly and happily spent the remaining time arranging his locker. That required making several trips to his car and back. Always there were the watchers. Silent, dark-faced people with, what seemed to him, hard, cruel eyes.

Standing at the big picture window in his home on Long Island, the huge, round-faced man felt the hot surge of his rising anger. He allowed it to surface as he rounded on the much slighter built, younger man who stood four paces behind him.

"Not again. I cannot go through all this again. Goddamnit, do you know how many markers I had to call in to cover your ass the last time?"

"But, I. . ." The gray-green eyes looked weak behind the large lenses.

"But nothing, damn you. You have to control yourself. This is it, final. If you can't keep that thing in your pants, perhaps I could arrange to have it cut off for you. I'm telling you straight now. There will be no more of these 'incidents.' I'm through covering for you. I don't want you to crawl in here ever again to whine about protection. If you do, I'll turn my back on you, you'll be history."

"But, Mister Baldu---."

Fury mounting, the larger man growled his outrage. "I don't give a shit about the people you work for. They're not my concern. I'm telling you; get a grip on yourself and don't let it happen again. Now get out of here, you make me fuckin' sick."

On the following day, his first on patrol, Michael Romano received an assignment to a radio car. The vehicle was painted with the old colors; black, green and white.

Mounted on the roof was a siren, (mechanical), shaped like a bullet, and a single rotating red light. Along with the radio car came a training officer, a black man with eight years on the Job, named Leonard Jones. He stood about 5'-8" tall. Jones was thin, maybe 140 pounds and appeared wiry. He wore his hair short and a neatly trimmed mustache under his nose. His gun belt and leather gear looked as if he had just polished it. His uniform shirt had been tapered and had military type creases. Jones stood ram-rod straight.

41

Mike gaped. *Holy shit, look at him, he's so neat. He should be on a poster.* With it came a new worry. How could he make an impression and show this guy that he wanted to be a serious cop? Then an idea occurred. Be friendly. That should do it.

"Hi, pleased to meet you," stated Michael as he nervously thrust his right hand forward, a rigid smile plastered on his face.

His training officer took his hand and smiled. "The pleasure is all mine, Mike. This is a first for me, too. I've never trained someone before. I'm looking forward to it."

Throughout their partnership, Leonard, or Len -- to him the name sounded stronger than either his given name or the more familiar Lenny -- remained the same meticulous man that Mike met that first day. He never wore a uniform twice. His clothing was always cleaned and pressed before he put it on. Len did everything by the book. In later years, Michael would credit his success to the early training he received from Len.

Shortly after 0800 hours (8 A.M.) the following morning Mike began his first tour of duty. As the new team walked down the front steps, Len said, "Mike I'll drive the first part of the tour. We're Sector Adam."

So excited at the prospect of "hitting the streets," Michael didn't care if he had to trot alongside the patrol car.

While Len opened the driver's door to RMP (Radio Motor Patrol) number 1489 Mike scanned the block to see if the other cops were watching. He made certain that he stood correctly and looked like a real cop. Pleased that he saw nobody staring at him, Mike then took further note of the car. The auto was a four door, 1968 Ford. The doors and the trunk lid were painted black, the fenders dark green and white. The roof was all white. The car's numbers were on the rear fenders and across the trunk. The doors had a shield much like the one he wore on his chest.

"Hey Mike, get in and relax. You've got a long way

to go," Len shouted over the roof of the car. Mike felt his face flush. "Don't worry so much. You'll do fine, Officer Romano," Len added as Mike tried to hide his embarrassment by almost launching himself into the seat.

When the engine started, so did the butterflies in Michael's stomach. *It's finally happening; this is it.* Len began to drive and showed Mike the precinct boundaries. Mike acted as the recorder (the passenger side).

Len's gentle litany began, "The recorder is responsible to do all the writing and usually handles the jobs for the team during his half of the tour. He is the spokesman and does all the talking initially when meeting a complainant. The driver is called the operator and acts as the back-up man. At mid-tour, usually after the meal break, the roles are reversed."

During the first few hours the team handled few calls for police service. Mike wrote his first summons, a red light. Romano attempted to relieve the monotony by absorbing his surroundings. He now understood what the orientation sergeant meant when he said that the buildings and houses were once good homes. He could see the fancy scroll work above the windows on some of the row houses. They even had front yards. The open entrances to some of the apartment houses allowed some of their past grandeur to peek out from under years of dirt and grime.

"All units in the 6th Division are to be alerted to look for a Sears truck stolen at gun point within the confines of the 34th Precinct. New York registration; 715889. The description of the perpetrators is as follows." The voice of the radio dispatcher prodded Mike to fresh alertness.

Mike snapped out of the boredom he had begun to experience. He spoke his thoughts to his partner. "There had to be more to this then sick calls and parking conditions. We're assigned a real job, real police work now. Let's find that stolen truck."

Angel with a Gun

"Whoa, now," Len advised, one long finger pointed to the radio speaker. "We gotta find out more first."

The voice from the radio continued, "The perpetrators, two male blacks. Number one is wearing a red, waist length jacket and black pants. Number two, is wearing a blue jacket and black pants. Both men are about 25 years old and are armed with handguns. Units are advised to use caution. The truck was last seen heading toward the vicinity of the Three-Two thirty minutes in the past."

Len spoke as he gently took Mike's hand as the rookie reached for the handset. "Listen Mike, it would be unusual for any RMP to locate the missing truck. It's over a half hour old and if the vehicle is not found or spotted within minutes, it's usually hidden away, especially during daylight hours."

Romano smiled to hide his mild embarrassment, "Got it Len, its 1100 hrs. I made an entry."

"Good boy."

Two minutes later, as Len rounded the corner of 5th Avenue and West 129th Street, there at the curb, about 20 feet off the corner on the north side of the street, sat a Sear's truck.

"Holy shit, I don't believe it," sprang from the surprised Len. "This would be too good to be true." Then he studied the registration number.

"Mike, read me that number they gave."

Mike checked his notes. "New York, 715889."

"Bingo! Mike, tell Central that we located the missing truck."

The novice cop maintained his decorum and calmly as he could notify the radio dispatcher. From the neighboring command, the patrol car that had the complainant (the truck driver/victim) aboard, answered. "Three-two, Unit 1489. Be advised that we are on the way."

Mike keyed the microphone. "Ten-four." He'd done it! He had actually used the Ten-Code, the police radio shorthand that conveyed a lot with a little. Man, this was really for real.

44

When the RMP bearing the truck's driver arrived, Len and Michael got out of their car and approached the other team. Len took the lead.

"It's unusual that we found this thing after so long a time. Let's open it so he," indicating the driver, "can tell us what's missing," Len said.

While Len talked with the other cops, Mike did what he thought to be appropriate; he looked into the apparently abandoned store front right next to the truck. It seemed vacant and closed. The black, expandable steel gate in front of it gave sign of good maintenance. The windows had been almost completely blocked with what looked like white glass cleaner.

It had rained the night before and the rookie noticed a puddle in a low spot right in front of the door. Exiting the puddle were several wet footprints. It appeared that a person or persons went through the puddle and entered and exited the storefront. There were numerous prints. Someone had been very busy. In addition, the gate across the front did not have a lock.

Reluctant tell his partner about his observations for fear of being ridiculed, Mike hesitated. What was he out here for if he didn't tell Len and possibly recover the guy's goods? He made a decision.

"Hey, Lenny," stated the exuberant rookie, "I don't want you to think that I'm nuts or anything, but look into this store. It's loaded with large cartons. You can see where the guys went in and out of the place. See what I mean?"

Len crossed over to his partner. "Mike, don't get excited. You must be watching too much television. Things like that just don't happen in real life. Why would they put the stolen goods so close to the truck where anyone could find them? Oh, and call me Len. Okay?"

"Sure, but Len, look at the puddle in the doorway. It has foot prints leading into the store. Let's go in. The gate isn't locked."

Angel with a Gun

Len gently offered sage advice. "Look Mike, you can't just walk into someone's private property like that. You need a search warrant, and to get that there has to be probable cause. As for the foot prints in the puddle, it can't be from the guys that took the truck. It's too long in the past."

Romano had grown impatient with his mentor. "But maybe they just got here."

The rear loading door of the truck was rolled up by now and revealed an empty cargo body. The cops all exchanged theories as to what happened after the driver was ripped off. Only the driver himself paid any attention to Mike's words.

Mike averted his partner's glance. He was embarrassed by the gentle scolding. His embarrassment was short lived.

With a sudden move, the truck driver stepped to the building and looked in through the abandoned shop windows. There he saw what he recognized to be the cartons he had loaded that morning. "Hey, this cop here is right. My merchandise is sure as hell in the store." After entering the store and making sure the cartons contained Sears merchandise the group returned to the sidewalk.

Now Len went along with the program. To allow his partner to save face, he asked, "Mike, do you think that maybe this panel truck behind us is loaded too?"

Mike studied the vehicle a moment. "I don't know Len, but maybe my luck is still holding. Let's look."

Behind the Sears truck sat an old, dark green panel truck. It too looked abandoned. It bore a thick coat of dust and road dirt, and it had no windows except in the passenger seat area. Oil and fluid stains marked the pavement under the engine compartment.

The driver heard Mike's remark and added, "Maybe it is, there's still stuff missing."

Mike found the rear of the truck locked. Len called the

Joe DeCicco

license plate of the vehicle in to the radio dispatcher. Mike was elated. He forgot himself for a second and slapped Len on the back. "All right," he said.

The dispatcher returned that the truck was stolen. Now they tried the doors. Finding the curb-side passenger door unlocked, Len leaned in. A moment later, he uttered a low, impressed whistle.

"Well Mike, I guess you recovered all or most of the property. This truck's loaded."

Len squeezed into the truck's rear and opened the doors so they all could look inside. The driver still had his bill of lading. Tallying up the merchandise found in the green truck and the store revealed that all but two items had been recovered. Both were televisions sets. Big screen ones, worth around $800 each.

Len turned to Mike. "Call for the patrol sergeant to respond to our location."

Mike keyed the radio and spoke briefly. Static squawked back at him, then the calm, flat voice of the dispatcher. Mike acknowledged and turned back from the car. "He says ten minutes."

"Good. We've got us one hellacious score here, partner."

Once the sergeant arrived, he realized there was going to be reams of paper work to complete this job. He called for two footmen to handle it.

Pleased with himself, Mike could not resist teasing his partner, "Well Len, it looks like the teacher can learn from the student."

Len produced a mock scowl and replied, "You just got lucky." Then a smile of approval burst on his face. Mike beamed back at him. Their relationship was cemented right at that moment.

In the weeks that followed the two men continued to work well together. One day some three weeks after the Sears truck incident, Len said to Mike, "You know Mike, it's good that you're the way you are, all vibrant and full of enthusiasm. I've grown complacent over time and you've brought me up. I'll keep you out of trouble and you can fire me up a little. We're gonna make a good team."

Mike basked warmly in the compliment. It fit exactly with what he had hoped for when he became a cop. He found the work exciting and constantly different. He had been bored working in an office. Sitting at a drawing board for eight hours a day made his back ache and brain fuzzy with boredom. As a new police officer, he found himself on a natural high. He spirits always soared.

All too soon, something would change that. An ominous relic of the past would begin to obsess Mike to the point of endangering his career.

CHAPTER FOUR

One month had passed since Mike first walked into the Three-Two station house. After a bright Saturday, the Romanos sat down to a late dinner. The children had been put down for the night in their room.

Betty had managed to happily make Mike's favorite meal, in between a phone call from her mother, a visit by the young housewife next door, and caring for kids that day. They would dine on calamari (squid) in spicy tomato sauce served on linguini. The squid had been brought fresh earlier in the day. Mike knew that it took hours to do properly. His mother had prepared the dish as a weekend ritual through all the years he lived at home. He appreciated Betty's effort to emulate the older woman. Mike spoke excitedly as he helped himself to seconds.

"Listen Bet," using her sometimes pet name. "Did I tell you about the drunk that always sits in the roll call room under the mail boxes?"

Betty sighed and covertly rolled her eyes. "Yes, you did Mike. Is that the guy that the men put a DOA tag on almost every day?"

"Yeah, a UF-95 it's called. That's the number of the form. Years ago it was a DOA tag; Dead on Arrival. Sometimes it was called a toe tag."

Somehow, that irritated Betty. Perhaps it was the result of her busy day. "Well, what's so interesting about the men teasing a drunk? It's disgusting," she protested, making a face.

He had her now. Wiping his mouth and swallowing a mammoth piece of calamari, he attempted to continue. It was extra spicy, that piece. His eyes watered. He chewed and coughed spastically. After regaining his breath he continued, "Listen, every time we have roll call and the old guy's there, the sergeants go right ahead and do their thing. The old guy just sleeps away. Well, yesterday, sure as shooting, he was there on a day tour and had a 95 tag on his coat. Nobody bothered him. The four-to-twelve tour saw him, and the midnight tour. When we got there for our day tour, one of the bosses went over to shake him awake. Do you know what happened?"

Betty sighed audibly. "No, Mike tell me."

Almost spitting out calamari, he tucked a piece back into the corner of his mouth using the back of his right hand and said, "The guy fell over dead. He spent three tours in the chair and nobody bothered to check him".

"That's terrible, Mike. Maybe he could have been saved if you guys paid attention to him."

"Betty, I only just returned from a swing when we found out he was dead. It's not my fault. There's over one hundred fifty cops there. I'm happy that I'm not the desk Sergeant on duty. The shits gotta hit the fan on that one."

She failed to see the humor in someone dying. "I guess you had to be there," she responded tartly.

Mike produced a pained expression. "You wound me, Betty."

Betty looked across the kitchen table and decided that she should make amends.

"Honey, I've noticed that you walk a little taller, stand a little straighter since you joined the force."

Mike acted embarrassed. He took her comment as criticism. Mike remembered her previous comment about the dead drunk. She had destroyed his mood. He became defensive.

"Are you telling me that I've changed Betty? That I've become another macho cop. It's just because Len stands so straight and if I do it too, we look professional together. Like a team. It's all psychology. If we look like no nonsense guys, then we get respect and usually nobody will give us a hard time." Again he asked, "Are you telling me that I've become one of those macho cops?" He felt insulted.

By now he had put down his fork. He continued, "Oh yeah, I felt bad about the old guy dying. It should have never have happened, but I wasn't there. The joke's on the cops for not realizing that he was dead, not him".

Betty tried to gain back some lost ground. "Listen Mikey, I didn't mean anything bad by that comment. I'm proud of you. Yes, you're different but it's a good difference," she assured her husband.

Indeed Betty Romano was proud of her husband. He had made several good arrests in his short time at the Three-Two. She had begun laying out his uniforms, neatly folded on the first day of each set of tours. Mike brought the soiled uniforms home when he swung out ---his days off after his five day work week. Betty sent the pants to the cleaner and did his shirts herself.

It made her feel more. . .wifely. Her secret voice whispered in her ear that she had the way to make amends. It worked, too. All through the long, mild night.

Things often happened in an odd way, Mike Romano soon found out. Mike had been in the Three-Two for about six weeks when he officially became a Harlem Cop. He had completed a day tour – eight - to - f our -- and entered his yellow, 1972, Dodge Colt station wagon. He gave a friendly wave to three other cops.

"See ya," he called out the window.

"Take care, Mike," one burly, bullet-headed cop threw back.

Funny, Mike mused. A lot of the old-timers believed that their greatest danger came in their off duty hours. Would he ever see it that way? He began the drive home by going east from the Station House on West 135th Street, made a half right as he crossed Fifth Avenue and a quick right onto Park Avenue. Another quick left put his vermilion auto at the entrance of the Harlem River Drive. Then, on to the Drive, and over the Triboro Bridge to Queens. He took the same route every day.

The afternoon seemed quite warm for the time of year, it being October 31st. Already, gaggles of children could be seen on the streets in Halloween costumes. Mike had the window on the driver's side open to enjoy the air. He had entered the curved entrance to the highway when he noticed two youths, about 16 years old, leaning on the railing. Behind them several younger kids played baseball on the gnarled lawn of a Department of Health building. Their shrill voices floated to his ears.

As he piloted into the traffic lane, Mike glanced over to his right to see one of the youths turn toward his on-coming car, reach over the railing and point in his direction. He saw something metallic glint in the punk's hand. Instinctively, he ducked. **Bang---Crack!** That sound had gotten his attention. Obviously the youth had been pointing a gun in his direction because now, staring him in the face, he saw a hole high up in the center of the car's windshield. The round went right out the open driver's window. Mike's instincts had kept him out of harm's way.

Romano automatically slid down in his seat. His heart drummed in his ears. *Damn it's loud,* he thought for a giddy second. Mike kicked open the passenger's door, gun in hand. Over the gun sights, Mike could see the two youths running away. *Slowly squeeze, don't jerk the weapon,* he remembered. He could also see the kids playing ball and did not follow his instincts. His thoughts became a mixed stew. Don't want to hurt the kids. Yet, Mike yearned to fire at the fleeing teenagers. *Mustn't, though, kids in the way,* he admonished himself.

But he sure wanted to blow that pair out of their shorts. They quickly disappeared over the crest of the knoll on which the youngsters played. "Damn!" Mike spat aloud.

Putting his weapon away, he drove off the next entrance

52

ramp against traffic and blaring horns to get to the Health building. Once inside the building, Mike phoned the 911 operator.

"Nine-one-one, what is your emergency?"

"Get me an RMP. I'm on the Job. I want to report a shooting incident."

"One moment, please. Do not hang up."

Mike rushed on, not wanting to be put on hold. "This is Patrolman Romano. I want to report shots fired. I was the target." He went on to report the incident as he saw it and concluded with descriptions of the youths. "Two assailants, black males, age approximately sixteen. Number One, the shooter: five-eleven, 150 pounds, wearing a blue windbreaker and faded denims. Number two: six-three, about 190, wearing a blue polka dot bandanna on his head, an OD army jacket, T-shirt, and jeans."

The receiver of the handset rattled in Mike's ear. "No, I'm not hurt. The shooting is over, but I do need a patrol car." He knew that shots fired at a police officer would bring an instant, urgent response. All responding officers would assume that the officer had been either shot or about to be.

In the time it took Mike to walk back outside at least six radio car teams arrived, lights flashing, sirens wailing. They mounted the sparse lawn, their tires spewing dirt. Yelling, the ballplayers scattered in every direction.

Once the respondents confirmed that he was unharmed and in control, the RMP teams began to drive off and return with suspects that fit the descriptions given by the radio dispatcher. One of their own had been shot at. It could have been any one of them. The "family's" safety had been jeopardized. The men in blue would find the guy quickly.

Mike formed images of old TV shows and movies he had seen, Round up the usual suspects men. Over the next half hour, his brothers in blue brought several dozen "suspects" to the scene to be viewed. No luck.

While this went on, Mike's sergeant, Louie Armini, a man who liked to ease the pressure of the job with a joke whenever possible, arrived. "Are you okay Mike?" asked the boss. Quickly taking note that his officer was fine, in an attempt to lighten the moment he added, "Did you get hit in the head? I don't see any injuries."

Mike smiled as he answered, "Sure, but look at my car window. Why would anybody just shoot at me like that?"

"Because you're here. Welcome to the Three-Two Mike. You're a real cop now and an official member of this command." The boss slapped him on the back and turned to leave.

"Thanks Sarge," Mike replied as the potential of the incident began to sink in. He hoped that they could not see his legs quivering as though they could no longer support him. Damn, his heart still roared in his ears. He continued, "You mean that here in the Three-Two people just shoot at other people for no reason?"

Sergeant Armini gave Mike a rueful expression. "Look Mike, things like that happen here all the time. You're driving a yellow car. Those little shits could see you coming blocks away. You did good. You're still here to complain about it. Come on back to command, there's reports to fill out."

Mike scrunched his face and groaned. "Oh, fine, paperwork. Which will thrill my wife when I'm late for supper."

On the ride back to the station, Romano's mind whirled. *Some archangel! Get a grip Mike.* His knees hadn't stopped shaking. He couldn't help little four year old kids if he lost it. Mike remembered the rooftop incident. It stayed always on his mind.

He remembered the outrage that he felt when he learned what had actually happened.

Romano felt a hole in his chest as remembered that Betty, too, was a victim of rape as a child. His blood pressure rose at the thought. He hadda go home and not worry Betty. He had two children now. The little girl's rooftop rape was the catalyst that changed his career and his life. Donald had probably been conceived that night. He smiled at the thought of their lovemaking that fateful August night. Glancing up at the bullet hole in his windshield had no effect now. The memory of their passionate tryst, combined with his determination to always do his best, stopped his knees from shaking. At least for now.

It took about one hour after returning to the station for Mike to do the appropriate paperwork concerning his incident. Officially interviewed by his sergeant and the responding duty captain, he felt drained when it was over. Sergeant Armini came to him then with his statement to be signed and assured his subordinate that everything that could be done to investigate the incident would be done.

"You shouldn't worry, Mike. I will personally assist in the investigation. After all you're one of my men. . .one of the best at that."

After he left the station house, as he began to enter the highway again, Mike relived the recent incident. He began to shake inside. During the ride home his eyes constantly fell on the hole in his windshield and his mind heard the gunshot with every glance. When he arrived home, upon entering his apartment Michael found Betty sitting on the living room floor with Anne playing with dolls.

"Hi Daddy," his daughter said as she attempted to hug him around the waist. Her curly brown locks just about reached pants pocket height.

Mike steadied his still shaking knees and bent to kiss his child while he asked, "Where's Donald?"

Betty responded with, "He's asleep in his crib." Feeling something amiss, Betty mimicked her daughter, grabbing him about the waist. "Where's my kiss?"

Angel with a Gun

"I love you too Bet", with that response, he gently broke free. Mike went into the kitchen, opened the fridge and looked for the bottle of Chianti wine that usually waited there.

By the time Betty walked into the kitchen to see why her husband was not acting in character, he had poured his third tumbler. "What's wrong Mikey? You look upset."

Instead of answering, Romano put the glass down on the counter top and pulled his wife to him, giving her a rib-crushing hug. He felt grateful to be alive. Mike knew he had to tell Betty. But how without causing undue alarm?

Fighting the worry lines off his face, he began with, "Betty come inside and sit down. I've got something to tell you about."

His ominous tone instantly made her fear the worst. Whatever that was. She went numb as tears welled in her eyes.

Mike told the story uninterrupted. Betty only stared at him and tugged at her shirt. After hearing the full account, Betty rose, moved slightly toward her husband and as if receiving an electric shock, took a step backwards and stood silent, staring at Michael. She never said a word. After seeing the terror in his wife's eyes, he tried to make light of the incident.

"Come on, Honey. It was a fluke. Maybe it wasn't a gun. Maybe the kids threw a rock. I'm fine. Let's play with the kids."

Betty smiled weakly and followed Mike as he walked Anne into the children's room. Later, when their delayed dinner had been eaten and the children put down for sleep, the couple retired to bed early. Mike took Betty in his arms.

"Come here baby, let me show you that everything's fine; . . .every. . .little. . .thing."

"Not so little," Betty cooed as she melted into him, soft as a cloud.

Good, thought Mike, *everything's back to normal.*

Everything was not back to normal. Beginning the next morning, Betty no longer took care of his uniforms. She quietly "let" him put the shirts into the dry cleaner along with the rest of his costume. So caught up in his job, Mike never noticed the subtle change in the routine.

He did make it a point to get home early the next few days, and on Friday he brought a bottle of Betty's favorite Vin Rose. Her eyes lighted at the sight of it and she quickly took out two of the footed, funnel-shaped crystal glasses they had received as a wedding present. She poured the chilled wine for them both and took a sip. Her face instantly crunched up and she squinted her eyes.

"It tastes sour."

"Why's that, Bet?"

"I don't know. . .it just does."

Mike lifted the bottle and examined the label. "Look. It says right here. 'A soft, medium-dry, red wine.' It's sure not Chianti."

Betty looked miserable. "I don't know, Mikey. It's just. . .that things don't taste right since---you nearly got killed."

Mike put his big hands on her shoulders and held her at arm's length. "Baby, listen to me. I didn't nearly get killed. Most likely, that dork didn't know it was loaded. Loosen up, Honey. I can live with it; you'll just have to, too."

Mike continued to make light of the incident whenever possible. It took seven weeks before he finally convinced Betty that the shooting on the Harlem River Drive was a fluke. He made his most impassioned pitch during the evening of the Saturday before Christmas, December 22.

"Honey, please believe me. The guys at the Three-two have gone over this like one of those things through wool." Mike pointed to a carding brush that hung on one wall. Betty had found in an antique shop on West 59th. "That shooting simply was not connected to me. They went through all my past arrests, checked out every punk and perp I collared. My boss personally double-checked their work. Nobody, not one single shithead that I have arrested, is near the age of the boys who shot at me.

"They were probably making a gun sale and I drove a bright yellow station wagon. That must have attracted the eye of the buyer. So he took aim and squeezed off. Like I told you before," Mike went on with forced sincerity, "He was probably too stupid to know if the gun was loaded, or even how to check to see."

Then he added for assurance, "The best that the guys on the Job can tell, nobody is after me and it will probably never happen again."

Finally, the incident closed in the Romano household one afternoon shortly before Mike went in for a 4-to-12 tour. He brought up the subject and once again told Betty, "The customer probably wanted to see if the gun worked and I conveniently provided a target."

After his comment, her response made him think. "I didn't want you to go to work after the shooting in your car. It was silly now that I think of it.

My reasoning was if you don't have clean uniforms, you won't go to work. You can't get hurt and I'll keep my husband."

"Come here you silly woman. You and the kids are never gonna lose me. No way." Betty moaned; her knees turning to rubber in his embrace.

That quickly, the rift healed, things returned to normal and Mike arrived late for work that day.

Slowly with the passage of time, Betty again began taking care of her husband's work clothes.

CHAPTER FIVE

Work continued for Michael along what was considered normal for the Three-Two. Winter blew in, cold and damp. Dirty snow piled shoulder high along the streets. By mid-December it had grown to twice the height of a man. The Command had the usual shootings, robberies, burglaries and the almost weekly homicides. They took reports on each one and turned the felony cases over to the Detective Squad on the second floor of the station house. Mike reflected on it and decided that he had become comfortable with being a Police Officer. About once every two weeks Mike would visit his resident station house and look up his friends; John Cutbert, in particular. Their bond had grown stronger since Mike joined the force. Sometimes those meetings would be in The Abbey.

From the outside, The Abbey looked like any other neighborhood gin mill. It had no window in the door. To the right of the entrance was the obligatory minimum sized window required by the State Liquor Authority. Painted dark green and white, the exterior had become grime-encrusted, the pigment faded and chipped. The interior, however, was another matter.

Lining the walls were photographs of past and present policemen. Interposed among the photos were reproductions of the shields worn by fallen members of the department. Not every officer that had passed on was represented, only those who ever took at least one drink in the place. The phone behind the bar was an old police call box. Stenciled in black on the door was; "110 Pct. EMERGENCY CALL BOX."

The bar itself was reputed to be one of those high, throne-like desks from an old police station, cut down to size.

Jim Behan, the owner, himself a former cop, claimed he didn't know where it came from. On either side of the cash register were green globes similar to those so familiar to Mike from the Three-Two.

The pull handles for the tap beer spigots had been made of night sticks.

Over each urinal in the men's room was what looked like a camera lens and a plastic sign; "Get a grip on yourself, I.A.D. is watching." Because I.A.D., the Internal Affairs Division, was the unit that policed the police, the Internal Affairs Division, practically every cop in every police department in the world despised Internal Affairs officers. They were looked upon as rats, "cheese eaters" who were either ass-kissing political climbers within the department, or turncoats, men and women who got caught at transgressions and became spies to get off. Glued to the walls of the stalls were lengths of black rubber hose. Over each one was written; "If it's tough going, use freely to beat the shit out of yourself."

Back out in the bar itself, three old wooden booths stretched along one wall and on the far side of the ever present pool table rested several small round tables. The walls had been done in municipal green, made tolerable by the neon beer signs scattered around the place. It was there in that silly, almost surrealistic atmosphere, that Mike Romano, the would-be archangel, learned more about the child rapist he had visions of someday capturing.

It happened at 0100 , on an achingly cold January night, after a four-to-twelve tour; his last one of the set. Mike was swinging out and decided to visit The Abbey in the hopes of finding a friendly ear to swap stories with. He was more than pleased to see John Cutbert smothering a bar stool when he walked in.

"Jim, let me have a scotch and water will you and give my little brother whatever he's having," Mike shouted while he pointed at his large friend.

"Michael my boy." Cutbert greeted warmly. "Please have a seat my young friend. There's something you would be interested in hearing." John was only ten years older than Michael, yet he always referred to him as "his young friend." He was also feeling no pain; Cutbert had been there since midnight.

"Hi, John. Let me catch up to you before we talk about anything serious, will you?" teased Mike.

"No Michael, you should hear this sober. After that you'll damn well have ample reason to drink".

Not convinced the sergeant had serious news, Mike put on a jovial mean. "What is it John? Did one of the poster girls in your office get apprehended? I hope so. Which one?"

After taking a healthy swallow from the fresh drink placed before him, John replied, "We know the name of the guy that raped the little girl last year around the corner from hour apartment. You remember? The incident that upset you so much. We think we know the name of his hook in the Job, too".

Mike's heart started to race. His pulse quickened in anger. Swiftly regaining his composure, he turned and called out. "Jim, give us two more," as he drew his bar stool closer to John.

The sergeant continued, "See one of the guys over in Queens Sex Crimes got drunk at a racket last week" – you know that party that I went to last week. "He shot his mouth off and gave it up." John looked around for imagined eaves droppers and continued, "The guy's related to a Deputy Inspector in One Police Plaza. You know, the Ivory Tower, the Puzzle Palace. His name's Bryan, B-R-Y-A-N."

"Is that his first name? Or is that the rapist's name?" came Mike's excited reply.

"Yes and no. You see, Bryan is the big boss' last name and the first name of the guy. The guy's last name is Wilkey, Brian with an 'i,' and Bryan's first name is Dennis. So the rapist is Brian Wilkey and the "hook" is Dennis Bryan, with a 'y'," came the slurred answer. John had begun to feel no pain.

"How did they find out the bastard's name?"

John took another drink, visibly embarrassed by his garbled answers. "I don't know, Mike."

"There's got to be something more to this John. Why would an Inspector risk his career to protect a dirt bag like this Wilkey guy?"

"The guy's supposed to be connected", was the reply, indicating to a cop "in the know" that Wilkey was involved with the Mob. "The little girl's father is a reported heavy gambler and owes 'the boys' a shitpot full of money."

"Then this boss, this Bryan, must be involved also. Right?"

John waved to the bartender for another round and continued. "That's one possibility my little friend. Don't go getting too nosey. You could get hurt." Then he offered sobering advice. "You have a long career ahead of you Mike. Don't blow it." After finishing his sentence, John gazed with what appeared to be guilty eyes down toward the bartop.

"Damn it John, there's more isn't there?" asked Mike.

Without raising his eyes, John answered his friend. "Yes Michael, there is. Some of the boys at sex crimes think that the little girl was raped because her father owed so much money and wasn't paying up."

Bile rose in Mike's throat. He banged his fist down on the bar causing John to jump. "Damn, which one of those two is the bigger piece of shit? Huh, John? Which one? I swear John, someday I'm gonna get both of those bastards. Now I have a reason to drink. Jim let's have two more."

Cutbert put one of his ponderous arms across Mike's shoulders and said, "Don't go getting too nosy. It's not just your career. If Wilkey is connected, you could get wasted. Keep it cool, man. Real cool."

Mike knew about being connected. He had watched as

guys he knew at Bishop O'Fallon High School dropped out to hang on the street corners doing favors for the numbers sellers, running errands for the Wise Guys, eventually becoming a soldier in one crew or another. Some of them even went on to become button men, or Bono Umo -- Good Fellahs -- as they were called in Italian. A few of them also got whacked out. "To live by the knife and the gun and to die by the knife and the gun." For some, it wasn't just an oath they took. Yeah, Mike Romano, descendant of generations of Italians, knew connected.

Sighing, he responded with, "Yeah, sure John, you're right." But he could not stop visualizing beating Brian Wilkey into hamburger meat. The two friends said good night several minutes later. Mike spent his entire two days off without saying anything to Betty about the new information.

January faded into February, then March. April came and before he knew it, Mike was looking at May.

Another swing ended and Mike returned to work on Sunday, May 12, 1974, to find that his partner had taken the day off. That disappointed Mike. He had become very uptight and wanted to discuss this problem this new information proposed with Len. Like it or not, John had been right. This could be extremely dangerous to him.

Romano was assigned to work with one of the more colorful men of the command, Gregory McAllery, or Mac as he preferred to be called. The events of the day were about to take Mike's mind off the rapist. Greg, like Len, had about eight years on the Job and was three years younger than Mike.

Equal in height, he was slightly paunchy, with a round face and medium brown straight hair. He always wore a smile.

The young centurion would soon find out that the stories he heard about McAllery were true. He would be able to understand why his partner for the day was affectionately called "Wacko Macko". It was said that Wacko walked to the tune of a different drummer. By the end of the tour, Mike was convinced that not only did Macko walk to the tune of a different drummer; he marched to a whole different band!

Their team was assigned to work Sector Eddie. Mike hoped that during this tour something would happen to inspire Greg's marching band to begin its cadence. Mac checked out the RMP, while Mike retrieved the rectangular, aluminum clipboard. He would be recorder for the first half of the shift.

"I hope you have a neat hand," Mac observed as they entered their car. "I've got a six-year-old who writes more legibly than a lot of these guys."

Mike laughed. This was his first taste of Macko's off-the-wall style. "Don't worry. I got straight A's in penmanship at Queen of Angels grade school."

Mac threw up his hands. "Spare me from mackerel snappers!" Then he went on to explain. "I'm not descended from Stuart Scots. Presbyterian tried and true."

An hour into the tour they sat in their patrol car off St. Nicholas Avenue and West 136th Street munching on coffee and doughnuts. As Macko downed his second powdered sugar-coated, cherry jelly doughnut, he turned to Mike and commented, "Just like real cop's Mike. Isn't this what cops do best?"

Michael verbally relived the night of the child rape and the fact that the ugly incident inspired him to become a police officer. He was prone to do this when he found a good listener. The radio dispatcher interrupted their snack.

"In the Three-Two, at 142nd Street and Lenox Avenue there's a naked man walking on the divider. He seems to have a leash around his neck and is being led by another male. Sector needed to respond." Macko grabbed the handset and stated, "Three-Two Eddie to respond, Central, K." Then to Romano, "Mike hold on, and cap the coffees."

Macko drove to the location given, lights flashing and siren wailing. It took all of about ninety seconds. Sure as hell, there was a naked man standing on the concrete road divider. He looked bewildered and hurting.

On the man's body, from head to toe, Mike could see small cuts and bruises. The man looked as though he had been pounded like a cheap piece of meat before it left the butcher's case. Around the guy's neck, tied in a noose, Mike saw what looked like the kind of rope used for clothes lines. However they did not see any person, male or otherwise, leading him around as the dispatcher had stated.

Mike keyed the microphone. "Sector Eddie 10-84, Central." On the scene. "No assistance necessary, K."

"Ten-Four, Eddie. Do you need a bus?" An ambulance.

"Negative, Central, we got it, K," came Mike's reply.

Exiting their car, the stalwart men in blue cautiously walked up to the man, night-sticks ready in their hands. They had no way to know if he was a crime victim or some psycho at that point. Mike eyed the nude figure thoughtfully. The world is full of perverts. *At least this guy isn't a kid,* surmised Mike. Then he looked around in an attempt to spot any lone male paying anxious attention to them. He saw none. Greg by now was in conversation with the naked man.

"What happened to you guy?" Macko asked as he began to pull out his handcuffs.

A bewildered expression on his face, the subject made an appeal to Macko. "Wakeem beat me up and took my clothes. The sucker tried to kill me. We're friends. Why would he do this?"

Macko turned to Mike. "Mike, take the sheet out of the car so we can cover this guy."

It was standard procedure for the men of the Three-Two to carry one or more bed sheets in the car trunk. They came in handy. Harlem Hospital was the sometimes unknowing source of supply.

Angel with a Gun

Once Macko had handcuffed the man and wrapped him in the sheet he was put into the back of the RMP.

As the junior, the curly haired Romano allowed Macko to begin the questioning. "What's your name and what the hell happened?"

Their prisoner, who smelled like an outhouse, screwed up his face as though about to cry. "I'm Joe Black, and Wakeem did this."

"Who the hell is Wakeem? Where does he live?" asked Greg.

"He was my friend, not really, but we know each other from the neighborhood, a long time, you know?"

Mike jumped into the interrogation, "No, we don't know. Now tell us what happened, Joe."

"Well, you see, there was this party last night, not really a party, but we were all hanging out and drinking and stuff, in Wakeem's house."

Mac took it up. "What does he look like?"

"He's about twenty-three and has short hair. He was wearing a fancy flowered shirt when he beat me before… you know, this morning. He's about big as you," pointing to Michael. "He got a bad street rep, man. He's offed three people." Joe meant that Wakeem had a tough street reputation and was credited with having killed three people.

Mike realized that Joe was being a good guy. That was his way of telling Greg and Mike to be careful.

"Where's his apartment?" the dark haired Romano asked.

"Two-five-four West 144th. Street, the second floor front." Black responded without prompting, "We were all partying and some people left about five this morning, but me and another guy stayed. We were friends with Wakeem and his old lady."

Black went on to explain that after the crowd left, Wakeem fell out -- went to sleep-- on the living room floor and

66

his wife on the sofa. He continued, "I couldn't sleep so I looked around the house." In the process, at one point, he stood next to the sofa and looked down at Wakeem's wife while she slept. The party host woke up from his drunken slumber. Through gaping yawns, Joe was accused of looking at Wakeem's wife in the "wrong way".

"I told him that I was doing nothing wrong and he fell back to sleep." The sheet wrapped "tenderized man" continued, explaining that about fifteen minutes later, Wakeem woke up and chased him down the long hallway of the apartment. He was struck from behind, across the back, with a chair. Joe Black also accused his assailant of beating him with a chair leg that came off when the chair broke as he was hit.

"I got knocked out. When I woke up, he held a gun on me. The bitch took all my clothes off me. Then she held the gun and he took the rope and tied me up. He put the rope around my neck and said he was gonna hang my naked ass out the window. He changed his mind and took me into the street and walked me up and down naked."

By the end of his story they stood in the lobby of the station house.

Sitting behind the wrought iron rail was the "precinct receptionist." In the seventies, in each station house, civilian volunteers acted as receptionists. A patrol car picked them up at their residence, and returned them after their "tour of duty." The Three-Two had one particular female receptionist who thought that she was the Commanding Officer. She attempted to make demands of the cops and bosses as well. At times, she even demanded to be driven for her grocery shopping. It was Department Policy to acquiesce to these volunteers. This woman was a real ball breaker. As Mike and Macko walked their charge into the precinct, this receptionist, Ruth, looked up with interest. In her mind these two officers were about to again abuse the poor man they brought in. She had seen the exposed marks on his body.

Angel with a Gun

Ruth squeaked like a soprano who had just been stabbed in some tragic opera, and exclaimed, "You men should be ashamed of yourselves. Beating him like that." Nothing was further from the truth. So, her comment was ignored by all.

The desk officer asked, "What is this man, the naked man run?"

"Yes, sir", Mike answered.

"Search him. Remove that cover," came the order, referring to the sheet that protected the public from seeing Joe's battered, naked body.

"But Lieutenant, there is. . ." Mike began.

"Don't give me any stories, you two know the rules, all persons brought here in handcuffs are to be searched before the desk."

With a flourish worthy of a stage magician, Wacko Macko removed the sheet in one fluid motion. From behind them, came a shriek and the receptionist's chair tumbled. It seemed that Ruth could not take poor Joe Black next to her so she scrambled over her desk. Her rapid move exposed her long legged underpants over hefty thighs. She now stood on the other side of the railing, where she danced around as if her feet were on fire. She tried without dignity to lower her skirt. Mike could see that she was frantic.

Was that a drum roll in the background? Wacko's band beginning its cadence?

Lieutenant Hanrahan stuck his head out of his office. "Romano, take that man into the muster room. And you, Mac, find a pair of old pants to put on the guy." To Ruth he snapped, "Get control of yourself woman. Haven't you seen a naked man before?"

Both men loved it and laughed as they passed her to go out to find Wakeem after taking care of Black. The event cured Ruth. Afterward, Ruth resolved, she would always give wide berth to cops bringing prisoners before the Desk Officer.

Returning to the street, and feeling a bit giddy, Mike and Wacko, drove to the area of West 144th Street looking for the elusive Wakeem. Greg turned east down West 144th off of Eighth Avenue. They proceeded halfway down the block when, there, walking on the left side of the street, Mike saw a male who fit the description given to them, complete with flowered shirt. With the man was a female.

"Hey, Wakeem, come over here a minute," Mike called. The woman stopped in her tracks. The man took several more steps before stopping.

As Wakeem turned and approached them, he looked into the rear of the car, apparently expecting to see Joe Black. "You guys come to arrest me for beating that nigger?"

"Yes," Macko replied.

"Okay, but you gotta arrest him too, because he tried to rob my house and was looking up under my woman's dress as she was sleeping."

Macko got right to the point. "So you tuned him up for that?"

"Yeah, I beat his ass."

The woman identified herself to Mike as Jean Davis. She followed up with her address. She was Wakeem's wife. She did admit to assisting her husband in removing Joe Black's clothes. The team decided that they would only take Wakeem back. If the woman needed to be arrested too, they could always come back for her.

Wakeem's real name turned out to be John Davis. He claimed to be on Welfare. He was probably dealing drugs. The damn shirt had to cost over seventy dollars, Mike surmised.

"Well it's was like this Officers. We had a party last night and Black was over too. There was lots of drinking and stuff. Some people left late, you know in the morning, like today. Black, he stayed to sleep. But he didn't. Instead he looked up under my wife's dress at her stuff, you know, poontang."

69

With a merry twinkle in his eye, Wacko asked, "Did she have panties on?"

"No she never wears them, man. Anyway he looks at her thing, you know, what all women got and I yell, 'Hey nigger, get out of here.' I thought maybe I was dreaming, you know? Then fall asleep again. When I get up again, for real, he's trying to sneak out the door with my stereo. I yelled, jumped up after his ass and took a chair and hit him over the head with it. He tried to go through the door but the stereo was too big. He got stuck there and I hit him good. Muthafucker fell and smashed my stereo. When the chair broke, I took one of the legs and beat him more. Fuck him."

Mike took up the questioning. "How did he get the rope on his neck?"

"When he was down, I asked Jean to take the rope off the clothes dryer. You know the old fashioned kind, over the bathtub. Then she helped me tie him and take off all his clothes. After he was naked, I took him out in the street and walked him like the dog he is. I told everyone that he was a crook and next time Wakeem was gonna kill him."

"He said that you had a gun. Do you? He said that's how you and your wife got his clothes off," prompted Greg. "You held a gun on him. Your wife stripped him. Did you like it? Watching you wife take another man's clothes off."

"Hell no, I ain't got no gun. When I hit him, I knocked the nigger out. First I thought he was dead."

Greg continued to taunt the suspect, "You didn't answer the question. Did you like watching your wife strip another man"?

"What's wrong with you, man? You fucked up, or what?" Wakeem whined an angry reply.

Macko cuffed Davis, AKA Wakeem, and he and Mike put the suspect into the patrol car. Macko softly whistled a weird tune all the way to the station. Mike wondered if it came from the band Wacko Macko performed to.

When the group entered the station, Ruth got up and went off somewhere. Mike chuckled. Once before the desk officer, Michael and Wacko Macko gave the Lieutenant the twenty-five words or less version of what Davis claimed happened. The boss ordered both men charged with the appropriate crimes that applied to them and had them both brought down to Central Booking.

On Joe Black's arrest report Mike wrote: Penal Law 145.05, Criminal Mischief in the third degree, an E Felony, for damaging the stereo, property valued at over $500.00, and PL 140.20, Burglary in the third degree, a D Felony. Mike knew that all degrees of Burglary were felonies. He was able to charge burglary because Black occupied the premises unlawfully by staying in the apartment after Davis told him to leave. He also took property without permission or authority to do so.   Mike also felt that Joe Black committed another unlawful act by peeking under Jean's dress. Mike knew that the courts would never press the charge of Burglary, but it got him "into the system." He thought of Wilkey, the child rapist. Why couldn't he be booking that piece of shit? Someday...

Taking a collar (arrest) Downtown meant several hours "in the system" for the cops. It meant overtime and that put Mike a few dollars closer to the "something more" he was always thinking about. He wanted to keep his promise and get his family a house. Felony arrests got cops Downtown. They were considered serious enough for the Legislature to affix penalties of over one year in jail upon conviction.

For John Davis, Romano wrote: PL 120.05, Assault in the second degree and PL 265.01 Criminal Possession of a weapon in the fourth degree (the chair leg). With the exception of the possession of the chair leg, all the charges lodged against the two men were felonies. In addition to the overtime, Mike knew that he performed a small service to society by charging felonies. Both men would be off the street for at least two days. In Davis' case, if the street stories were true, some street person might remain alive.

After he had put the men in the main holding cell within the bowels of the court building's basement, Mike sat in a large room littered with old wooden desks. At each decrepit desk sat an Assistant District Attorney. Mike's turn finally came up and he was interviewed as to the circumstances of the arrest.

A bored-looking ADA, who looked to be in his mid-twenties and fresh out of law school, glanced up and peered over his wire-rimmed, octagonal glasses at Mike Romano. The nameplate on his desk read: Sampson. "What do we have here, Officer? Criminal Mischief in the Third Degree, and Burglary in the Third on this one," he went on as he scanned the paperwork. "Assault in the second and Criminal Possession, for the other. Couple of desperados you've got there, Officer-- ah--Romano."

Mike responded eagerly, "Yes, sir. Subject Black tried to steal a stereo. Subject Davis slammed him over the head with a chair and then beat hell out of him with a leg that broke off."

Sampson shoved his spectacles up on his nose and forced a smile. "Why don't you go over it, point by point, Romano? Give us some idea why I should waste the judge's time over this."

Mike launched into a detailed narrative, aware that over the next several hours, the charges would be evaluated, properly worded, typed, added to the myriad of necessary forms, correlated and docketed. He then sat in the courtroom designated for arraignments and waited his turn. After waiting for what seemed like days, his name was finally called. The next step called for Mike to retrieve his defendants from the Tombs where they had been sent after the initial processing downstairs.   Prisoners were routinely sent to the City Jail to await arraignment.   It could take days if the system was over-loaded.   Mike brought both men through the tunnel from the old Tombs to the holding pens behind the court room.

The "Tombs" was the common term used to refer to the jail house attached to the Criminal Court Building.   It used to look like a huge grey mausoleum.   It had been constructed of large granite blocks.   For the most part, the building remained a dark chalky grey even though it has been renovated and an addition constructed since the early days.   A new facility was scheduled to be completed and occupied in late 1991.   No doubt it would still be referred to by the more senior cops as "The Tombs."

Mike patiently waited in the court room.   The two cases were finally called, together, because they were companion cases and actually cross complaints.

In the court room, the Assistant District Attorney working arraignments turned out to be a dark-haired female, Jane Farefine.   She had firm ample breasts above a slim waist.   Her hips missed being too wide by a couple of hands.   Looking at the sheath type dress she wore, Mike found her attractive.   He thought her figure resembled a cello.   She was the topic of much discussion among the male police officers.   Jane had what could be referred to as a wholesome sexuality.   Over the years she had risen to a prominent place in the New York County District Attorney's Office.   When asked for a quick rundown of the case, Mike jumped at the chance to speak with her one-on-one.

At last, the judge asked for the reading of charges.

Farefine added that the circumstances of the arrest be recorded for the record.   When the judge heard the story he responded with, "No shit, I couldn't think of a better punishment myself."   The court room broke up.

Then the judge added, "Case against Davis is dismissed."

"Thank you Your Honor," Davis' Legal Aid attorney replied.

Turning to the other Legal Aid lawyer, the judge asked, "Counselor, how does your client plead?"

Black knew that he was in serious trouble with Davis. Deep Shit, as they say on the street. He felt safer in jail right then. He held a muted conversation with his attorney.

"Guilty Your Honor. Does The Court wish to impose sentence now? My client will accept."

With an air of consuming indifference, the judge pronounced, "Six months in Riker's. Next case. Lodge the prisoner."

Mike wasn't sure if Justice had been served in that court room. He kept remembering that Davis was reputedly a miscreant, a piece of shit, a drug dealer. Here he was Michael Romano, sworn Police Officer, protecting the rights of this wart on the ass of Society. An archangel would have slain them both.

CHAPTER SIX

Over the weeks that followed, Mike Romano found himself becoming even more obsessed with thoughts of Brian Wilkey and what he did to little girls. Wilkey was scuzz. A dirt bag that did not deserve to live. Time and again, Mike swore he would bring an end to the career of the disgusting pervert. His compulsion spilled over onto Betty.

One night they sat at the kitchen table, over plates of scampi, it being a Friday. Mike had just wound a forkful of fettuccini and lifted it to his mouth. Chewing thought-fully, he had a sudden flashback of the night last August when Wilkey had paid a visit close at hand. He swallowed and reached across the linen cover to put a hand on Betty's forearm.

"Betty, I want you to promise me one thing. Be careful. Keep on watch at all times. Don't ever get separated from the kids when you are out."

Betty studied him a moment. "It's about that man, isn't it? The pervert? What's his name?"

"Wilkey. Brian Wilkey. And, I'm going to get him. Fix him good."

Betty paled. She recalled what had been said about a threat to Mike's career. "Do you remember what you told me about the possible danger to your future with the Department? I want a life for us, a future for me and the children. For God's sake, Mike, enough is enough." Donald began to make a fuss and began to wail loudly. Betty came to her feet and started for the living room. "Donny needs changing. It's your turn," she fired at Mike over one shoulder. Potty training was under way, but there were always little accidents, for which the boy remained in diapers.

Mike joined her and retrieved a fresh diaper from the ever-present bag. Then he bent over the couch. He went about the task of re-diapering his son. It did not stop their argument.

"Don't you see? It's because I do want the best for all of you. If I nail this bastard, it'll probably mean a promotion. That's another reason why I want to fix his clock for good and sure."

Quickly, Betty digested this. A look of horror washed over her face when she thought of one aspect that apparently Mike had not. "You said Wilkey was connected to the Mob. What if he finds out who you are and that you are after him? What if he comes after us? Think of Anne. Do you want her to have the same experience as that little girl and me?"

Mike almost dropped Donald. Hadn't she been listening at all? "But, you don't understand." Shakily, he sat down, put his son on his lap.

"Yes I do. I've heard you tell Lenny that you want to be like Saint Michael. You want to right the injustices in the world. You're even willing to do it alone if necessary. But, I'm begging you. Let it go."

Mike felt the heat rising in his head. "Listen, Betty, you just don't understand how a man feels about his daughter. About little girls getting hurt. Especially if he's a cop, a good cop." His voice had risen, which startled Anne and caused Donald to begin a wriggling attempt to escape his father's lap.

"Give me the baby before he cries again. If you can't lower your voice, go see your cop friends in the Abbey." Sneering, she added, "Maybe there's another one like Lenny. Maybe someone else will tell you to stop this terrible meddling, too. Maybe somebody can get into that thick skull of yours. I can't." With Donald in her arms, she stormed to the children's room at the back of the apartment, followed by a sniffling Anne.

A stricken Mike stood alone on the worn carpet. Sure, he had gotten hot under the collar, and upset at what he thought to be Betty's lack of understanding, but he didn't like to argue with her. He felt aching guilty. Grudgingly, Mike wondered if he was doing the right thing, as he dialed John Cutbert's home number.

Joe DeCicco

John picked up on the second ring and Mike tried to sound cheery. "Hey, John, what are you doing? Feel like meeting me for a couple of drinks?. . .Sure, in about thirty minutes, the Abbey."

He tip-toed down the hall and called softly to his wife. "Betty, I'm meeting Sergeant Cutbert for a couple of drinks. Be home early." He received no response and winced.

Before leaving the house, Mike entered the children's room and gently kissed both of the youngsters. As he walked past his spouse, Betty automatically held up her face to him. Then, remembering her anger, she turned her head, allowing only her cheek to meet his lips.

Mike stifled a groan. "Don't be angry, Honey. I know what I'm doing," he offered apologetically. He sensed her anger and her hot glance, even though he never turned to look back. He quickly and quietly closed the apartment door and double locked it before walking away.

Only when he arrived in front of the Abbey did Michael's guilt at angering his wife subside. He silently vowed not to provoke her again.

The Abbey thronged with people. The usual din assailed him; the juke box shouted out some worthless sounds, and the babble from the bar sounded like angry bees. Some big off duty cop, who still wore his uniform shirt, struggled to lift a female onto the bar. As he placed her into a sitting position, Mike smiled appreciatively at the exposure of her long, trim legs. Someone whistled. Mike continued into the depths of the watering hole to the far end of the bar. There he noticed a new addition.

Mounted on the wall next to the pay phone hung a porcelain commode. A neatly lettered sign had been placed in the center of the bowl. It read: "One Police Plaza." While Mike shouldered his way through the crowd, he heard the familiar voice of John Cutbert.

"Yeah, you see, there's this guy, my friend that you should meet. His name's Michael. We've known each other for a long time." Sitting next to the large sergeant, Mike saw a somber man in a business suit. "Hey, Mike, you're the last man I expected to find here tonight. How come?" Cutbert exclaimed excitedly.

Sight of John's pensive companion instinctively made Romano excited to be there. He ignored the turmoil behind him. John was conning the man next to him. But, why? Whatever the case, Mike would play along.

Romano asked, "John, are you going to introduce me to your buddy?" He leaned to his right and pulled over a barstool. Then he turned back to the bar.

By now, the girl stood on the floor. Mike shrugged and asked, "Jim, let me have my usual scotch and give John and his friend whatever they're having." It could have been anything. John had an eclectic taste in alcoholic beverages. Mike sat on the edge of his stool, eagerly awaiting an introduction.

Extending his glass, John began, "George Cali, Mike Romano. Mike Romano, George Cali." After draining his glass, he continued. "George works in Queens Sex Crimes, Mike. You two should have a lot to talk about."

John's voice held a veiled hint, instantly acknowledged with a nod from Mike. John continued, tongue-in-cheek. "Maybe after you have a couple of more years in the street, you can apply for the detail."

That idea had its appeal. "Very happy to meet you, George. Any friend of John's is definitely a friend of mine." Suddenly it struck Mike. *Hot damn, this guy is John's source of information about Brian Wilkey and that asshole of an Inspector.* Mike hoped he could manipulate the conversation around to his pet project. All he had to do was get this guy a little more tipsy. He'd get some answers. Could he pull this off?

John came to the rescue. "Do you guys remember one

night last summer? This happened on 90th Street, just off 34th Avenue. On a roof top. Some little girl got raped. They never found the guy. Mike, you live around the corner from the scene, right? George, maybe you heard about it, being in Sex Crimes?" John did not let on that he had leaked any information to Mike earlier. *Bless you, John.*

Romano took a good look at the man in the business suit. He looked about forty years old, average in height, although sitting on a barstool did not give any hint to his real stature. His suit was a sedate, blue-gray plaid. George had two of the bushiest eyebrows Mike had ever seen, that hovered above large, round eyes. His hair was peppered with gray and slightly disheveled. All together he looked like an unhappy owl.

"Hey, George. Why so glum? Have a bad day?" weak, but the best Mike could think of.

Cali replied, "It's just another shitty day in court. We thought we had a guy locked in. Good enough to get a conviction, and he slipped through on a technicality. The Judge declared a mistrial. Seems that when the jurors were in the corridor, some of them overheard two guys from my office discussing the case. They told the foreman, who told the Judge. Now we gotta do it all over again. It's gonna be tough."

"What kind of case was it?" Mike almost choked on his drink in anticipation.

"Nothing too unusual. Some guy was doing his fourteen-year-old daughter since she was eleven. We get them all the time."

For all of George's bland revelation, the head of Romano filled with visions of an innocent girl, her body only beginning to metamorphose through puberty, being forced to submit to some swarthy, overweight, pervert. Spaced between her feeble protests and soulful sighs, her father would implore her not to tell Mommy.

Scotch-flavored acid rose up in Mike's esophagus. It burned fiercely and caused him to grimace. His mind instantly raced back to the rooftop, the four-year-old girl, and the hot summer night that changed his life. He could contain himself no longer.

"George, did you work on the case John asked about? The one that happened on 90th Street, just off 34th Avenue last August? Some guy raped a four-year-old girl and got away. I hear he's been identified and nobody can touch him."

George made a sour face. "Yeah, we know who it was." Cali bided his time, allowed himself time to think. He yelled, "Let's have another round. Will you, bartender?"

It became obvious to Mike that the detective could not decide if he should discuss so sensitive a matter. So he prodded, "Who was he and why can't you guys do anything?"

Slowly, Cali discarded his apprehension and began to become agitated while he gulped his drink. Mike signaled for a back-up round for the trio. At last, Cali made up his mind and spoke through a pained expression.

"His name's Brian Wilkey. We think he might know the kid."

"How did you find out who he was?" Excited now, Mike pressed further. His voice became a whispered shout. "Why can't you arrest him? The bastard raped a kid. You know that I was out with my dog when it happened. If only I had heard something. He would have been given flying lessons from the roof."

George smiled at Mike's youthful enthusiasm, remembering his own. A wistful thought whispered through his head. *Someday, kid, you, too, will calm down and not want to cure all the world's ills. Some day you will only want to do the job and go home.* He answered instead, "Whoa-up, kid. One question at a time. Fact is, it was old fashioned detective work. You know, lots of hours and leg work. Interviews and re-interviews, records checks, that sort of thing. We were lucky, too. Yet, it doesn't matter how we got him. We can't do anything because he's hung downtown in One PP. You know, kid, someone's taking care of him."

Romano blurted, "Who?" His mouth went dry in anticipation in spite of all the drinks.

"Listen, kid. The guy's hook is a high powered Inspector. He's a guy on the rise. You sound like you wanna go after the guy. Don't. You'll get hurt. This guy Bryan is a bastard."

Mike's mind spun. *Shit, this guy sounds like Lenny.* He forced out words. "Brian Wilkey? He can go to hell. Too bad I can't help send him. He's a perverted sleezeball."

"No, Mike. I mean his hook. Dennis Bryan, the Inspector."

An archangel's imaginary wings twitched. That's it. He finally heard it for himself, from a guy who worked on the case. Now he had to know why.

Mike feigned a casualness he did not feel. "Yeah, I heard he's tough. He used to be in I.A.D.. How or why would a police boss protect a rapist? It makes no sense." Careful, pick his brain. He could not let out how much he knew.

An unexpected answer came. "Because they're related and the boss is on the Pad. He's getting dirty money. Sleazeball's a bag man and works for a wise guy. He's a collector. We think the little girl's rape was a message. Her father gambled heavy. Bryan protects Wilkey. Wilkey makes payments to Inspector Bryan."

"Holy shit!" came Mike's quick retort.

George continued, "That's why we got veiled threats of transfer if any arrest got made. We were about to close in on this guy. You know that once Bryan found out Wilkey was identified, he reached out to our office." The detective had the full attention of both men.

With another swallow of whiskey, George continued. "The squad commander got a personal visit from Bryan. You can't do that shit on the phone," he explained parenthetically. "Anyway, Bryan told my boss that the men had better be sure about the evidence before they looked up his cousin. Smart bastard. He was careful to say that if the guy was really guilty to lock him up anyway."

John nodded. "I guess even a dirt bag like Bryan covers his ass in case the walls have ears."

George continued his tale. "You got that right. Then he went on to say not to screw up, because the guy's family and Bryan didn't want any grief from the Job or relatives. He told the boss that if they were sure, go ahead and arrest Wilkey, but don't screw up, only don't make waves, 'cause if he, Bryan, got embarrassed, there would be transfers."

Mike probed deeper. "Is Inspector Bryan really his cousin?"

George worked on gulping his fifth drink since Mike entered the Abbey. "We don't know for sure. Nobody will give it up. Some shit, huh, kid?"

"Yeah, but George, there's gotta be a way. Maybe the guy could be followed?" Mike pressed his luck.

George shook his head in rejection. "Not by any of us in my office. We're not crazy. Nobody wants to go toe-to-toe an' nose-to-nose with an Inspector. Let alone Bryan." Cali signaled for another round. He was growing tired of Mike's apparent obsession. "You can do it, Mike, if you're so hot on it, and don't care about your career. Me, I got three kids and an ex-wife to support."

"Yeah, you're right, George. No use steppin' on your weenie." Mike wanted Cali to believe he made light of it. "Hey, Jim, another round." A dark conviction buzzed in Mike's head. *This guy, Wilkey, is going down someday. Maybe there's some way to get Bryan, too.*

After the drinks had been put down, the furry-eye browed detective attempted to stand. He felt tired and wanted to go home and sleep. John assisted him, while he groped the man's pockets unsuccessfully for his car keys.

"I'm okay, John, I'm okay," George told his large friend. He was too far gone to drive.

Joe DeCicco

"Where's your car, George?" queried the big sergeant.

"It's---it's back at the office. I got a ride to court today and to here. I'm gonna take a cab home. I'll get my car tomorrow."

Relieved, George steered his friend to the door. After they saw George safely into a taxi that Jim had phoned for, the two friends went inside and sat down again.

"Listen, Mike," John urged over the yammer of the juke box. "Don't go getting yourself in trouble. I see the look of the hunter in your eye. You can't avenge all wrongs."

"That's okay, John, I know that. Anyway, look at the girl leaning over the pool table. In those tight maroon pants, her ass looks like a heart." A sudden expression of contrition flashed across his face. "Betty's waitin' for me. Gotta go."

John turned a long, hungry, speculative gaze on the girl at the pool table. Mike slapped his friend on the back and nodded toward the girl in question as he added, "Happy hunting."

Mike made it back home in less than five minutes. As he approached his apartment door, he heard the faint drone of a late night talk show host's monologue. He knew that Betty would probably be awake. He felt almost sober. Mike hoped that she wouldn't be too upset with him.

He held tight to one conviction. The trip to the Abbey had been worth it. Now all he had to do was get Betty to understand. She would probably still be upset. Should he tell her what he had found out now, tonight? Why not? She was his wife and she did love him. *It's gonna be all right,* Mike assured himself as he began the unlocking process..

Mike found her in their bedroom, propped up in bed. "Hi, Hon." Mike cupped her chin as he leaned down to kiss her.

Angel with a Gun

Her nose wrinkled. "You smell like too many scotches. And don't get too noisy. The children are sleeping." A slight chill still edged her voice from earlier in the evening.

"You're still pissed off."

"No, I'm not," Betty denied.

Mike turned away. After removing his off-duty two-inch" barrel, .38 caliber revolver from his waistband, he put it on the top shelf of his closet. His eagerness to tell her his revelations caused him to slam the door.

Betty quickly said softly, "Mike, slow down, damn it. The kids."

"You are pissed off," he began. Then, "Wait until I tell you who I met tonight." After a short pause and no encouragement, Mike barged on. "The guy who had the case involving the little girl who was raped on the roof around the corner, that's who. You remember?"

"How can I ever forget? That's all you talk about. Don't get me upset again about that Wilkey guy, Mikey. It took me hours to calm down. Keep it down to a quiet roar, will you? You're getting wound up." She shook her head, then relented and gave Mike a quick hug. "What guy?"

Mike's hands moved along with his mouth as though they shared the same muscles. "When I walked in, John was with a detective, this guy George Cali, from Sex Crimes. He told me why they can't lock up Wilkey. Deputy Inspector Bryan, the guy John said was related to Wilkey is on the Pad. And he's Wilkey's cousin. Wilkey actually pays Bryan Mob money." He spoke as he peeled off his clothes. Absently he threw them against the closet door. Betty pulled a face.

"Tell me quietly, damn it."

Once he had lowered his voice again, Mike related the entire conversation from the Abbey.

Knowing her husband's strong morality, Betty began to soften. "Please, Michael, don't push too hard. This Bryan guy might be dangerous."

Upset as she was at Michael's obsession, she could never go to sleep angry. Her archangel now lay in bed. Grabbing the remote, she switched off the television and snuggled against him, running her fingernails up and down his naked flanks. His response caused the bed to moan in protest.

"Sshhh. You'll wake the kids."

Mike relaxed again. . .almost. "Next time I'm in One PP, I'm gonna check out Wilkey and find out what his record is like."

She grabbed his hand and guided it. "Check this out."

"I intend to. Thoroughly, might I add," came Mike's murmured reply.

CHAPTER SEVEN

"Hey Len, let's get some lunch early for a change." Mike had the RMP wheel for the first half of the Wednesday day tour.

"Okay, Mike. Stop at the deli on Lenox between One Thirty Second and Thirty First Streets. Their food's always good. Besides I feel like a fresh ham sandwich, and they make one that's terrific".

As the duo entered the shop, Mike slightly ahead of his partner, ice gripped their hearts. They had walked in on a hold-up. Two young punks held the clerk and four patrons at gunpoint. One was deep in the store, at the end of the service counter. He had not seen the officers as he was shouting directions to a second clerk stacking shelves.

They had no need for words. The two guardians of the peace simultaneously drew their revolvers. Each man knew what his partner thought without saying a word. The stickup men had no idea that cops had arrived. Mike slid further into the shop and moved left against the wall. Only a rack filled with potato chips and other similar snacks gave him partial cover.

His back to the street, the gunman closest to the door brandished his revolver. "Gimme all your cash. Empty that register an' git yer stash."

Len's thoughts raced. *These two are dangerous; they must be new at the game. No self-respecting Harlem robber would stand with his back to the door without a backup man.* Lenny began to flatten himself against the door jamb hoping to avoid detection. *This is stupid,* he thought, *if the guy turns around, he'd look him right in the eye.* In case there was another guy outside, he decided to stay put. The door frame would give some protection against a possible third gunmen.

Directly to Len's right stood the long service counter. On the other side of it the shop keeper had his hands in the air. He looked pleadingly at the officers. His lips moved rapidly. It suddenly came to Len that he was counting seconds. After waiting for what he believed to be an appropriate length of time for the officers to set up, he dropped flat to the floor.

Blinking, the gunman looked startled and glanced to his left in an apparent attempt to say something to his partner.

In the split second that the closest gunmen hesitated, Len yelled "Police! Freeze! Don't move or you're dead."

Too late, the gunman began to turn and saw Len's revolver about 12 inches from his nose. His face went gray as he froze and dropped his weapon.

At the same time Romano had his man directly in his gun sights. *Slowly. . .the target must be directly above the sights in the center. . . controlled breathing*, Mike remembered the instructors drone. The second gunman cast a bewildered look at his partner. His jaw began to tighten. He appeared to be thinking about trying to take Lenny.

Mike's growl sounded from behind the potato chips. "Drop it you son of a bitch or you're history."

Features blank, the desperado's jaw slackened, "Where are you man?" asked the puzzled gunman, his head oscillated like a desk fan.

"Up your ass, and about to kill you. Drop it now. One. . .Two."

Had he not been so focused on the punk with the gun, Romano might have been startled when the clerk struck his head on a trash pail as he hit the floor. He yelped and remained motionless.

"Okay---okay." The second gun hit the floor.

Slowly, the counterman got up off the floor and peered over the ledge. Seeing everything was over, he leaned against the shelving, shaking like an aspen in a gale. His voice came out low, and entirely sincere. "Thank God---thank God."

Len had his man by the shirt collar and walked him to the rear portion of the shop where he found a clear section of wall. Mike had his perp on the move also. Roughly the two policemen shoved their prisoners against the wall. After the men had been handcuffed, Mike retrieved the guns. They were both revolvers containing six live rounds.

Slowly now, the previously prone store clerk shakily got up. Blood trickled down from a cut over his eye.

In an attempt to ease the tension in both the store and himself, the counterman quipped as he wiped the blood from his eye, "Well at least the pail ain't damaged." He held it up.

After Mike and Len herded the suspects into their patrol car, Mike realized that his knees shook violently. It sometimes happened like that after a tense moment. The rush of adrenalin, the brush with potential disaster, the after-shock. *What good would potato chips do against a gun?* he silently asked himself. *It worked though, just like they taught us in the Academy; use any cover available to gain the advantage.*

Following the custom of most radio car partners, credit for arrests was taken alternately. It was Mike's turn. He took the collars. But, damn, how he hated the paperwork. Both men would be charged with robbery and criminal possession of a weapon. Len drove as they transported the punks Downtown for booking and arraignment. Once the prisoners' papers had been processed and the lethargic wheels of justice set in motion, which took the rest of their shift time, and several hours more, Mike returned to the Three-Two, changed into civvies and went over to Police Headquarters. Regardless of the time, he had things to do.

When the elevator door closed, Mike pushed the number six. The Bureau of Criminal Identification, or B.C.I. as it was more popularly known, was in room 606. That was the tenacious cop's destination.

Taking a UF-90 (Request for Records Check) form off the stack on the service counter, Mike wrote in the name of Brian Wilkey. He guessed at Wilkey's age and height, since he had no idea of either. Then he crossed over to the counter and handed the request to the clerk.

"You forgot to sign this."

Sighing, the persistent centurion signed his name and exhaustedly sat down to wait. He had begun his tour of duty at 0800 hours that previous morning; he looked at the wall clock and saw 0200 hours. It was tomorrow. The ebony haired cop calculated that he had been awake over eighteen hours now.

Through eyes heavy with sleep, he looked around in an effort to remain awake. The enormous room was filled with row upon row of file cabinets containing hundreds of thousands of fingerprint cards.

On one side of the cavernous room ranked a bank of FAX machines used to send fingerprints to Albany. Next to them sat several noisy Teletypes that clicked out criminal records in response to the print inquiries. The complex actually occupied most of the Southwest quadrant of the building. Included in the numerous cabinets were the records of every arrest within New York City, the famed "Rap Sheet"

Inquiries could be made nationwide. The system was almost 100 percent accurate.

"Police Officer Romano, your RAP Sheets are back".

Startled, Mike jolted awake, striking his head against the wall behind him, offering, "Sorry I was dozing; too many hours, you know. Thanks". Mike accepted the papers from the clerk's hand and stared, bleary-eyed at them.

WILKEY, BRIAN DOB: 02/03/45
HGT: 69", EYES: BROWN
HAIR: AUBURN
NYSID: 3274902Z   FBI: 7282102 NCIC: 0018828

....

....

```
NYCPD:06501002      P L  225.10 PROM GAMB 1 DEG. E/F
114/ QNS01002       PL 225.20 POSS GAMB RCDS 1  E/F
04/02/65            PL 265.02/4 CPW 3 DEG.         D/F
NYCPD:07211323      PL 130.60 SEX ABUSE 2DEG    A/M
114/ QNS11323       PL 245.00 PUB LEWDNESS      B/M
07/15/72
```

....

RESIDENCES: 04/02/65 3545 86 STREET, JCK HGTS QNS

RESIDENCES: 07/15/73 3545 86 STREET, JCK HGTS QNS

THERE IS NO FURTHER INFORMATION AVALIABLE REGARDING THIS PERSON AT THIS TIME

He was pumped up now. *Son of a bitch, he's a gambler or bookie, and a pervert. He lives right in the neighborhood, in Jackson Heights.* Somehow he would nail him. Next stop, Photo Unit.

At the window in the basement the clerk said, "Please submit a UF-90 and sign it."

Mike did as instructed. The clerk studied the sheet and gave Mike a bored expression. "Come back in half an hour or forty-five minutes."

Romano nodded in resignation; always the hurry up and wait.   His next stop would be OCID (Organized Crime Intelligence Division).   He would return in about forty five minutes for the photos.

Romano had never been in OCID, nor did he know if they would help him. He decided to take a chance. Mike found the office closed.   It was not manned during the Midnight

90

tours. He checked the posted hours and decided to return after 0800.

Aching from the need to sleep, Mike returned to the Photo Unit where he retrieved the photos and returned to an empty court room to catch up on some sleep before a new day began. An old hand at the court system Mike knew it would be hours before his men would be arraigned.

Promptly at 0801 that morning Mike entered the offices of OCID. The clerk, an attractive redhead with a generous smile looked up at him.

"Good morning. What can I do for you?"

Mike gave her back a morning-fresh grin. "I want to check if you have a jacket on someone."

"The name, please?"

Romano gave her the name and vital statistics on Wilkey, which she noted on a form on her desk. At least here one did not have to do the paperwork oneself. "One moment. I'll see if we have him."

She returned in four minutes. "Luckily there is some current information on your man. This Wilkey seems to be a bad character."

Mike took the intelligence sheet and read it eagerly. It stated that Brian Wilkey was reputedly a bag man, making the rounds of the gambling locations to gather betting slips, and collecting porno parlor kickbacks in Midtown Manhattan, mostly in the 42nd Street area. Included in the package was a note regarding the possible sexual molestation of a debtor's family. Wilkey had recently been, for a short time, the suspect in the sexual molestation of a 9 year old boy. He functioned as collector for the Costello Crime Family's vast gambling business. He had never taken a collar for any of it. Mike got nauseous at the thought that the rumors about Wilkey's double perversions had proven true.

OCID also had some background information about the younger Wilkey. He had been born on the west side of Manhattan, Hell's Kitchen. It turned out that Mike's obsession had been in trouble since his early teens. The jacket listed several arrests as a Juvenile Delinquent, now sealed. Mike knew that all JD records were sealed after the youth reached his or her 16th birthday. He could not find out what they contained.

Included in the file he found notes concerning Wilkey's formative years. He had been an abused child. The courts took him away from an abusive mother at the age of ten. The report went on to say that Wilkey's mother would deny her young son use of the toilet and when he would release body fluids, she would punish him severely. Punishment ranged from mental abuse to savage beatings. Then, beginning at the age of ten he was in and out of group homes. Reading between the lines, Romano surmised that sometime during these years, Wilkey had himself been sexually molested. The report listed the fact that Brian had a sister. She had been fortunate enough to be raised by a foster family from the age of 12. Her name was Elizabeth. There was no mention of his father.

Mike made copies of the file, thanked the clerk and returned to a long wait at the court.

Golden beams filtered through the canopy of green above. Unusual for New York City, the warm, moist breeze had a refreshing salt tang. But, then the park was right on Jamaica Bay. Brian Wilkey breathed deeply and looked around with practiced, studied indifference. A plethora of playground equipment dotted this portion of Spring Creek Park. It was one of Brian's favorite hunting grounds. The chirp of children's voices filled the air with cheery sound. Brian's gaze arrested at last on two particular youngsters.

A sweet-faced, white-blond haired boy, of about ten,

and his little sister, some two years younger, climbed the ladder of a set of monkey bars. A profound ache expanded in the chest of Brian Wilkey. He had caught absolute hell from that fat slob brother-in-law over the last incident. But, Dennis Bryan held his future, hell, his whole life in his hands. Wilkey had done as told, had been celibate for nearly two years now. How much could a healthy man be expected to endure? He was no damned priest. Yet, he had been compelled to suppress and repel his natural appetites. It would have to be soon now. He could not endure this much longer. Perhaps, one of these two? Both? Brian stifled a deep groan as he watched the boy and girl opposite from the bench on which he sat.

Across the way, on the monkey bars, the boy moved with such lithe grace that it took Brian's breath away. His energetic movement had hiked up the little boy's shirt, to reveal his navel, and an expanse of a flat, smooth, sun-browned abdomen. Behind him, his sister swayed from side to side in her effort to keep up with her brother. Her wriggling had raised the hem of her overall-strap halter to display an ample swath of lightly tanned skin. This visual feast caused Brian's groin to ache and he felt himself swell in response. The intensity of it forced him to bend double.

He couldn't help it. It wasn't his fault. He was... what he was. He had always been like that. His litany of self-assurance, devised long ago, washed over his mind. It had started so long ago. He only dimly remembered that day when he had still been a baby just emerging into boyhood. How old had he been? Four? Five?

He had been in their back yard with his sister, only two years older than he. In his memory, Brian saw himself dressed in the pair of baggy, brown, knee-length shorts and sandals over bare feet. Elizabeth wore a pair of red shorts, with a white, frilly, bare-midriff halter top.

It had seemed so innocent; it still did. Elizabeth had come and sat cross-legged with him on the grass. Without the least indication of it being a conspiratorial endeavor, she had placed one hand on an exposed portion of his thigh. She smiled at him encouragingly and slid up to the top of his shorts, all the time smiling so sweetly. After that. . .well, after that it had been a confused jumble of delightfully delicious excitement.

They had not stopped with that first encounter. Brian had no vivid memory of how often, yet he knew it happened with some regularity. Now and then, Liz would come to him and ask, "You wanna play the game?" And he always would. So intense had been his enjoyment that at the age of seven he reasoned it would heighten the sensation by sharing his pleasure with some of his friends.

Then had come that painful and humiliating day when Brian was in the third grade.

One afternoon, Brian's mother had burst into his room to catch him and his best friend, Jimmy, doing. . .the most delightful things.

"Pervert," she had screamed at Jimmy, a word Brian had never heard before, and sent the boy home in tears. Then she had turned on her son.

After a long lecture, in which she used such words as "impure," and "depravity," she hadn't simply spanked him. Far more vicious than the many other times, she beat him so violently that Brian believed he would never be able to sit down again. His buttocks remained a collage of sickly black, green, and blue for a week. A smudge of yellow-green ringed his upper left arm from where she had held him down.

His degradation and pain made it easy for him to promise his mother that he would never, ever, do those things again. But, it all felt. . .so wonderful. He could. . .never really.

... stop. Not. . .after three years. Not. . .after all. . .that. . .fun.

Yet he had tried, hadn't he? Years later, while attending City College, he had met Martha. He had been studying accounting at the time. They met, fell in love. Brian made a conscious, albeit difficult, effort to put behind his preoccupation with children. He really concentrated on projecting a romantic aura around Martha. Hadn't he? They had married right after Brian graduated with an AA degree. It lasted 18 months. That's when Martha had confronted him over the breakfast table. Brian's present, tormented memory replayed the ugly incident.

"Brian, I'm leaving you. I want a divorce."

Stunned, Brian had gaped at her. "Wh--but, why?"

"Face it, Brian. There's something. . .missing inside you. You aren't capable of satisfying me. We haven't been husband and wife and lovers for over a year. And when you do manage to perform, you often call me by other names; Lacey, Crystal, even Liz. My God, Brian, your sister's name is Liz. More than once, you even called me. . ." she finished with a shudder, "Shit. What's with it with you?"

Within three months, Martha had her divorce. After that, more and more, his hunger, Brian realized now, centered around, and concentrated on, children. Little girls in particular; and always his pleasure was taken with force and ended with the girl being hurt. With a start, Brian Wilkey realized that the boy and girl he had been watching stood directly across the paved walkway, staring at him.

Brian smiled his, "I'm just a kid at heart," smile. "Hi, I'm Bri."

Slowly, a winning smile spread on the boy's tan face. "Hi, I'm Tommy. This is my sister, Ashley." Then he began to shyly smile, his chin down, cobalt eyes staring at Brian through long, blond lashes. Anticipation clutched the heart of Brian Wilkey. Was this it? Was it going to be now?

Joe DeCicco

It was 1500 came before the two stickup men were arraigned. Mike felt like he had gone ten rounds with Sonny Liston, yet he was required to be present before the judge. Mechanically the proceedings progressed.

"Officer Romano, please answer the question," came the gentle scolding from the presiding jurist. The judge continued, "I realize that you had been here for many hours but, please take note of the arrest time. The court asked you if the defendants were any trouble at the time of arrest. Did they resist in any way?"

Mike snapped his brain from the lure of Morpheus and responded with a brisk, "No, Your Honor. When my partner, Officer Jones, and I ordered them to drop their weapons, they did so in a timely manner."

From the bench came, "Thank you officer. Is there anything you want to add?"

"No sir," came Mike's lazy eyed reply.

"The defendants are held over until Friday the 12th, one thousand dollars, cash or bond. Put them in inside Bailiff." As he slammed his gavel down, the judge shouted, "Next case."

Mike reached home at 4:30 p.m. Tired as he was, he could hardly wait to tell his wife what he had learned. "Betty, here's a photo of Wilkey. If you ever see him on the street get away and call 911. Look at this sheet. He's a pervert. Never let Anne or Donny out of your sight."

"Take it easy Honey. You're getting all wound up again. Why would I ever let the children out of my sight? You're getting nuts about this guy again." Betty appreciated his protective instincts but felt that he treated her as if she was a child. She was getting annoyed. *"Stop it!"* she wanted to yell.

Almost as though he had read her mind, Mike hastily responded. "Goddamnit, he's a pedophile!" Mike saw the hurt enter her eyes first, then spread over her face.

96

Hastily he modified his attitude. "Okay, Okay, but please keep the picture."

Mike showered and hit the bed about 5 p.m. that afternoon. "Don't wake me for supper, Honey," he called to Betty, who stood at the kitchen sink, peeling potatoes. "In fact, don't wake me unless the building is on fire."

"Mikey!" Betty squeaked.

He slept through the night like a dead man. In fact Betty put her hand on his chest several times to make sure she still had a husband.

It dawned warm the following day. And it got hotter before Mike went to work on the four to twelve. Now in late spring, the interior of the Three-Two station house registered ten degrees hotter than the surrounding air outside. Mike felt as though he sat near a dry cleaners' big pressing board, the steam-fed suit presser type. His collar chaffed his neck. The fact that he sat near an open window afforded little relief. At least not until a cool can of Bud flew into the room through that very window, just as roll call began. The can landed at Michael's feet with a dull metallic thud.

He still felt heady over his discoveries of the day before and bent down to grab the chilled cylinder. With a flick of his thumb he pulled tab from the top to allow access to the golden liquid. The resulting hiss was heard by Sergeant Burke. Burke, a fair man with eleven years in the command, attempted to conduct roll call from the front of the room. He knew the pressures of being a ghetto cop. The men worked hard and played hard. Burke also knew that often it was difficult to separate the time distinction. The guys on the Job generally considered him a tolerant man.

"Get rid of that Mike, now."

"Yes sir. Right away," he replied as he took his second swallow.

Immediately, the men in the room erupted in feigned jealousy. "Hey, Serge, it ain't fair. He's got a beer an' we don't."

"Yeah, it's 1600 and it's still over eighty out there," another mumbled.

"What is it, favoritism that Mike's got a cold brewski and we don't?"

Their antics caused the sergeant to walk to the window, just as Mike dropped the almost empty can down to the men below. Amid cat calls from his subordinate officers, the Boss pulled down the ancient sash after shouting a warning to the men outside.

Adjacent to a short alley next to the building that housed the main portion of the Three-Two was the precinct garage. Access to the garage was either from the large overhead doors, a small door at the building's rear or a cross-over from the rear of the cell area. The cross-over, combined with the alleyway, resulted in a covered area where the men gathered even in the rain. In place under that canopy lay an old fifty gallon oil drum that had been split lengthwise, fitted with a grill, and placed on a stand constructed of cinder blocks. During the Spring and Summer season, one could find a barbecue going and some "cold ones" at almost any hour. The cold beer in roll call was not unusual. Reprimands were given tongue in cheek.

Back at the front of the room, Burke lifted his clipboard. "Let's get back to where we were. Bronkowski, Carstairs, Cramer, Edson. . ." he continued through the roll call. With that concluded, he called their attention to the new Hot Sheet. "There's too damn many cars gettin' boosted out there. We ain't talkin' punks out joy-ridin' here. You check the year and make on these entries. Some of them are expensive jobs. An' they don't turn up abandoned when the kids took 'em run out of gas. They're goin' somewhere. So, keep a sharp eye.

Maybe one of youse clowns can pull a coup like that Sears job Romano did."

Three hours into their tour it was still hot. In a futile effort to cool the interior of their auto down, Lenny piloted the vehicle toward the upper end of the command at high speed along the East River Drive. Their vehicle, along with most on patrol, had no air conditioning. To get out of the glare from the setting sun, Len drove under The Macolumbes Dam Bridge on West 155 Street. The ancient structure spanned a narrow part of the East River connecting Manhattan to the Bronx.

Romano could not contain his fetish any longer. "Hey Len, look at this. It's Wilkey's photo," as he thrust it in his partner's face, blocking his view momentarily.

Len almost struck a pillar. "For Cripes sake, I'm driving. You nut."

Mike did not look the least contrite. "Sorry. But now I know what he looks like. Len, someday I'm gonna get him. You'll see."

In an effort to avoid any further close encounters with immovable objects, Len headed down Eighth Avenue. The team approached West 145th Street.

"In the Three-Two., Man with a gun at the corner of West 145th Street and Eight Avenue. Male black, dark red shirt, black pants. No further description. K," crackled the voice of the division dispatcher.

Mike automatically scanned the area. "Awh, shit Len, there he is."

"Slowly, Mike, slowly."

"Three-Two Adam on the scene Central. Will check and advise."

"Use caution Adam. Backup on the way." The men knew that other cars would respond automatically. Everything would be all right. Other teams got into shit, not us. We are good and lucky too.

Joe DeCicco

The subject stood on the eastern sidewalk about twenty feet south of the inter-section. When Len brought the auto to a stop about fifteen feet to the man's rear, Mike exited. His right hand extracted his service revolver. Mike quickly scanned the area in the oncoming twilight as a safety precaution, comfortable in the knowledge that his partner would alert him to any trouble. After seeing no additional impending problems, Romano turned toward the front of the RMP.

Len burst out, "Shit he's got a gun", and thrust himself upon the man. Mike holstered his weapon and jumped to assist his partner as the two men tumbled to the soiled pavement.

Bam! Bam! Were they dreaming? Gunshots whistled above the combatants. Shards of red brick stung their skin. Bullets struck the store front next to them. "Where the hell is that coming from?" shouted Mike as he drew his gun again.

Shots had come from across the street. The team had been fired upon by another person. *The guy's got a partner; this has got to be a dream. I'm gonna wake up now,* Mike told himself. As he rolled, a black revolver slid next to him. Reaching out his left hand to grab the weapon, he thought, *My god, this can't be Len's. It better be the guy's.*

Mike hoped he was correct when he shouted, "Len, I got his gun."

Two more rounds flew from across the street in the cop's direction. One of the rounds bounced off the sidewalk in front of Mike. His forehead stung from chipped concrete. Attempting to keep low, afford a small target, Romano jammed the recovered revolver under his prone body. He was surprised to see that he still held own weapon. Looking across the street, he saw a figure take a combat stance and fire in his direction. Even from that distance, the shots roared in his ears. Romano saw no parked cars, no fleeing citizens, no buildings. He saw nothing but the human form across from him. That figure held a gun and studiously attempted to kill him. Mike's reaction was immediate. Pointing his revolver as if it was an extension

100

of his index finger, Mike fired twice. His mind raced. *Did he fall? Did he even get hit? Did the son of a bitch perp go down?*

The sound of his own gunfire still echoed in his ears when Romano heard his partner shout, "Mike help me. He's got another one."

With Len still shouting, he was thrown backward by his larger adversary. The man stood and began to yank another handgun from his waistband. Three rapid shots cracked from police weapons. One of them from Mike, in response to his partner's two rapid discharges. The man lay motionless.

Saint Michael, thank you, thought Mike. "Len, you okay?" he asked as he looked at the front of his shirt for blood. He felt no pain so he must have been OK. On the other side of the street, staring up at the sky, lay the other shooter.

Heaving deeply, the blue warriors caught their breath as backup cars began screeching onto the scene. It was over. Both officers now began the shaking that resulted from the rush of adrenalin.

"We're okay, we're okay," was all the men of Sector Adam could say for the first few minutes, as they leaned against anything solid. Within three minutes the scene became controlled mayhem.

They were a sight. Mike's trousers had ripped at the knee, to expose shredded skin. His shirt hung out of his pants, filthy with street grime. His equipment belt had spun around so that his right handed holster hung on his left side. Len looked similarly disheveled. None of the responding officers commented on it.

Emergency Service arrived with their "Battle Wagon," one of three large two ton trucks outfitted with a myriad of equipment including sub-machine guns. They were there to give any assistance necessary. On this run, after the fact, they began illuminating the area with large floodlights.

Two ambulances arrived to transport the wounded. There were none. Both assailants lay dead. The original suspect had been hit three times in the upper torso. The gunman on the west side of the avenue had been struck in the head and under the armpit of his right side. His hand held a 9mm semi-automatic pistol.

Mike's patrol sergeant conferred with a duty Captain. "It was a righteous shooting, Cap."

The Captain, the ranking officer on duty, and covering the 6th Zone, in which the Three-Two was included, long with the neighboring Two-Eight and the Two-six. "All right, Tim," he told the sergeant. "But the ME and I.A.D. will have to confirm that."

Several uniform officers attempted to rope off the scene. At the same time, the area quickly filled up with gawkers. Cars driving on the streets stopped at the intersection. Not one of them made a U-turn. Their drivers added to the curious, quickly gathering crowd. The patrol sergeant looked their way. "Fuckin' ghouls," he spat.

Detectives arrived. The squad began interviewing witnesses and made sure there were no innocent bystanders struck.

Avoiding a cadaver, the captain stepped over to where Mike and Len sat on the front seat of their squad. "Okay, who fired at which perp and how many rounds?"

Mike looked up. He had the appearance of having been run through a thrashing machine. "I fired three rounds, sir. Two into him." He pointed across the street. "And one into him."

Len spoke up. "I shot this one here by the car twice."

After determining who fired how many shots, the captain ordered Mike and Len to be transported back to the command. Before they departed, he advised them, "All right, you know the routine. Standard procedure dictates that there will be in-depth interviews of both of you. Further procedure, resulting from your union negotiations, requires that you men be afforded the right to seek medical treatment for shock trauma. You will also be given the right to discuss the incident with a union delegate, along with medical treatment, before giving statements to the Department."

Len spoke for them both. "We don't need treatment for shock, or any other medical stuff. But we would like to exercise our right to speak to a delegate."

"You agree, Romano?"

"Yes, Captain."

"Go on, then."

After three hours of having to tell the story again and again, the men were excused and allowed to go off duty. The Duty Captain once again offered them medical services. Mike suspected he wanted to take no chances with their union. Mike and Len declined for the second time. Standard procedure required that their service revolvers be forwarded to the Police Academy Lab for ballistics checks. Hell, the guns work. Well too, thought Mike as he handed his over to the boss. The Job would soon know officially who shot whom. The following day would have been their last work day of that set of tours. As Mike and his partner signed out, they both filled out the forms to take it as a vacation day. Coupled with their normal swing, they would have three days before returning to work. Their service revolvers would be back and waiting for them upon their return. Neither man would be unarmed, they both owned off duty revolvers.

Just before the men of Sector Adam left the station house, Lieutenant Henry Ludge, commander of Sixth Detective Division Homicide, dropped in on the team in person. "For what it's worth, I'll tell you that I believe it was a good shooting. I also believe that they were probably going to hold up a local shop when interrupted. The dead stickup team was wanted for several shootings and suspected in three homicides." Ludge paused in the doorway. "I want you to know that I will write you both up for Department Recognition."

Len grinned. "That's great, Loo." Then he cocked an eyebrow. "Even if it don't come back a righteous shooting?"

Ludge waggled a finger at him. "Get outta here, Jones."

As they left the station, Len asked, "Hey, Mike, are you ready to stop off at the Abbey for one or two?" It was a minor detour for Len. He lived in Laurelton, Queens. He had never been there with Mike and was mildly curious about the place.

He quickly accepted the invitation. "Are you kidding? It may help stop my knees from shaking."

"Are you going to tell Pat?" asked Mike. He had started to calm down at last. His humor was returning. "By the way, it's nice to know that even 'Peter Perfect' can get his uniform dirty."

The answer came quickly, "Up yours, Mike. Yeah, I'll tell Pat about this thing tomorrow or later if I'm not too drunk. Good thing we told the girls we made arrests instead of the real reason we're late and gonna be later yet. Come on, let's go," Len urged.

Later, at the Abbey, they verbally relived the incident over again. Inevitably, Mike commented, "Too bad one of those guys wasn't Wilkey. It would have been real justice."

Len quickly chastised his friend, "Listen, there you go again. Today we were like any other Harlem cops. In the right place at the wrong time. Just another day in the Three-Two. This time we were there. Let's toast Saint Michael; he was with us today." Holding his glass high and staring at Mike, Len smiled broadly and said, "To the archangel, Drink up."

Close to 2 A.M., in walked a familiar face. It was John Cutbert. John was surprised to see Mike there. After introductions were made, the reason for the slurred speech on

Angel with a Gun

the part of his friend became apparent.

Before he started the recounting of the close brush with Death, Mike shouted, "Hey Jim, help John catch up to us will you? He got a late start. Don't take his money tonight. We're celebrating being alive."

The trio closed the place.

Late the following day, the men told their wives about their close encounter with Death. Betty took the news by staring off into space and hugging two-year-old Donald to her chest. In the Jones household, Pat gave a short cry and told Len that if he was out with his partner, he should just say so and not concoct a story like that one.

"You had better not ever tell me another tale like that Leonard Jones or I'll beat you to death in your sleep," shouted Pat.

Len made no attempt to argue the point. She was in denial.

Before the men could telephone each other, Anne and Pat monopolized the phone for hours. Each man allowed his wife as much privacy as possible during their conversation. Neither cop wanted risk overhearing anything nor witness any sobbing. They might have been asked to leave the Job. No way.

Dennis and Liz Bryan sat at the trestle picnic table under the patio canopy in their back yard. They torpidly looked over the ravaged remains of a barbecue pork rib dinner. Dennis had prepared them in the smoker and felt justifiably proud of his accomplishment. They had been tender, juicy and delicious. Too bad Elizabeth's parents had been unable to attend. Then again, maybe not.

Dennis had a later night appointment. He had made arrangements with his office to call him and summon him from

105

home at 9:45. By 10 p.m., he would be in a mid-town hotel room with his latest sweet, toothsome thing. But, if Liz ever found out, or even suspected he had something on the side, she would make life a living hell. He could kiss the Deputy Commissioner's job good-bye. God, that woman frightened him.

CHAPTER EIGHT

A week went by before the archangel and his partner received good news. Sergeant Burke brought it up at the end of roll call. "Oh, by the way, Jones, Romano, we just received word that the Grand Jury officially made your shooting justifiable."

More good news came several days after that. Burke was again the bearer of glad tidings. "I want you two to know that Lieutenant Ludge wrote you up for the Police Combat Cross."

They would proudly wear the gold trimmed breast bar with its solid green field.

After their harrowing experience, the team became very cautious. Summer rapidly approached. The nights grew fairly warm. The back alleys began to have an odor all their own. One evening on a four-to-twelve tour they answered a "Burglary in Progress" call in the rear of 252 West 140 Street. Two other teams answered the call as backup units.

While the undaunted buddies, being the first to arrive, moved to the rear of the building, Mike began to mumble, "Damn it, this place looks like a garbage pail. Look over there, old food covered with what looks like white mold. It stinks too. Don't step in any dog shit." He gave a short chuckle. "Although it would smell better than some of this stuff."

"Shhh, we don't know where the guy is. Don't alert him. Keep quiet," came Len's muffled retort.

Scanning the void, across the litter, Mike saw an old lady gesturing toward the back of a building. The same one they had responded to, 252 West 140 Street. He snapped his fingers to alert Len. When the woman saw that she had both their attention, she excitedly began pointing toward the rear of number 252.

Realizing that she was attempting to tell them where the burglar went, Mike and Len climbed the wall of the building with their flashlights, one floor at a time. The old woman almost fell from her lofty perch, as the circles of light struck the fifth floor. She motioned to the left with her arm and guided the men to focus on the center apartment. There, at the fire escape landing, they saw an open window. The old girl gasped in her excitement and almost toppled out in happiness.

Romano, being the taller of the two, reached up and pulled down the retractable ladder. It rattled loudly as it descended. Mike winced and they immediately began to climb. They made slow progress. Each man kept motioning to his partner to go easy. They found it difficult to climb the steel rungs and whisper into the portable radio alerting the backup teams as to their progress. It was paramount to remain as silent as possible. The adrenalin rush, compounded by the fact that neither man wanted to fall into the debris below, made holding control of their voices almost impossible. On rare occasions, the old fire escapes had been known to come loose and deposit people in a ruinous condition below.

Those rear yards bulged with things that boggled the mind. Dirty diapers, cans, bottles, used condoms, needles, and not the kind that a loving Grandmother used to mend socks either, and a hundred other things littered the ground. In addition they contained clothing, broken furniture, metal pipes, discarded toilet bowls and all too often dead human beings, or their parts, which remained undiscovered until Chance intervened. As Mike had observed, this yard was knee deep in the stuff and gave off an unearthly odor. Either man would rather face another gunman then fall into this odious quagmire of broken bits of people's lives.

Once on the fifth floor landing, they heard from within the abyss before them what appeared to be a painful moan.

Next came a rustle, the sound of a bird's wings. Maybe the archangel hovered nearby. Mike drew his revolver and looked at Len as if to say, "Let's get this sucker, he's hurting someone."

Using hand signals, Len managed to tell his partner, "On the count of three turn on your light." Mike nodded.

As the men turned their hats around, to prevent the white shield cap devices from glistening and giving them away; Len held up first one finger, then two. Mike thought Len took five minutes before the third finger came up.

"Freeze you son of a bitch, one move and you're dead." There in the beam of white light sat a man on the toilet, his pants around his knees. His face contorted in pain. He groaned miserably.

"Who the hell are you?" demanded Len.

"Hey, I live here man. Don't shoot, please."

Mike prodded him. "Do you have any identification? Throw it over." Immediately, Mike got nervous as the man reached down to his pants. "You better come up with a wallet."

"Here," came the response. He tossed the tossed to the team.

"You see officers. My name is Charles Borrows and I live here. Couple days ago my wife found out that I got a woman on the side. You know, I'm a man. But anyway she started all kinds of shit. Throwing things and all. So I left. Tonight I feel sick, feel all clogged up. Gotta use the can. My key don't work. She must have changed the locks. Anyway, it's my place and no skinny woman's gonna keep me out. So I climb the fire escape and come in."

"Central, Three-Two Adam here. Thank the other units for the backup. We have proper ID, K."

"Listen sir, would you mind if we climbed in and took the stairs down?" asked Len, polite as always.

A big white smile flashed in the ebony face. "No problem."

While the team passed the still sitting Borrows, Len handed him his wallet. The man proved he had one hell of a sense of humor when he added, "And thanks, gentlemen, for scaring the shit out of me. I feel better now."

The rest of the tour went rather uneventfully. They responded to the usual family fights, disputes of all kinds. Near the end of the tour, the radio crackled, "Violent dispute within the confines of the Three-Two. Sector Eddie; respond to 147 West 149 Street, apartment A3. Acknowledge, K."

"Three-Two Eddie, ten-four, K." It was Wacko Macko.

"Three-Two Adam on a backup, Central," Mike added quickly. "Hey Len, maybe I can get to see him work again."

Once in the third floor apartment, it became apparent that no further units would be needed. Greg had the situation under control.

"No further units needed at West 149th Street, Central. Sector Adam will remain with Eddie until completion, K."

"Now listen you guys," shouted Greg. "We got to either end this shit or lock someone up. Your choice."

The adversaries proved to be husband and wife. The husband, John, was employed as a truck driver and spent days away from home. His wife Millie had worked her way into a rage, claiming that he had a woman on the side. At least that's what she believed. "Why else would he stay away for days?"

John shouted his explanation, "Listen woman. I'm driving trailer. Sometimes I go across to other states with a load. It takes days. To make more money for you, I wait maybe another day to get a load to drive back. You got everything you want. Don't you?"

"Listen you lying' nigger. You can't fool me. I wasn't born yesterday." With that remark she picked up his CB radio and threw it out the open window. It splattered when it hit the ground.

"Bitch", John replied as he put his foot through the television screen. "That radio is part of my job. No radio, no

110

money. You go peddle your ass to buy yourself a new T.V."

Millie jumped on him arms flailing. Walter, Macko's partner, and Len pried the women from her husband. Greg was braying like a Jackass.

"Listen folks. If you want to break up the place, let me help. The police are always ready to serve," stated Wacko. With that remark, he put the front half of a small sofa over the edge of the window.

"You keep breaking up things and we'll empty the place so you won't have anything to fight over. Then we can leave."

Millie took her husband's duffel bag containing some of his clothes and whipped it towards another window. It was closed. Mike stared in fascination. *She's really getting into it,* he thought. The glass exploded allowing the bag to plummet to the ground below.

Wacko Macko really brayed, caught fully by the spirit of it. "Ok, here goes," he calmly stated and gave the sofa a final push. It landed with a thud on the pavement.

Hard to say whom he surprised more, Millie and John, or Len and Mike. Walter had long ago gotten used to his partners antics. The dispute ended at that moment with both parties looking at Wacko and laughing. "You some crazy mother, Officer," John said through a chuckle. "Now take all those guys and let us alone. We got some cleaning up to do and some things to take care of."

"Sector Eddie to Central, K."

"Eddie."

In the Three-Two, 147 West 149th Street. Condition corrected." Wacko drummed his fingers on the handrails and whistled as the men in blue walked to the street. It was now end of tour.

Mike had never gotten used to the free and frequent use of that most prejudicial of epithets. Once behind the wheel of Sector Adam again, he decided he and his partner had gotten to know each other well enough for him to ask. "I can't understand it, Len. I mean, how often some of your people use that word."

"What word?" asked Len, only half listening.

"You know--uh--nigger." Mike said it hesitantly.

Len grinned. "Oh, sure. Nothin' unusual about that. The way a lot of us see it, me included, there's always been niggers in this world. It don't matter the flavor. Vanilla, chocolate, strawberry, they're all the same. Anybody who expects a free ride, who lies around on his or her back and whines for a handout, is a low-life nigger. No matter their color. Webster's defines it as, 'a worthless person.'"

That left Mike stunned into silence.

Back in the locker room, Mike asked, "Hey Len, how does Greg get away with that? Nobody ever gets mad or angry. Those people laughed. Their couch went out the window. It's history now."

Len shook his head, equally puzzled. "Mike, I've been here about four years now and to my knowledge he's never been in trouble for that sort of thing. There's no explanation for it. I'd say the man's got a guardian angel."

When he got home, Betty was waiting up. Since the shootout on West 145th Street, Mike often found her sitting in the living room watching late night television.

"Hi, Honey. How was the night?" She reached up to kiss him as he past her chair.

"Great Bet. Let me first see the kids and I'll tell you about it." Mike planted a big wet kiss on his wife's lips. She giggled.

Both of children lay in their beds, sound asleep. Mike crossed to his son's side and pulled the cover up over his shoulder. Returning to the living room he sat down next to her.

Joe DeCicco

Betty snuggled into him as he related the events of the evening.

"What do you think of that Wacko Macko, Hon? Any guesses on how he gets away with doing things like that. The guys say he's been doing it for years."

Betty carefully held a bank expression. "I don't know. But if you throw something of mine out of any window when we argue, you'll go right after it."

At that point he scooped his wife into his arms and feigned an attempt to open the nearest window. They tumbled to the floor in laughter.

"Mikey, be careful, you'll rip my blouse." Betty wore one of Mike's old shirts. It was threadbare.

Maybe she's feeling sillier than could be hoped for at this time of night. That's not a blouse. "Really," he responded as he made a grab at the collar and gave a gentle tug. Betty arched her body away from her husband. The first button popped as though responding to his wishes and flew across the room.

Betty squealed softly, ever mindful of the sleeping children. By now she had yanked Mike's tee shirt up over his head. She left it there to block his view, while she ran her fingers through the swirls of hair on his chest. "See, now you've done it."

"That's it woman." Swiftly, the remaining buttons disappeared from her shirt, assisted by his groping left hand. Mike's right hand pulled his shirt away from his eyes. His groin swelled with delight to see the battered shirt reveal rock hard nipples on her now jiggling breasts. *Don't stop now, guy.*

He continued to playfully paw her. She giggled false protests. Claiming that her voice would wake the sleeping children, Mike smothered her with kisses. "It's the only kind way to keep you quiet," he murmured.

Soon thereafter they both lay on the floor spent and exhausted, cooing like two pigeons. Their discarded clothing soiled with the pleasures of their love tryst.

Angel with a Gun

"Betty, not again. I'm too tired," moaned Mike in response to a wet tongue on his face. Only half awake he heard, "It's not me Mike," followed by a giggle.

Opening his eyes saw the Abigail, their dog, eagerly awaiting a late night walk. His face flushed in feigned embarrassment, Mike put on some clothes and reluctantly took the dog for a quick walk.

When he returned, Betty lounged seductively on the bed. "Come here you nice man. Abigail can't say thank you, but I can."

Later, Mike slept like a dead man.

CHAPTER NINE

Following the late night romantic athletics, Mike had off for the next two days. He planned to leave the children with his mother-in-law late in the day. He wanted to catch a movie and relieve Betty from cooking for one night. Playing at a local theater was a highly rated film about the trials and tribulations of a small group of survivors trapped inside an overturned ocean liner. The film was highly rated in newspaper reviews. Dressed in a "tanker" undershirt and ash-gray fleece shorts that bore the logo of the NYPD Academy, Mike sat by the open kitchen window and discussed it with Betty over morning coffee.

"Sweetheart, there's a really great flick playin' at the Rialto. I thought we might park the kids with your Mom, take in an early dinner at the Privateer, and see the movie. Sound okay to you?"

Betty didn't even hesitate. "Sure." The Romano's enjoyed the relatively inexpensive food at the Privateer Diner on Astoria Boulevard and visited often. Some-times they brought the children.

"Get me some more coffee, Bet. Then, how about some of those dollar-sized pancakes? I picked up some bulk polish sausage on the way home last night."

Betty patted her belly and rolled her eyes. "Yum. You gonna make it into patties and cook it on the grill?"

Mike left the table, headed for the charcoal cooker on the small, rear balcony. "Easy, sweetheart, you spoil me much like this and I'll have to buy new uniforms."

A stricken expression blossomed on her face as Betty responded tartly. "What about me? I still haven't lost all the pounds I gained when I carried Donald."

Mike grinned hungrily. "On you, it looks good, Baby."

Angel with a Gun

At a minute shy of 6 p.m., Mike and Betty walked into the diner. The owner's son, Charley, manned the register and greeted them each by name. He snagged a pair of menus and led them at a booth in the large rear portion of the diner.

After they had seated themselves, and opened the menus, Charlie excused himself with a cheerful, "Enjoy your food, Mike, Betty."

Mike ordered his favorite, Twin Romanian Steak. The dish consisted of two strips of flank steak, marinated in a "secret Greek sauce," cooked over an open flame, and served with French fries.   Betty, gastronomically a conservative, ordered Pot Roast with mashed. They both ordered beer.

"Let's hit the salad bar," Mike suggested.

Betty nodded agreement. "Sounds good. I hope they have that super Green Goddess dressing this time."

Their entrees arrived while they still worked on the greens. Two bites into his steak, Mike excitedly announced, "Bet, that guy over on the other side. It's Wilkey. Look!"

Betty glanced at him, puzzled. "Mike, you're nuts. Why would he be here?"

"I told you he lives in the neighborhood. Right at 3545 86th Street, here in Jackson Heights. That's him. Look in the mirror."

Brow furrowed, Betty studied the image in the glass. "Yes, it could be him, but it's too coincidental. You're so obsessed with the man. It only looks a little like the photo you insisted I keep."

"Where is it? You're supposed to carry it all the time. I wanted you to know who he is for the kids' sake."

"I keep it in the bag that I carry Donny's stuff in. Its home," came her reply.

Reaching for his wallet, Mike Romano excitedly pulled out a photo of Brian Wilkey and slid it across the table to Betty. She looked at it, then the reflected visage. Yes, she reluctantly agreed. There across the room was indeed his obsession, Wilkey.

The man that Betty Romano saw did not match her preconceived notion of a child molester. He did not look like a pervert. Wilkey appeared to be about five-foot-ten. He was clean shaven and had sallow skin. He had a slight redness to his cheeks, which emphasized the pale orange ghosts of boyhood freckles. Betty thought it might be because of his fair skin. Wilkey wore his hair cut short, though not so close that it hid the natural waviness. He seemed to be a rather thin man, maybe 150 pounds. The hands of the man in the mirror were rather large, with long fingers. He could have been a piano player.

When she began to turn to speak to her husband again, Betty's eyes once more fixed on the man's hands. She shuddered. Michael's obsession looked like an ordinary man. Well almost, the hands bothered her. The hairs on her neck bristled. If she didn't know who or what this man was, Betty now believed that she would feel the same upon seeing him, even by chance. Mrs. Romano began to hope that her archangel would indeed avenge the little girl.

Shaking her uneasy feeling Betty saw that Wilkey had a woman with him. She had shoulder length strawberry blonde hair and was fairly attractive. Her clothing denoted a comfortable income. She appeared to be about forty years old and had noticeable freckles.

Curiosity prodded Betty to ask, "Hey honey, who do you think she is?"

"Shh, why don't you keep quiet and listen? Maybe we can hear something," Mike answered brusquely.

Try as he may, Mike could not overhear any of the conversation. He and Betty remained at their booth until the couple left. Wilkey and his companion drove off in separate cars.

Mike looked after them with a scowl. "Damn, I should tail them, find out where they're going."

Betty drew a pained expression. "Honey, we have a movie to see, remember? This is supposed to be our night out."

Chagrinned, Mike nodded his surrender and signaled for the check. He paid Charlie and they left for the Rialto.

During the movie, Mike spun plans through his head on how he would find out more about the man he considered an abscess on the face of society. Little did he know that fate would soon provide the opportunity.

On the return from his swing, Mike began a set of mid-might-to-0800 tours. On the first tour the hand of Fate, or perhaps it was St. Michael, threw the first roll of the dice.

"No other Sectors available in the Three-Two, Sector Adam, K," crackled the voice of Central. Mike checked his watch. Five minutes short of 0200.

"Len answered, "Three-Two Adam, K."

"Respond to the front of 450 St. Nicholas Avenue. Anonymous complainant reports two abandoned children in a black Caddy in front of."

"Three-Two Adam, ten-four. Will check and advise. K." Parked right in front of the building entrance they found an old, four door, black Cadillac. Mike judged the year of the car to be somewhere between 1960 and 1963. It was apparent to the men of Sector Adam that someone or several someone's had been living in the car. The interior was littered with clothing, empty cereal boxes, soda cans, beer cans and curiously enough, dolls and empty milk cartons.

The radio car team could not readily determine if any children occupied the auto as claimed. The doors had been locked. Len asked, "Three-Two Adam, at 450 St. Nicholas, Central. Is there a call back or further information, K?"

"Negative Adam. The call is five minutes old. Any

disposition?"

"Will continue to check and advise, K."

Mike thought he saw some movement. "Hey Len, the coats in the rear moved. Maybe the kids are under them." He began knocking on the window of the auto. He received no response.

"Mike, on the chance that you're not seeing things, let's rock the car. If there are kids in there maybe they'll wake up. By banging on the car, we'll scare the crap out of them."

Rocking the vehicle caused the children to stir. The coats covering their faces fell away. Now the men shined flashlights in the youngsters' faces. They looked like two little girls, one, being much younger than the other. Mike's heart beat heavy. It happened every time he found a child in trouble. He thought of Wilkey and the rooftop. Wilkey, the serpent under the foot of the archangel.

While they rocked the ponderous vehicle to near exhaustion, the team noticed that the young children began to open their eyes. Once more the officers illuminated their little faces with their flashlights. The kids shielded their eyes at first. *Cute little things,* Mike observed. After realizing that two cops stood outside their makeshift bedroom, their faces took on the expression of wide-eyed, ebony "Kewpie Dolls" as their eyes opened in amazement.

When the door of the vehicle finally opened, the stale odor that drifted out caused Mike to comment. "Whew, ooff." He stated the obvious, "They were in here a long time."

Len nudged him to keep his comments to himself. "Shh, these kids must be scared," he whispered.

"Hi, kids. Are you okay?" asked Len, as self-appointed spokesman, thus taking the lead.

"Yes, thank you officer," came the polite response. "Did we do something wrong?"

"No girls. Someone called to have us come see if you were all right. That's all. Small ladies should not be sleeping all night in a car. What are your names? Do you have a Mommy and Daddy?" Jones continued.

"Yes, sir, we do," replied the older girl. "I'm Denise and my little sister is Salina."

At that point the younger girl began to whimper. "Its okay, Salina, these nice cops are not going to hurt us. They're here to help."

Denise continued, "Our second name is Johnson. Is there anything else Officer?"

Mike thought, *This kid is far beyond her years. She's already grown up.* Denise, put a comforting arm around her younger sister.

"Why are you sleeping in a car girls? Where's home? Where's your parents?" Mike asked.

Denise beamed up at him. "Mommy and Daddy are out for the night. We live here in the car for a couple of weeks now because we don't have a house. It's okay though. Mommy says we gonna have one soon."

"Excuse me girls," stated Mike as he guided his partner to the side. "Listen Len, we gotta send the kids into the house and wait for the parents to come back. I wanna lock the shits up. We can charge Endangering the Welfare of a minor, maybe Abandonment. The kids could be killed out here. Or worse. Remember, there's Wilkeys in Harlem too."

Jones mused over the situation. *My partner's nuts.* He sighed and responded with a wave of his hand and, "There you go again, my friend. Take it easy."

Mike knew by his partner's response that he was going to get nowhere in his effort. He led them back to the children. Once again with them, Len said, "Listen girls, we're going to have two lady policemen take you to the station house to wait for us. We'll see you later."

Mike called for Sector David to respond to the scene to transport the kids. They were a female radio car team. An experiment at the time.   Faye Hill, the shorter of the two women, stood about five - foot - five and weighed close to 160 pounds. She wore the neck of her uniform shirt open. Mike had even seen hair on her chest at times. Some of the men said it was sexy. To Mike, dark curly hair, poking out of a women's shirt, was a turnoff. He shuddered as he thought of her naked.

Christine Blaine, or Christie as she preferred, stood about five-foot-nine and a knockout. She wore an Afro, popular at the time, and weighed maybe 125 to 130 pounds. She was built like Diana, the huntress, from Greek mythology. Christie resembled a television star of the time that played a private detective. She also took Karate lessons.

Christie   could   model   as   the   proverbial   "Brick Shithouse" that men fantasize about in locker room discussions. Mike had seen the team hold their own against men on the street. When they arrived on the scene, Mike was amazed how "Mother-like" they were with the girls.

"What do we have here, Romano?" Faye Hill growled at the young officer.

"A couple of little girls, all alone," Mike responded.

Christie came out of the car and crossed to the Caddy. "Oh, you poor dears," she cooed to the sisters. "Come on, we'll take you to a place where you can be comfortable. Do you like cocoa?"

Guided by her impeccable, adult manners, Denise responded politely, "Yes, ma'am. But don't you think it is too hot for cocoa?"

Laughing, Faye squatted beside the girl. "You're right, Honey. More like a soda, huh?"

"Yes, ma'am. Or ice' tea. We both like ice' tea."

Faye did not even blink. "All right, then. Iced tea it is. With maybe a nice, big, gooey doughnut?"

Denise's eyes grew large. "Oh, yummy."

"Get in the car with us and we'll take you to a safe place," Christie suggested.

After the lady cops took the girls away, what was to be the only rift in their long partnership began. "Listen Len, we gotta lock them up."

"Mike, don't be too hasty. This is Harlem and things other than what you're used to are common here. People are poor. Sometimes they sleep in their cars for a few days. They can't afford hotels."

"Yeah, but the girls were alone. There was no adult with them. It's night time damn it. They were not with their parents. You're not even a father. You don't know how I feel." Raw anguish could be read on Mike's face. "Wait until you have a kid. Wait until your kids grow on you. Then you'll know why I'm ready to put them away."

Len thought that his partner was way out of line. He loved his child and cared for her, though he never saw her, what with his ex-wife moved clear the hell to Texas. He tempered his own rising anger with moderation; *He's talking out of his ass. Someday he'll learn to control his emotions.*

"Let it go, Mike. We can't stay here until who knows when. And, we've got a whole Sector to patrol, right?"

"Sure we got the Sector. But, this is worse than negligence. What if they've abandoned them?"

Len had an answer for that. "If they have, they ain't comin' back, right? So we'd be spinnin' our wheels, right? I tell ya, Mike, you've just got to let this one slide."

Mike persisted in the argument. After a couple minutes, the ardent expression of their differences was interrupted by, "Excuse me Officers. I'm the super of this building. I called."

He had been watching unobserved from the dark shadows alongside the building entrance. The shadows were formed by columns holding up a portico. He looked the stereotype of a building superintendent. The man was only five-foot-six. He wore a torn, dirty graying white tee shirt under a dark brown leather vest. The man's huge belly pushed his

122

paint-splattered pants down to the verge of falling. From his jaw hung a half smoked cigar. He badly needed a shave.

Mike turned to him, eager to learn what he could. "Oh, sure, thanks. What's going on? Have they been here long? Where are the parents?"

"Those kids and their folks have been here for two nights now. Today at about 7 p.m. the car pulled up and a man and woman got out. They said that the girls were their kids and asked if I could watch them for a few hours. The children would stay in the car and sleep. They would be back about 10 o'clock."

"Yeah, go on," Len impatiently urged.

Pausing to hitch up his pants and attempt to light the cigar stub, the disheveled man continued, "Now I remembered the car and them, so I said okay. They swore they would be back about ten. They said they were going out with friends. They promised to give me something for my trouble. They been gone too long. That's why I called 911."

"Len, see that's why we gotta lock them up. Let's wait for them to come back", was Mike's excited reaction.

Gently pushing his over-eager partner aside, Len spoke to the building super. "Sir, do you have a phone number if we need you?"

"Yes, it's 333-4578."

"Name, please?"

"John Washington, apartment 1B."

"Thank you. We'll be going now. Mike, let's go. We have a lot to do, partner." Len lead the way to the RMP.

Once in the patrol car, Mike Romano remained highly annoyed at his partner. Flexing his imaginary wings, Romano, jabbed his index finger in his partner's face and added, "Then I'm coming back with another partner and wait for them."

Arriving at the Three-Two, Sector Adam found the two girls lounging in the Commander's office, the door opened, a television set on.

Christie and Faye stood outside. Faye spoke up, "There's no place set aside for kids in this house (station house) so we put them inside. The boss isn't in. Besides, there's a television there.

Once again becoming the tough female cop that Mike knew, Faye said, "They're all yours. We gotta go back out on the street. We ain't no mothers. If I wanted kids, I'd get married."

Mike laughed and called after them. "Up yours, Faye."

Faye snorted and loosed one of her deep-throated growls. "That'll be the day."

While the female team negotiated the corridor and lobby, both Len and Mike appreciatively turned to watch Christie until she walked out the door.

The men of Sector Adam returned their attention back to the girls. The younger child, Salina, was watching an old black and white movie. Denise sat, reading a newspaper to keep busy.

Mike was dumbfounded. It was the New York Times. "Can you read that, Denise?"

"Sure," and she proceeded to read a paragraph with halting accuracy.

My God, she is far beyond her nine years. Mike felt his emotions well. He turned his back on his partner and stated, "Len, you stay here with them because I'm going out to wait for those bastards to come back. I'm gonna lock them up."

Walking through the station house in search of a temporary partner, the would-be avenging angel found a lone police officer in the cops' lounge. The guy's partner had gone down to court with an earlier collar. The man, Jack Baker, was free. He had stretched out on a second hand couch and watched the same movie that had little Salina's attention.

Mike approached him, his face alight with his sense of urgency. "Jack, listen, Len is busy with two little girls that were abandoned in a car on St. Nicholas Avenue. I want to go

124

there and wait for the parents to come back. When they approach their car, I'm gonna cuff them. They're gonna take a collar. Will you go with me?"

"Sure, Mike, no problem. What started this? What happened?"

"Tell you on the way."

After hearing the entire story, Jack agreed with Mike. The kids' parents should be arrested. Plain and simple, Len was wrong. The two cops waited for several hours. It would soon be dawn and the kid's folks never came back. At about 0600 the dispatcher stated, "Three-Two sector Adam, ten-two and acknowledge, K."

"Ten-four Central," Mike replied. Their squad was being called in for something.

Back in the station house, Len had made ready to transport the two girls to a shelter in Far Rockaway, Queens. "You still upset, Mike? Or will you make the ride to the shelter with me? If you still insist on arresting their parents, we can discuss it on the way back. I'll show you that I'm right."

"Sure Len, we're partners. Being pissed off is like being married. I'll just make believe you're Betty and we had an argument." Mike tried to ease the tension between them by adding, "I might even try to make up to you by trying to take you to bed. How's that?"

"Up yours, Mike. Let's just go."

"No Len, up yours. That's the whole idea."

Both men laughed. They were friends again.

It was 0930 hours when they got back to the Three-Two. The desk officer, Lieutenant Fondalar, was reaming two civilians. They turned out to be the parents of the two girls.

"Just who the hell do you think you are? What possessed you to leave two little girls alone on a Harlem street?

If my men didn't take them in, maybe they would have been hurt or worse."

Mr. Johnson, the father, claimed that he knew the kids would be all right because he asked the building super to watch them.

"They're okay now guy," stated the Lieutenant. Then he went on. "Officer Riley, place these two under arrest." He motioned for the station house security man to come forward. "Charge them with Abandonment and Endangering the Welfare of."

As Riley put cuffs on both of them, Mike smiled and said, "See, Len, I told you so."

Jones responded with, "He's as crazy as you, Mike. Let's sign out. We'll finish this tomorrow."

CHAPTER TEN

On the following day, Len and Mike sensed tenseness between them. The tension was almost tangible. Mike knew it was mostly his doing but he could not control himself. He could not let go of the night before. "You know Len; I was thinking all day and decided that you could never appreciate how I feel about those kids because you're not a father. When you have your own children you'll know."

Shortly after turning out the team made an arrest. They had responded to a dispute and busted one of the adversaries for possession of a gun. They went to the arrest processing room at 0030. Record speed for a bust, even in the old Three-Two.

Mike sat at a desk and prepared the finger print cards for his partner. He overheard Len telling another officer, "Yeah, Mike's a great guy but sometimes he's nuts. This is Harlem and he grew up in an affluent white neighborhood. He just doesn't know how things are in a poor black neighborhood."

That angered the would-be archangel all over again, that his partner didn't understand how he felt. Mike rose quickly and strode across to his partner saying, "Hey, Len, I'm still pissed about yesterday. Here's your cards. You can process the papers for this collar alone. I'm just gonna sit here."

Feeling stupid at his outburst, Romano sensed the rush of blood to his face. He quickly added, "Unless you really need me." He knew it to be a feeble attempt to save face.

The usually cool, soft spoken Leonard Jones felt his own ire growing within him. "Fine, Smartass. I won't."

With the partners at an impasse, Fate would once again touch Police Officer Michael Romano.

Angel with a Gun

The telephone rang. Mike picked it up answering, "Hello, Three-Two, Police Officer Romano here. Can I help you?"

A weak voice from the other end answered. It was female. "Yes, I'm a witness to a crime and I'm gonna get killed."

"Calm down. What crime and who's gonna kill you. What's your name?"

From the other end, the woman spoke like someone who had run to catch a train. Her words collided with one another. Mike barely deciphered her message. "My name's Mary Atkins. All the cops know me there. I used to be an Auxiliary Cop. You know, one of the volunteers. There was a bar robbery about ten months ago. In White Plains, and I was there. They shot two off-duty cops. One died. Back then I tried to tell people but they wouldn't listen. Now you gotta."

As he listened Mike tried to visualize her situation. *She sounds like a nut, but what if it's real? Damn, I have to get her in here.* Mike's heart began to beat like the trumping sound of a large bird's wings. The avenging angel syndrome had taken hold of him again.

Mike forced himself to speak calmly. "Mary, do you know the name of the man who's trying to kill you? Is it the same guy who shot the cops?"

Panting with anxiety, Mary continued. She spoke like a sprinter ran; fast as she could. "Yeah. His name is Roger Hays. The White Plains cops think he's Spanish. But he's not. He's a black guy from Harlem. He was arrested in the Amol Bar last week." As she continued to answer Mike's questions, he learned that Hays had not been arrested, only detained and released.

Mary explained, "But the cops didn't take him to the station house. They frisked him and he had a .38 in his underpants. The gun was under his balls. They missed it and let him go. That night Roger left behind a shotgun without the

128

wooden part. I got it. It was the gun that killed the cop in White Plains. I wanna help. I'll talk to you but come and get me. Please, I'm scared."

Mike could not believe his ears. If this woman was telling the truth, he was about to help catch a cop killer.

Not wanting to get in another tense situation with his partner, Mike decided to remain in the station house if at all possible. He began with, "Mary, I'm in the middle of processing arrests now and can't come over to get you. Please call a cab and I'll meet you in front of the station house. Have the driver beep the horn. I'll come down to get you."

Her response came coated in fear. "No. Maybe he'll be outside and he'll shoot me. You come for me."

After several minutes of the same, Mike was surprised to hear her say, "I don't know if I can get a cab now. If one will take me to you, I'll call you and then you look for me. Okay?"

"Absolutely, Mary. I'll be waiting."

At that point Mike gave his partner the twenty-five-words-or-less version of his conversation with Mary. Len listened, his eyebrows rising as the tale unfolded, then informed Mike that Mary was well known in the Three-Two. She could be a bit of a nut also. She worked a bar maid in the Amol Bar.

Mike went right into the Precinct Detective Squad office that was adjacent to the arrest room. Only one man sat there. He appeared to be a seasoned detective. He was slightly overweight and chewed on a cigar stub. The man had his tie open, his jacket off, a large, gold, and pinky ring on his right hand. He wore his graying hair slicked back, and his slightly swarthy face hosted a bulbous, crimson nose. *My God, he's right out of an old movie,* thought Mike.

Detective Old Movie bent over and closed one of the desk drawers. On the chipped, dark oak desk, was a placard, Det. Flynn. Never looking directly at Mike, he asked, "Yeah. What can I do for you kid?"

Mike sniffed the air. It smelled of whiskey. "This woman called and said that she had information on a cop killer. Some guy named Roger Hays."

"Don't know any cop killers, Kid. Don't know anybody named Roger Hays. Flynn leaned back and his chair squealed in protest. The old detective asked, "Is the guy white or black?"

Romano replied, "My informant claims that the police are looking for a Spanish guy and the killer, Hays, is black."

"Roger Hays, Roger Hays. Wait a minute." Flynn slowly rose from behind his desk. Sloth-like, he crossed over to a lectern stand next to the office door. On top of it was a large black ledger labeled Telephone Message Book.

Once he had the book open, Mike could see large red numbers in the upper right hand corner of each page. The detective turned to page number 152; the entry was hand written on page 153. Flynn tapped an entry with his pen. It had been recorded earlier that same day at 1130 hours. The message came from Lt. Ludge, CO 6th Homicide, asking for any information on one Roger Hays.

"Seems like Hays was arrested earlier today, kid. The boys at 6th Homicide wanted to know if anybody else wanted him too. But Hays is a black guy."

Flynn closed the ledger with a vengeance. It sounded much like a gunshot. Mike felt the impulse to duck.

At once, the old cop began to return to his desk. Smiling he said, "Hold it a minute, maybe there's a wanted poster for the cop killer."

Flynn then began a cursory inspection of the various clipboards hung on the walls and the flyers they contained. He put a note of ridicule in his voice. It was a slow night for him and Mike provided some entertainment.

Mike was becoming annoyed at the attitude of this rude old-timer. He held his cool, feeling inside that he would show up this man and others like him in time.

After being assured that there was no such poster, Mike

decided to look through the clipboards himself.   Under the mocking silent, eye of Detective Flynn, he took his time.   One clipboard that rested against a cabinet, he found what he was looking for.   An artist's rendering of a suspect listed as a male Hispanic, wanted by the White Plains Police Department.

The man in the poster was being sought as the killer of a cop.   The dead police officer had been a New York City Detective. The face in the poster, and his unknown accomplice, also shot a White Plains cop.   On the bottom of the sheet a telephone number and the name of the Detective in charge of the investigation in White Plains, New York, had been written. The incident happened almost ten months before.

Mike wrote down the phone number and replaced the clipboard.   *Fuck this old bastard; I'll make the call and the points, if any.*

Shortly thereafter, two White Plains Detectives left the Detective Bureau, on their way to the Three-Two Precinct. Grinning, Mike told his partner.

Len was skeptical, "That's terrific Romano. But what if it's a wild goose chase? You put wheels into motion here. I can't bail you out. You'll be on your own."

Mike's enthusiasm could not be dampened.   "Don't worry, Len.   It's good info.   The guy's in the 6th Homicide holding cell or Central Booking. We can get him."

The telephone rang. It turned out to be Mary. She had found a ride with a car service and was on her way over.

Mary arrived within five minutes.   She came upstairs without Mike having to go down for her. He prompted, "Listen Mary; tell me the whole story again."

Mary went through the story again for Mike. He found it impossible to take notes. Mary continued to speak as fast as a runaway freight train. She had been present in the bar during the shooting. The two officers who had been shot were friends, sitting together when two gunmen entered and pointed shotguns at everyone.

After cleaning out the cash register, they began robbing the customers. When they got near the two cops, the officers attempted to draw their guns and got shot. She guessed that the robbers became too excited because one guy, Hays, dropped his shotgun and a wooden piece broke off. He picked up the gun, but left the missing part behind, and both men ran out. Mary recognized Hays as a regular patron of the Amol Bar. Hays also recognized her.

Several days after the shooting he sent a warning to her never to say anything or he would kill her. He was now blaming her for "dropping a dime" on him --- causing his near arrest. Word on the street reached her that he was gunning for her. Mike showed her the "Spanish man" in the poster.

Mary's eyes went wide and round and her lower lip trembled. "That's him. That's Roger Hays."

At 0300, the two White Plains detectives arrived. They introduced themselves and Mike filled them in.

The older of the pair, Walt Furgeson, turned his level, gray gaze on Mike and spoke thoughtfully. "Yes there was a piece of a gunstock recovered at the scene. You've done a good job, Patrolman. Developing this witness has given us a real break." He flashed a warm smile on Mike and then Mary. "Who'd you say is running this on your end?"

"Sixth Division Homicide, sir."

Furgeson reached for a phone. "We'll give them a try." They received no answer.

Karl Jaeger, the younger detective, shrugged. "Well, that was a bust. Let's call Central Booking."

At the far end of the line, the phone was picked up on the third ring. "Central Booking, Dwyer."

Walt Furgeson spoke through a slight strain. "This is Detective Sergeant Furgeson from White Plains. Do you have a Hays there? Roger Hays? Might be listed as a Hispanic."

Papers riffled over the phone. "Yeah. Hays is still here. Due to be arraigned tomorrow morning."

Relief echoed in the voice of Furgeson. "Keep him for us, will you? We'll be right down. Thanks." Walt Furgeson hung up and turned to Mike Romano. "I want to thank you for all the help you have been. And, I'd like to take this young lady -- Mary is it? -- Downtown with us."

By that time Len had finished with his paperwork. Grinning, he looked at his partner, shook his head, and said, "Only you Mike, only you. Step in shit and come up smelling like roses. Maybe you do work for God."

Mike did not mean for his reply to sound flippant. "It works for me because I'm a nice guy. That's why", Mike replied, feeling like he just won a million dollars. Detective Flynn grumpily closed the door to his office, and remained inside. Gotcha, Flynn, rejoiced Romano.

Mike drove Len and his prisoner downtown. He returned to the Three-Two, while Len remained to complete the booking process and take the man through court. Mike fell asleep in the lounge awaking just in time to sign off duty at 0800. Happily he drove home and told Betty about the night, before going to bed at 10 a.m.

"Mike get up, there's a boss on the phone." Betty shook him awake at about noon.

Sleepily, Mike took the receiver from her, "Hello, Mike Romano here."

His supervisor was on the other end. "Mike this is Sergeant Armini. You're being rescheduled to work a four-to twelve tonight instead of another Midnight. It's your last one in this set. You get a longer swing this way. Sign in at the Three-Two and after suiting up report to 6th Homicide in the Two-Six Precinct. Report to Lieutenant Ludge. Got that?"

"Yeah Sarge. How come?"

Angel with a Gun

"Because you did good last night. That woman, Mary identified Hays in a lineup just a couple of hours ago. Good work Mike. Proud to have you as one of my men. See you later."

Mike remained awake for the rest of the day. He excitedly relived the entire incident with Betty. At 2:00 p.m., Mike left home for the Three-Two.

Mike walked into the offices of 6th Homicide Division at exactly 1615. They expected him. He was asked to wait a few minutes. While he nervously looked about the room, Mike spotted a short distinguished looking man, who walked out of a small, rear office. It was Lieutenant Ludge.

"Officer Romano, we meet again," he stated, extending a smile and his hand to Michael.

"Yes, sir, we do. Is everything okay? Are there any problems? Was it the right guy last night?"

"Yes Mike, everything is fine. You did an excellent job. He was the right man. Please step into my office with me will you?"

Once inside the lieutenant closed the door. "Sit down, Mike. Make yourself comfortable. Please tell me how you got involved in this."

Over the next twenty minutes, Mike told him the whole story. When he concluded, Ludge leaned forward and spoke with candor.

"You see Mike; in this office one of my men is a detective assigned as liaison between the White Plains and New York Police Departments. He's got that assignment because he lives next door to a cop who is assigned there. It's strange that we had this guy Hays in our custody and never knew he was a cop killer. We took him in for stabbing a man as he stole the victim's bicycle.

"Hays was brought into our office yesterday. The

134

arresting detective paraded him around to see if anyone wanted him." Ludge gave Mike a sharp, meaningful look. "This particular liaison detective was present. He never said a word."

"I didn't know that, sir," Mike said apologetically, as if it might be his fault the detective didn't know who Hays was.

"I'll talk to him later," Ludge continued.

Mike felt the irony in the Boss' voice. *That guy is in deep shit,* he thought.

"Now you have to go into another office and be interviewed by I.A.D. on tape. Tell them the story as you told me. You'll be fine," stated the Lieutenant.

Romano didn't know the reason for the taped interview. He sat through it anyway. Lt. Ludge was pleased. That's all Mike cared about. It was going to be fine. After the sergeant from I.A.D. had finished, Lt Ludge called Mike into his office to say good-bye.

"Mike, thank you for your help. You'll hear from me."

Mike started to turn from the desk when he saw a photo laying there. It was of Ludge and another man who Mike recognized from past encounters, the boss from the Police Academy. With the men were two women. One of the women in the photo he recognized as the lady from the diner. The one they saw with Wilkey.

Mike decided to use the Lieutenant to check his own information on Bryan. "Excuse me Boss. Who's the folks in the picture with you? Nice looking people."

"Thank you Mike. The lady in green is my wife. The man standing next to me is Inspector Dennis Bryan, next to him, his wife. Our wives have a cursory friendship through the Job. That photo was taken at the Captain's Endowment Association Christmas Dinner two years ago. Why do you ask.?"

For the moment, Mike's mind sped elsewhere. Bryan looked even bigger in the photo. *He's tall, and with his fat, round face, and big stick-out ears, topped with that red hair, he*

*looks like a great big pumpkin. That's it! His new name; The
Great Pumpkin.*

"Just admiring how good everyone looks. That's all.
Where does Bryan work, Boss?"

"In the Chief of Department's Office. He's one of the
men in charge of personnel allocations."

"Big guy, huh?" Mike thought; *Bingo in the,
Suspicions Confirmed department.*

"Yes. You could say that. I stay on a friendly basis
because of my wife. He can be tough, though. Good man to
have on your side. Anyway, thank you again Mike. Take care.
The Job needs men like you."

Their interview had ended. Mike thought, *Thanks Boss.*
Now he had a good make on what that shit-head looked like,
too.

While Mike drove back to command all he could think
of was what he had learned. That son of a bitch. Mike recalled
Bryan from his graduation. The woman they had seen at the
diner with Wilkey was Bryan's wife. She is really that bastard's
sister. That's the tie. It's real. That means that Deputy
Inspector Dennis Bryan is dirty. Someday he'd find out how
much. The archangel's wings twitched again.

He couldn't wait for the tour to end so he could go
home and tell Betty. In celebration of the new information, he
would take the family to the Privateer Diner. The kids too. He
thought that the wife of such a lucky guy should not have to
cook.

CHAPTER ELEVEN

Following his swing, Romano returned to day tours. During this set Michael learned a little about politics in the Police Department. Sergeant Armini congratulated him again for his work regarding the cop killer. Armini handed Mike a clipping he had cut out of "Police Beat," from the City's most popular tabloid newspaper. It noted the arrest and indictment of Roger Hays for a bar stickup that resulted in the shooting of two police officers and the death of one of them. The article continued, "An unnamed police detective was demoted to the rank of police officer, transferred to the Bronx and returned to a foot patrol as a result of the investigation. Reliable sources indicated that patrol gathered evidence in the case, independent of the detective assigned to lock Hays into the crime, resulted in the suspect's identification and eventual conviction."

Stated as the reason for the detective's demotion was that, "It was later found that the detective in question had the same information patrol had uncovered. It came in the form of notes in his desk draw. The official reason for his being removed was cited by the Public Information Office as 'failure to take proper police action.' He was also put on three years' probation within the Department. Mike knew who demoted the guy. Lieutenant Ludge. He spoke to him later like he said he would. Now Mike knew why the I.A.D. interview had been tapped.

Armini also had more information for Romano. "Mike, I want you should know that Lieutenant Ludge has recommended you for a promotion to the rank of Detective Third Grade, as a result of the Hays incident."

Stunned, Mike stared at the sergeant. "My God, that's incredible."

Mike's elation was short lived. "Yeah, a little too incredible. The request is not going forward due to the lack of an endorsement by the Manhattan North Borough Commander. He cited the fact that you did not have full tenure on the job, to wit, three years in rank."

Mike was crushed. "Shit, Sarge, it would have been better if I never found out about the possible promotion. It's nice to hear that the guy that had the same information I gathered, and didn't act on it was punished. He deserved it."

Mike folded the clipping and put it into his wallet, then said, "Thanks for the article Boss, it helps."

His tour went rather uneventfully with the usual disputes, aided (sick or injured) cases, and past robberies. Nothing spectacular. Not until he got home did Mike find any excitement.

June had arrived, full summer. The days grew longer. Mike reached his apartment by 4:45 p.m. He found the place empty. Betty and the children had gone off somewhere. After walking Abigail, he telephoned her mother's house on 93rd Street. Betty often walked to her mother's with the children. Sometimes he met her there and the family would eat together and then play cards. His mother-in-law informed him that Batty had telephoned earlier and said that she was going shopping along 82nd Street.

Mike watched a news film about the latest moon landing when Betty burst into the apartment. Abigail, the family dog gently nibbled the big toe on Mike's right foot.

"Michael." She often called him by his proper name when upset or angry. The dog sensed her excitement and became overly playful. She jumped on the kids triggering a game of tag. Donald and Anne began to run through the apartment after the dog. Then she chased them. *If only we could get a house,* Mike thought. *There would be a back yard for this sort of thing.*

Joe DeCicco

"Michael I saw your car downstairs and couldn't wait to tell you what I saw today." Betty paced the room as she spoke. He had never seen her so agitated. The dog barked, and came galloping past her, the kids yelled in delight. The situation rapidly approached mayhem.

"Betty, Honey, please sit down in the kitchen. Let me pour you something cool. Orange juice, soda or some of my all curing scotch?" *This is going to be something. Betty's rarely this excited, he thought.* He'd have a scotch and water.

"Orange juice with lots of ice, thanks."

Smiling, he absently verbalized his last thought, "Except in bed," he said aloud, thinking about what it's like when Betty got excited during love making.

"What the hell are you talking about? Are you listening to me Mike? It's about Wilkey."

The magic word; Wilkey. She now had his undivided attention. Mike poured her juice, mixed himself a large drink, and sat down. He knew that she would continue without prompting.

"Mike, I was walking around after getting the kids some clothes and decided to see where Wilkey lived. It's somewhere on 86th Street? The 3500 block. Right?"

"Yes, 3245 to be exact. What made you look for him? You always tell me to leave it alone."

"Maybe it was the way he looked when we saw him in the Privateer Diner. He made my skin crawl. Anyway, I had the picture you gave me and I took a walk. The block is full of those big apartment buildings. The complex with the security booth and the nice landscaping. You know where, right?"

"Yeah. Tell me why you're so wound up. Did he threaten you or what? Did he approach you or the kids?" Mike had started to get nervous. The avenging angel syndrome began to grow again.

"No nothing like that. Better."

He's dead, thought Mike.

139

Betty excitedly continued, "Bryan's wife came out of the building. It was 3245. See, I wrote it on my hand along with her license plate number." Betty extended the palm of her left hand to prove her statement. Mike saw two numbers there. She had used a blue ball point pen.

"Anyway, the woman we saw in the diner that night, you said it was Wilkey's sister, Bryan's wife. She came out of the building, almost walked into me and the children. Then she went into a large blue car, a Buick I think, and sat behind the wheel. Now I was getting more curious so I stopped to rearrange some packages in the stroller. Donald was uncomfortable anyway. We stopped right next to her. On the dashboard of the car I saw a union card from the Captains Endowment Association. She reached in her purse and took out an envelope full of money. It was full of Fifties and Twenties. She counted it quickly, right there in front of me. Then she put several bills into her wallet. The rest she returned to the envelope and put it back into her purse."

Now he knew how he sounded to Betty when he ran on and on. He attempted to slow her down with, "Bet, maybe it was money from or for a bank or something. After all they're family, brother and sister." For all his objections, Mike hoped the transaction was of the "or something" type.

"No Michael. She had at least one thousand dollars. You told me Wilkey was involved in gambling and paid Bryan. Maybe his sister brings Bryan the money. Maybe today, Monday, is when she collects. Now we gotta find out why."

Mike could not help but chuckle. "What do you mean 'we' woman? You're constantly telling me to leave it alone. Now it's 'we'?"

"Well, you know what I mean. Why does he give Bryan money? You're the one who told me. Check with that detective from Sex Crimes again. Maybe he knows the reason. But you be careful anyway because I love you, you big shit. Oh, damn it, I'm getting just like you." Betty bit her lower lip.

Abigail and the kids had finally been corralled back in their room. Peace had returned to the Romano household.

"I love you too, Honey. Thanks. This is something to work on. I'll run the plate and see if it's Bryan's.

Back at work the following day Mike found a few minutes to log on to the station house computer. After completing the various access codes, he punched in: RVEH; RZ-2424, NY, the license plate Betty gave him the day before. Betty was right, a blue 1974, 4 door Buick was registered to Elizabeth Bryan, 02/22/43F, 122 Figurea Street, Staten Island, NY. His heart began to pound.

Checking further into Motor Vehicle records, revealed that Liz Bryan first received her driver's license in the name of Elizabeth Wilkey! *My God, here's proof. Now to find out why The Pumpkin is taking money,* thought Michael.

While Romano dug into the Wilkey/Bryan connection, a dialogue between Dennis and Elizabeth Bryan went from warm to acrimonious. The Bryan residence on Figurea Street was a split-level ranch and, like its neighbors, built in the late 1950's. It had a brick facade with the usual white shingled sides. The front was modestly landscaped. The rear of the house however, gave a hint to the financial abilities of the Bryans.

Here an in-the-ground swimming pool sparkled invitingly. A redwood deck surrounded the pool, with the adjacent area inlaid with red bricks. It might be possible that a Deputy Inspector in the New York City Police Department might have such a yard if he was handy with his hands, and there was a second income in the home, or if he was independently wealthy. In the Bryans' case there was an extra income. "Gifts" from his brother-in-law. Organized Crime money.

Angel with a Gun

In their well-furnished living room Elizabeth Bryan said with a seething hiss, "Listen you cheating bastard. You keep telling me that you're working late. I've been married to you long enough to be friendly with some cops. I know that you have girlfriends." Liz concluded by screaming at her Inspector husband.

Dennis raised his hands in mute appeal. "Please Liz. Don't go on like that. You know that there are jealous cops around. They make up stories. Believe me, I'm not running around on you."

"Well, if you are, you had better call it to a screeching halt. Not only will I file for divorce, but my brother, Brian, has instructions to bury you. Remember, you've been protecting him for years. He's been giving us money for years, too. Wouldn't the Police Department like to know about that?"

Paling, Dennis reached for his wife in an effort to pacify her. "Calm down Liz. Don't do anything foolish. If I got fired, you wouldn't get a nickel. There would be no pension. No money for you to get a piece of, "Dennis retorted. He rapidly grew more nervous as the realization struck him. This woman was not a Police Department subordinate. He had no power over her.

"Think about what I said, you bastard."

Beads of sweat began to form across his forehead and in the numerous folds at the rear of his more than ample neck. His blood pressure climbed. "Take it easy. We can work this out. Don't worry your brother about this. I may not like him, but he's your brother, and we're stuck with him."

"Take your smug, holier-than-thou attitude and stick it up your ass, Dennis. You straighten out or I'll have your ass."

Bryan attempted to answer her. His lips began to move without making a sound.

Liz continued, "You began to look out for Brian because he's my brother. When I started to suspect that you had other women, I made sure my brother began to say thank you with small amounts of cash. You liked the money. Sort of an insurance policy." In a threatening gesture she picked up a small figurine.

As Liz began to swing the hand holding the figurine, she continued, "Sure, you probably spent it on those bimbos. Now that the money is bigger, you're really in it up to your undersized prick. You better straighten out or else. I want it stopped." Her arm ceased swinging.

She had enough of talking. The porcelain statuette whooshed past his head and splattered against the wall behind him. He had no time to react.

"Okay, okay," he blurted the only response he could think of.

His whale of a body shuddered now. In retaliation, Dennis thought of telling his wife about the fact that her brother was a child rapist. Perhaps her anger would re-focus on him. Realizing such a revelation would only infuriate her more, he remained mute. Elizabeth would never believe such an accusation and accuse him of making it up. What annoyed him the most, now he would have to protect Brian even better and longer. If anything happened to that piece of shit, she would blame him.

That same afternoon, Mike Romano, telephoned his friend John Cutbert at home. His avenging spirit had been rekindled by the by the new information spawned by Betty's chance encounter.

"John, how the hell are you? It's Mike. Listen I have proof of the relationship between Wilkey and Inspector Bryan."

"Mike, what are you talking about? What proof?"

"Listen, I'll show you when I see you. But, before that try to arrange for me to meet with George Cali. I need some background. Can you set it up?"

143

Angel with a Gun

"My little friend, you're gonna step on your dick over this. Sure I can set it up. But you better meet me tonight and tell me what you're talking about."

"Sure John, my house or yours?"

"Our office, the Abbey, 2100 hours."

"Fine, see you there."

That night, Mike arrived on time and settled in at a corner table beside his friend. "Okay, here's what I've got," said Mike enthusiastically. Then he quickly brought John up to date. He began with the chance encounter in the diner, and then told of Betty seeing Liz Bryan at Wilkey's residence. He ended the story by showing John the printout of Elizabeth Bryan's auto registration, and the old name on her driver's license.

John considered that a minute, then nodded. "All right, I'll contact George and have him visit you. Make it here at the Abbey soon as possible."

They met two days later.

At 2150, their usual office hours, Romano walked into the familiar Abbey. He spotted the two men he came to meet, seated at a small round table in the far left corner of the room. Cali wore 'soft clothes' (regular street clothing). However, he did still look like an owl to Mike because of his slightly messed hair and bushy eyebrows above his large lens-covered eyes.

Mike walked directly to the table. He extended his hand toward Detective Cali first. "George, Mike Romano, remember me? We met here a few months ago." In the same breath he added, "Hi, John. Thanks."

Taking Mike's hand, Cali replied, "Mike, happy to see you again." In an attempt to add humor to the conversation Cali added, "John filled me in on your quest for the 'Golden

Fleece'. He also explained why you're hot on Wilkey again. How can I help?"

Mike ordered a round of drinks. After a snappy looking little part-time barmaid, named Lynn, brought their drinks, and a wicker basket of popped corn, Romano began a more detailed account of the recent developments.

"George, a few weeks ago I visited OCID. I picked up some interesting things there." Mike went on to lay out his discoveries, and then told of Betty's experience, concluding with, "And so she sat there, right before my wife, counting money." George allowed him to continue uninterrupted.

Mike ordered more drinks as he continued to speak. "John told you about the tie-in to Inspector Bryan's wife." Cali nodded. Mike kept going. "What I'm looking for is more background on Bryan. What's he all about? What's the story on him? Rumors or truths, I want it all."

Before Cali could answer, Mike continued, "Is he a closet queer? Does he chase girls? Is he a gangster? Besides Wilkey, does he take money from other sources?"

"Jesus, Mike you don't want much, do you?"

Mike grinned self-consciously. "Not really George. I'm trying to build a mental background file on him. In case God ever gives me the opportunity to screw with him, I wanna be ready. Someday I'm going to get Wilkey. If The Great Pumpkin ever tries to hump me because of it, I want to be ready to back him off or maybe take him down."

George leaned over and asked, "Great Pumpkin. Who's that?"

That question brought a chuckle from John, who ordered another round, "Inspector Bryan of course. Did you ever see him? Michael saw his picture in an office and christened him with the name." Clapping Mike on the back, John said, "I might add that I agree with my friend."

Lynn brought their drinks and winked at the now-gawking George. Cali was taken by her bright, almost white, blonde hair, worn loose about the shoulders. It framed her heart-shaped face in wisps. Above and below her big, childlike blue eyes she had silky lashes, so perfect, that George wondered if they could be real. Her petite stature was accented with an athlete's body, not one drop of unnecessary fat.

Mike saw that the man had been smitten by her, and his eyes indicated that his mind had gone somewhere else. Not even he knew where. Cali jerked back to reality as Mike knocked his knuckles on the table. "Hello, George? Is anyone home?"

George responded by asking Lynn if she had to go home right after work. She replied, "Cops", and sashayed away.

George's stare was accompanied by, "She moves like a well-oiled expansive watch."

Cali went back to addressing the men at his table. "You know Mike; you got a way with words. Yeah, I've seen him many times. He's about six-foot-three and weighs about 350 pounds. His ears stick out from the sides of his red topped head like Alfred E. Newman, and when he smiles, he shows big front teeth. 'What, me worry?' " George quoted the famous logo from 'Mad Comics'. "Yeah, you got that right; he does look like a great big pumpkin. He does. Anyway, you're good, kid." Then he gave Mike a mocking pat on the head.

"Thanks, Poppa," quipped Mike.

Laughing, George pulled his ears away from his head, stood up on his toes and forced his belly out in mock emulation. "Look at me guys, I just gave myself a big, fat promotion."

"Good thing you don't have red hair like he does. The impulse to kick you in the balls would be almost uncontrollable," choked Romano over guffaws of laughter.

"You should be a detective kid," continued Cali, as he sat down again. "We all thought that Wilkey was Bryan's cousin. You showed us that we were wrong. He's the guy's brother-in-law. Holy Shit."

Joe DeCicco

Although Mike had a good time with such nonsense, he didn't want to lose the reason for the meet. He got back to business and asked, "Thanks, but can you help me? I still need background."

"Sure, but this is only hearsay mind you. No proof that I know of. Okay?" prompted George in a confidential tone.

"No problem George," came Romano's expected reply.

"Guys have seen him at rackets when men get promoted or retire. Things like that. You know, no wives, 'Goomaddas' only." Mike knew that was cop slang for girlfriends. He nodded his understanding. "Well, they claim that he always leaves with a woman. No one special. Just any broad that appeals to him and he can get to leave with him." To let Mike know his own personal morals, he added, "I say, if you're happy at home, you don't have to have other women."

"Maybe he's just a friendly kind of guy, George." Mike had started to chuckle again. "From what I hear, he's as friendly as a sailor in a whore house with a fist full of fifty dollar bills. The man's a real coxswain. He considers himself a swordsman. Personally if I was a broad, I'd rather do without than hook up with him."

"Jim, another round, please," interjected George with a belch.

As Lynn brought the drinks, both John and Mike waited for another exchange between their friend and the barmaid. There was none.

John, who had remained quiet up to that point, felt it time to caution his friend again. "Mikey", the name he used when he was feeling the liquor, "remember, Bryan can hurt you. Be careful. Don't initiate anything. Remember; let God give you the opportunity." *As if He ever will*, thought the Sergeant.

Mike, seeing that the mood was about to change and become too serious, asked, "Hey do either of you two guys know why a boss is like a diaper?"

147

Angel with a Gun

Both George and John answered, "No." As though they rehearsed it, they said in unison, "But, please tell us."

Mike could hardly hold back his own laughter as he responded, "Because they're both always on your ass and usually full of shit."

Mike gave the punch line as George had his glass to his lips. Cali spit out half of his drink as more of it ran up his nasal passages. John belly laughed, sounding like a dyslexic thunder clap, first the roll of fading thunder, then the loud noise.

The ice broken, silly cop jokes continued until almost closing. Lynn had worn down the floor between her station at the end of the bar and their table. As the trio stood and exchanged the equivalent of good-byes, Lynn walked over and nuzzled George behind his right ear. She had to stand on her toes and put one hand on his shoulder to do it. In doing so the short bolero type blouse she wore exposed most of her midriff, hinting that the next thing in sight would be even more interesting. Mike and John attempted to put money on the table. George stopped them.

"You guys go ahead. Tonight's on me. We'll worry about next time, next time. Thanks for calling me down here." George's face looked like a kid's at Christmas. It was 4:00 a.m.

As the Abbey closed, Deputy Inspector Dennis Bryan pulled into his driveway at 122 Figurea Street on Staten Island. He had been out most of the night too.

The following morning, John Cutbert passed the front of the Abbey as he drove to work. George's car was still parked near the bar. Lynn lived around the corner. He thought, *Mike'll get a kick out of this. Gotta let him know.*

What John Cutbert didn't know was DI Dennis Bryan was engaging in conduct that would be much more interesting to Officer Romano.

148

CHAPTER TWELVE

As a Deputy Inspector, assigned to the Chief of Departments' Office in One Police Plaza, Dennis Bryan enjoyed the luxury of having his own Department vehicle. In the capacity in which he served, a personnel officer, the car was necessary due to the fact that he might have to meet with commanders throughout the city at a moment's notice.

Dennis, however, used the car to have liaisons with female paramours, while on duty. He didn't often spend time in the vehicle, but would sign out to allegedly visit a command and drive to meet his latest conquest. Beside the pending trouble with his wife, Elizabeth, Dennis hovered on the edge of a fall from grace which would have calamitous impact on his career.

It happened by coincidence, on a Wednesday, "Cheater's Day", in some of the local bars. Bryan got caught during one of his "command visits."

Earlier that day, the big-eared redhead had signed out from his office on the thirteenth floor of Police Plaza with the excuse of a visit to the Crimes Against Persons Squad on Staten Island. On the way out of his office, he had paused to tell his secretary, with whom he had slept half a dozen times, "I'll be at the CAP Squad on Staten Island until at least 1600. So, I won't be back to the Puzzle Palace until after end of tour. I'll sign out from the field and go on home."

Coolly, his secretary answered him. "Very well, Inspector." She did not even look up at him. Cast-offs were history with Dennis, and she knew it.

Dennis Bryan left One Police Plaza in a happy mood, a smile on his face as he thought of his up-coming liaison.

For the past several months, The Great Pumpkin had been seeing a Senior Police Administrative Aide, named Grace Grant. Grace worked in the Stolen Property Section and was married to a Sergeant assigned to the Police Academy. She had taken a vacation day for their assignation.

Bryan would not have been so contented had he known that Sergeant Bill Grant had suspicions that his wife was seeing someone. He needed no private investigator to check it out. Grant believed that he could handle his own investigation. Once a week he took a vacation day to check on his wife when he was supposed to be working. Bill used a different day of the week each time.

The Grants lived on Staten Island along one of the more rural roads on the south end of the Island right off the West Shore Expressway. At 1330, Grant parked his personal car about a quarter of a mile from his home and approached on foot. His heart pounded as he saw what he recognized as an unmarked department auto in front of his home. He knew that nothing was amiss at home, no emergency situation or police matter due to the lack of a marked vehicle. Besides his wife's car sat in the driveway, with no other cars around.

She was supposed to be working. *Damn her, the bitch is screwing around,* he confirmed his suspicions.

After noting the Department plate number, he silently walked up to his home. He found no signs of life. Instinctively, he retreated to a phone booth alongside the expressway. He phoned in for a plate check. It stunned Bill to find out that the car in front of his home had been assigned to the Chief of Departments' Office. The department vehicle clerk would not give him the name of the assignee. After retrieving the information provided, he then phoned Grace's office without identifying himself and asked for her.

"I'm sorry, sir," came the reply. "Mrs. Grant has taken a vacation day. Some family emergency, she said."

"Not yet," Grant muttered darkly after he replaced the handset. "But there will soon be one." Next he dialed 911.

"Hello, operator. At 1922 Bloomingdale Road." His own home. *She's screwing someone else in my own bed. Damn her.* "There is a woman and a high ranking police official being held hostage. I believe their lives are in danger."

Calmly, as they are trained to do, the operator asked, "Sir, who are you and how do you know that there's a police officer inside?"

Grant responded, "The plate number is YET-912, that's a department car assigned to the Chief of Departments' Office. Never mind my name." He then quickly hung up and went into the trees near his home to watch.

He knew that the operator would naturally notify the Chief of Department's Office. She sure did, because after about seven minutes, police vehicles began arriving sans the usual sirens, including Emergency Service. Holding riot shields in front of themselves, two ESU officers approached his front door and rang the bell. They received no response. The officers banged on the door. Still no one came. Grant's heart pounded. The cops waited.

"What the hell," Grant heard one of the ESU men say to another. "We got a false alarm here?"

"Don't count on it," his sergeant responded. "The Loo said the guy that car's checked out to don't live here. An' he's checked out of his office to visit the CAP Squad."

"Huh! This sure's hell ain't Crimes Against Persons."

"You got that right, Phillips."

Five minutes went by without any change in the situation. Then the duty Captain arrived. Grant fought his desire to rush to the cops. He remained secreted. *They're probably getting dressed and straightening everything out, Grant reasoned.* His mind raced.

After another 20 minutes of waiting, one of the Emergency officers climbed the telephone pole alongside the Grant's house. Grant knew that the bosses ordered a line attached to his home telephone. It was standard procedure to make telephone contact with hostage takers. As far as the responding police officers knew, they had high ranking brass inside and at least one civilian. There would be no errors on this one.

Grant never knew for sure if telephone contact was made. It must have been, because after several minutes, the front door opened, his wife stood in the doorway. Several officers went inside. Shortly thereafter, they came out and rejoined their fellow cops.

"All right, pack it up," the lieutenant in charge of the ESU squad called to the officers around the house. "Nothin's wrong in there. Some friggin' crank call."

They aborted the operation and everyone left. The unmarked auto remained. Sergeant Grant stayed where he was, too.

Grant watched the front door for what seemed like hours. In actuality only ten minutes after the police had left a large man wearing a grey suit departed also. Sergeant Grant did not know the identity of his wife's big red-headed lover, except that he was attached to the Chief of D's Office.

Bile tasted foul in Grant's mouth as he returned to his car. After heaving up his guts he drove to a bar and tried to get drunk. With shaking hands and hate in his heart, Grant telephoned his wife to say that he was stuck and would not be home until late. He then telephoned the local newspaper and gave them what information he had on the incident. Then he went back to drinking.

By Friday of that week, the local newspaper printed the entire story including the name of Deputy Inspector Dennis Bryan. Someone had recorded the incident at Headquarters. And someone else had, inevitably, leaked it. The Staten Island newspaper had somehow retrieved the information. The article quoted a "reliable source," who stated that the Inspector had only been visiting a sick friend and was not guilty of any impropriety. Bill Grand continued to read, while a cold fury wrapped around his heart.

"Occupants of the house claimed that they did not hear the doorbell, nor did they know police had gathered outside. They told our reporter that they were watching television." *Yeah, the Hump of the Week Club no doubt,* Grant thought angrily. The column ended with the usual assurance to the public. "According to the Public Information Office at One Police Plaza, an investigation into the incident is under way. Police sources claim that the caller of the cruel hoax will be found and punished."

Back in the Three-Two they had a few men who resided on Staten Island. They brought the newspaper clippings in to show other members of the command. Most of the cops weren't too interested. It just confirmed what they always thought, that rank certainly did have its privileges. Michael Romano however, found more than passing interest. He pointed it out to Len.

"What do you think of this, Len?"

Len took the clipping and read it rapidly. Mike suspected that his partner had taken a speed reading course. When Len concluded his perusal, and handed the article back to Mike, he worked full lips. "Just proves that the higher up the rank tree one climbs, the more exclusive the humps one gets on the side. Rank has its privileges, partner."

Mike did not agree, confident that this event would bear fruit eventually. He saved the clippings.

Deputy Inspector Dennis Bryan had brought a hint of scandal to the Job. Accordingly, he was quietly transferred back to a position in the Manhattan Borough Office.

"The bastard," Dennis growled as he cleaned out his desk. "It had to be her fuckin' husband. I'm gonna grind his balls into dust." Along with the transfer would come the loss of his Department car.

On the first Monday after he had been caught, his first day in his new assignment, Deputy Inspector Dennis Bryan sat in his new office and reflected over the past week. How could this have happened to him, a senior police officer? Now that he had his forays exposed, he had the sinking feeling that this would prove to be only the beginning….

It had been last Wednesday night, the same day he had been caught, that he knew that there would be problems. After returning home, he began his excuses. "Damn this job, Liz. I just got word through the grapevine that I might be transferred." Bryan, with over twenty years on the Job, knew that his bosses would probably take some kind of punitive action because of what had just happened. He wanted to cover his ass with Liz, although he was totally unprepared for the turmoil that followed two days later. . .

Liz Bryan enjoyed entertaining during summer evenings. They had the pool, barbecue, and yard to enjoy. The back yard could accommodate their all of their relatives and some close friends easily. On Friday, Dennis told her he would be home early and she had planned a get-together.

Liz had invited her brother-in-law, Jim Bryan, an attorney, and his wife, Connie; her foster parents; Dennis' mother and father. Also the Staten Island Borough Commander, along with his second in command and their respective wives. She also, without asking her husband, fatefully extended an invitation to her brother, Brian, allowing him to bring a date if he chose to.

Shortly after noon, Liz returned from last minute shopping for the evening's repast. She had stopped at the liquor store and picked up some wine to go with the canapés she had prepared; stuffed mushrooms, caviar, and the like. For her barbecue, she stopped at a gourmet delicatessen where she bought potato salad, coleslaw slaw, fresh pickles, cream cheese and chive dip to go with chips and pretzels. While she was out she also bought the local newspaper. After going over her check list for the evening, Liz telephoned her butcher. She had ordered one dozen, inch and a half thick, Delmonico steaks, one dozen half-pound hamburgers, two dozen loose hotdogs and three pounds of hot sausage, Dennis' favorite. Liz requested that the order be delivered by 4:00 p.m.

While the meat dealer read back the order to her, she glanced at the newspaper. On page two, in bold type, she read, "Police Deputy Inspector, Victim of Hostage Hoax." The article continued, "Last Wednesday, at approximately 2 p.m., Deputy Inspector Dennis Bryan, assigned to the Chief of Departments' Office of the New York Police Department was the alleged victim of hostage takers."

Liz quickly scanned the article and knew that her philandering husband had finally been caught. Her mind was raced. She finally heard the butcher calling in her ear, "Mrs. Bryan, Mrs. Bryan is the order correct?" Her reply was an uncaring, "Yes, fine, thank you." Then she numbly replaced the receiver.

After drinking half of the contents of one of the wine bottles she had just purchased, Liz telephone her brother Brian.

"Brian, are you coming over tonight?. . .Yes... Good. Come early. I have to talk to you about Dennis. Come now! The cheating bastard got caught and it's in the news-paper." Liz hovered near hysteria.

Wilkey, pedophile and child rapist, gambler or whatever loved his sister. "Liz, calm down and tell me what happened. Slowly."

Liz gave him the twenty-five-words-or-less version of the column in the newspaper. After a long silence, Brian's only comment was, "That bastard. I'll be right over. Don't worry, we'll think of something."

Angel with a Gun

At exactly 1:15 p.m., Brian walked into the kitchen through the patio door. He liked this room. Bright and airy, with a breakfast island separating it from the dining room, a butcher's block sat in the center of the open floor space, pots and sauté pans hung French chef style from overhead tracks. The cabinets glowed with a rich, pale lemon color. Tile covered the counters. He found Liz busy. She had resigned herself to continuing her preparations for the evening's gathering. At the sight of her brother, her eyes erupted in tears and she ran to him.

After hearing the entire story including, her past suspicions, Brian vowed that he would handle Dennis. He reassured his sister that everything would be okay. He would assure her future.   Without Dennis, if necessary.   Liz understood the veiled threat.   "No Brian. I know you have underworld connections, but I want to remain married to the son of a bitch if at all possible. His rank opens doors for me. There's also his pension. If he's fired, it's gone. If he's gone, then there's only the insurance. I want him around to make him miserable."

Brain gave her a shark's smile and responded, "Okay, Liz, you're calling this one. Remember, he's hurt you and I'm here to help make you feel better." He then went into the yard and found a comfortable corner from which he could observe his brother-in-law as he arrived.

While Liz continued getting ready for guests, she decided that if anyone asked about the column that night, she would let Dennis answer them. She would go along and reinforce any answer he gave. She planned to save her confrontation for the following day.

Dennis arrived home at 5 p.m. From his vantage point, Wilkey watched Bryan pull into the drive. From his stunned reaction as Dennis exited his car, Wilkey knew that Dennis had almost filled his shorts. He had just noticed his brother-in-law's car.

While at the office, Dennis had been informed that his "Hostage Incident" had made the papers. *She knows,* he realized with a start. *Liz can be handled. She must have told Brian. The weasel will be a problem.*

When her husband entered the house, Liz knew he had to have been drinking; his nose glowed a cherry red and perspiration dotted his brow, always a telltale sign. She knew why. Liz had hidden the newspaper. Despite her apparently calm facade, inside she quaked with anger. Dennis never knew.

Let him sweat, she thought as she said, "Dennis, glad you're home. Please do what you have to, we have guests coming tonight. Hope you remembered?"

Dennis began to tug at his clothes, remembering their last bout. Liz had implied that she might "drop a dime on him" with the Department. He wondered if she was responsible for his trouble. With nervous energy, he crossed directly to their well-stocked liquor cabinet and poured himself a double bourbon, straight, without ice. He gulped it down. Then a second. He knew that there would be trouble, probably tomorrow. The now cherry faced Inspector looked pensively at his wife. *Be nice to her, maybe it can all be smoothed over.* Maybe he could lie.

Trying to sound as though nothing was wrong, he replied, "Sure Honey, I remembered, that's why I rushed home. Sorry, be ready in a few minutes. I was deep in thought." He continued thinking, *Where's that weasel, Brian? Gonna have to deal with him too.*

After he had showered and put on loose comfortable clothing; a garish flowered shirt and tan Bermuda shorts, that did nothing to flatter his beer-barrel belly and tree-trunk thighs, he padded barefoot outside. It was now 5:45 and he wanted to find Brian before the other guests arrived. Dennis was surprised that his wife still didn't mention the newspaper. Maybe she hadn't seen it. No chance. She had her deviate brother here without advance notice. He knew there would be fireworks later.

Dennis found the serving cart loaded with liquor and began pouring his third bourbon since arriving home. He looked up and spotted Brian. Dennis had built a sort of arbor in a shaded corner of the yard and outfitted it with a wooden bench. The settee rested on a platform surrounded on three sides by lattice panels to ward off the sun on bright days. The bench now lay in shadows. Had Brian not shifted his weight, Dennis would have missed him.

"Hello, brother-in-law," Brian yelled, and produced a sardonic grin. "Been waiting here for your arrival for some intellectual conversation. Tried to talk with my sister for hours, but she's preoccupied."

Even though Dennis saw Brian, he jumped as the man spoke. Feeling like an ass, he responded, "Yeah, I see all the preparations."

Deputy Inspector Dennis Bryan's mind spun a web of misery; *I know he knows, he knows that I know he knows. This is stupid and childish. Might as well face the bastard and get it over with.* "What brings you here Brian? You're usually too busy to attend our little backyard functions."

"Well, you see Dennis, Liz telephoned earlier in the week and asked me over because we see little enough of each other. We're all we've got, you know."

Bryan knew he was being toyed with.   The look on Brian's face told him that. No matter, he was a tough seasoned cop and he would endure this man's taunts. He might even find a way to get away from accepting his "gifts." Liz might try to carry out her threats and tell I.A.D. about them. If she did, he wanted them to be able to prove nothing.

Two car doors slammed in the driveway. Their guests had begun to arrive. Dennis looked at his watch, a Rolex, another "gift" from his brother-in-law three Christmas' ago. The hands showed 6:20 p.m.   Dennis walked to the gate adjacent to the driveway.

"John, Mary, good to see you. Liz is inside the house. Come on in and relax," he said as he opened the gate and stood behind it. The Borough Commander of Staten Island and his wife cordially returned his greeting without any hint of the newspaper report.

Bryan looked across to the corner where Brian sat. *The cheeky bastard is coming to meet them. He knows. He's gonna screw with me all night.*

As the Commander and his wife entered the yard, Bryan transferred his drink to his left hand, extended his right arm in Brian's direction and said, "John, Mary, this is Brian Wilkey, Liz's brother." He was careful not to mention their last name or the Boss' title in front of his crooked brother-in-law.

Dennis thought that Liz may have told her brother who was coming, but he would be damned if he would chance giving his brother-in-law more ammunition. Indeed he felt damned already. This social deviate was his brother-in-law and he was locked in to protecting him. To make matters worse, he was here in the presence of Police Department brass.

John and Mary exchanged pleasantries with Wilkey and allowed Dennis to guide them to two comfortable chairs; first stopping at the bar cart to make them each a drink. The chairs were nowhere near the corner to which Brian had returned. Dennis felt some relief in the fact.

The party host looked back at Wilkey to see a scheming smile take form on his face. *If he starts up tonight, he'd find a way to kill him.* As his mind raced, Dennis felt his knees begin to shake.

The entire introduction and settling in process for the new arrivals took roughly five minutes. Dennis found his glass empty. Noting a lack of bourbon on the cart, he had not been aware that his last drink drained the bottle; Dennis excused himself and left his guests to go into the house and try to regain his rapidly slipping composure.

Once inside the kitchen, the Great Pumpkin saw with relief that Liz was not present and continued   into the living room and   straight to the liquor supply.   He poured himself another bourbon, ice, no water, and shouted, "Liz our guests are arriving. Come on out, Honey."

When he heard his own voice, Dennis shuddered.   It sounded nervous and shaky. *Holy my God, he sound like shit. Gotta maintain myself. It's gonna be bad enough later when Liz and I are alone.*   If anyone notices, he'd blame it on the bourbon.

From inside the bedroom came Liz's voice, "Sure Dennis, I'll be right out.   Try to act like a gracious host, will you? They're your friends too."

Deputy Inspector Bryan thought *if she did knows, she's the best actress I've ever seen. She would make some undercover cop.* "See you outside", he shouted as he turned to go through the house to the patio.

Entering the yard, Dennis asked, "John, Mary, are you okay?   Need anything?."   Crossing over to them, he added, "Another drink?"

John answered, "No thanks, we're fine.   We know where it is. How are you Dennis? You look shot. Maybe we should talk later."

That put the big redhead's brain in a whirl. *Shit he knows, now I'm gonna hear it. Shit. Then Liz, too.* He took a big gulp of bourbon as another car entered the driveway, followed by two others.   Dennis watched as the vehicles emptied their contents. The Chief's Aide de Camp, Lieutenant Bill Dali and his wife, Joan, parked right behind his boss' auto. Starting a second row in the spacious driveway was his brother, Jim, his parents and Jim's wife, Clair.   The last car was occupied by his in-laws; Pete and Kathy Sims.   The Sims's were Liz's foster parents, and had always kept in touch.

While the newly arrived company entered the yard, Dennis glanced over his shoulder at Wilkey. The nervy bastard had already climbed out of his seat and headed their way. John and Mary remained where they were even though John now stood.

One thought filled the mind of Dennis. *"If he acts up, I'm gonna kill him."*

Introductions were being made as Liz entered the yard. Dennis noticed her at once. He was both relieved and fearful at her entrance. The evening would now progress and end. As soon as he found out whatever his wife had to say about the day's revelations, he would deal with it. Yet he remained worried about his guests' interaction and subsequent reaction with his brother-in-law present. He was willing to bet the bastard had something planned.

To the surprise of Dennis Bryan, the evening went along well by anyone's standards. All the guests apparently got along well together including Brian Wilkey. After all, he was not totally illiterate, and had a reputation as a decent conversationalist. Everyone ate and drank considerably. Especially the host. By 10:45 that evening, even his huge hulk could not absorb further alcohol without adverse effects. Dennis was about to lose control.

Tension in Dennis' mind and worry about whether or not Wilkey would screw him that evening, and the impending confrontation with Liz, finally took its toll. It all pivoted around something totally innocent.

Wilkey it seemed enjoyed the company of Mary all evening. They both liked to dance and spent most of the night doing just that. The Commander himself gave his OK. Rising, he waved off Wilkey's protest that he must be monopolizing the Commander's wife.

"I'm not a dancer. If Mary wants to dance, it's fine with me. You two enjoy yourselves. It's only harmless fun."

Their dancing proved to be the evening's catalyst. It began as normally harmless flirting, or so the dancing couple thought. Dennis, upon observing it, became annoyed. Maybe he remembered his own indiscretions. Whatever, it struck home. That's how he had started many of his own affairs. He did, however, keep his thoughts to himself. Dennis, alert to the fact that Liz had noticed it too, decided to make an attempt to get her brother to tone it down. After all, he thought, *John is her friend too.*

Liz walked up to her brother as he attempted a dip with his partner after a complicated step. From some of the company came mild applause. Wilkey assisted Mary in regaining her stability and turned his attention to his sister.

Liz put her mouth next to her brother's left ear and said, "Brian please behave yourself. Mary's husband is the Borough Commander. He's not someone to have pissed off at you. Please behave." In an effort to assure him that she was not angry, she quickly added, "I love you; you're my brother."

Liz began to move away from him. Cat-quick, Brian's arm shot out and he grabbed a handful of her left buttock. Roughly, he shook it, saying aloud for all to hear, "It's okay, Liz, nobody minds. We're all family here." Both Brian and Liz chuckled. To most of the onlookers it seemed harmless sibling contact.

To Dennis Bryan, guilty of many sins --- the personification of some of them standing before him in the form of Brian Wilkey --- it became too much. In his current state of mind, he saw that act of physical contact as perverted. Brother and sister sex: incest is how he saw it. A disgusting, filthy act. His mind confused by the large amount of alcohol consumed that night, he snapped.

Dennis launched his six-foot-three , 350 pound, bulk across the patio. He grabbed Wilkey's arm and shook him violently, while he shouted, "Leave my wife alone you pervert! Don't play your games in my house, you Goddamned, incestuous pedophile! You bastard."

Dumbfounded, the guests stared. Mr. and Mrs. Sims sat staring in disbelief. The senior Bryans were equally disbelieving. Jim Bryan came up out of his chair almost as fast as Dennis had moved. Wilkey saw him rise and smiled, as if everything was fine. Then he motioned for him to stay away.

Jim felt grateful. His brother was far too big. He fought on paper, not with his hands. Only the Commander and the Lieutenant were not surprised. They knew the stress that Dennis labored under. They had read the newspaper. Dennis' civilian lover was under John's command, in his own Borough Office; he had also received several significant calls from One Police Plaza.

Liz, within arm's distance of Dennis, struck him across the face and without a word, turned away, taking Mary with her. Dennis let go of Wilkey. The stinging in his cheek cleared the effects of the alcohol and returned him to reality. Now he suffered visible embarrassment.

In a gesture that would appear to be understanding to the other guests, Wilkey took Dennis by the arm and began to move him toward the secluded corner that he had enjoyed so much earlier in the evening.

Once they had seated themselves, Brian began to threaten his brother-in-law. "Listen you fat, pompous ass. You've hurt my sister. You've taken my money. You've hindered several official police investigations." At the stricken expression on the face of Dennis, Wilkey quickly added, "Not that I mind. Some of them were against me. You've been paid for it. Don't fuck with me or my sister. Remember you're a criminal, too."

Maintaining his guise as the helpful counselor, the smaller man kept glancing up at the guests across the yard and smiling as if to say, "It's all right. I'm taking care of things. He's just a little drunk, that's all."

Deputy Inspector Bryan regained his wounded pride and responded. "You shit, you're a child molester. I'll tell the detectives in Sex Crimes to go ahead and lock you up. You'll get raped in jail." He then challenged, "Fuck you and your money. Prove I took any." Dennis got hotter by the second.

Angel with a Gun

Wilkey retorted, "I kept records, Liz took some of the money and put it the bank. The account reads, 'In trust for Dennis Bryan.' The records can be matched. I'll do whatever my sister wants me to. I read the paper today. Step out of line and, so help me, you'll be divorced, fired and probably in jail. Won't the cons just love to have a Deputy Police Inspector in with them? You're not too big to hold down. I may even take a stab at you myself."

The last remark pushed Dennis over the edge. He stood up and pulled Wilkey to him. He then held him by the front of his shirt, lifted the man off the ground and punched him in the face, as he flung him into the pool. The resulting splash wet the other guests who had become transfixed by the scene.

John stood up, followed by Bill.   In the most authoritative voice he could muster, he said, "Dennis please come with me for a moment." When Bryan held fast, he added, "Is it necessary to remind you who I am?"

Bryan had been shaken to his core. Did the boss want to speak as a friend or a superior? He just nodded and nervously followed him to the driveway gate.

While John opened the gate, he spoke, "Dennis, we've been friends for some time now. As your friend I've come to overlook your sexual indiscretions. However, the last one hit the newspaper and involved a civilian under my command. Downtown gave me the courtesy of informing you that you will be transferred back to Patrol Borough Manhattan, effective on Monday. If you have no comment, I'll say good luck and Mary and I will excuse ourselves. Good night Dennis."

Dennis observed that Bill stood behind John and that they had turned to gather their respective wives. Once together, the foursome said their good-byes and left. Even though family remained, Dennis left totally alone.

Jim assisted Liz in pulling her brother from the pool. He had a swollen eye by now in addition to a broken nose.

Dennis was a physically powerful man. However, right

that minute he felt weak and emasculated.

While Liz took Brian into the house to tend to his wounds and get him some dry clothes, Jim said to Dennis, "I'm not sure what's going on here, but remember, I'm a lawyer. Call if necessary. The folks and I are leaving now." With that, Liz's foster parents departed also.

Dennis felt alone, really alone, for perhaps the first time in his life. He took the bourbon into a guest bedroom and later slept the sleep of a drunk.

When he awoke the following noon, Liz and her brother were gone. He found his clothes piled in the hallway and a note pinned to them that read: "That's your room from now on. Don't come to mine unless you're invited." It had no signature. It wasn't necessary.

Elizabeth Bryan had forced Dennis to move out of their bedroom. He had no choice. No second chance. He had been confined as surely as if he had been jailed. He had to sleep in one of the guest rooms. He felt as he had just had his genitals removed with a rake.

Dennis remained at home the entire day and remembered the preceding night. Later that evening, even though Liz returned, with only his bourbon bottle to keep him company he continued his mental penance in the guest room. .

Manhattan South proved more than a living hell to the disgraced Deputy Inspector Dennis Bryan. Every day he saw the faces of men, from Captains to Sergeants, whose asses he had taken extreme pleasure in chewing in the recent past. He knew they had to be sneering at him. Their smug expressions, the conversations cut off as though by a switch when he entered a room, the side-long glances as they passed in the hall all told the story. Sergeant Bill Grant confronted his wife over the breakfast table a week later.

She looked at him warily as he stood before her at the stove. "I want a divorce."

She did not protest. Unfortunately he continued drinking and brooding.

"Goddamn that woman," Dennis Bryan cursed aloud one hangover-blurred Monday morning in the security of his new office. *Not Liz. No, certainly not,* he reminded himself.

That stupid Grant woman. She had clung to him like fucking glue. She had been demanding in the extreme. And she had the poor taste to have a suspicious husband. Now, him, he could take care of. *I will*, Bryan swore to himself. *Damn soon.* His secretary interrupted him.

"Inspector, Rabbi Walzman is here about the police patrol for the ADL block party."

"Show him in." The fire began in his belly. Was he getting an ulcer? When the religious leader entered, Dennis willed the bourbon fog to disappear and forced a smile. "Rabbi, so good to see you again. Sit down."

Once seated, Rabbi Walzman reiterated his needs. Dennis Brian listened with only half of his attention, and then made short reply. "You understand, these policemen will have to be off-duty volunteers, naturally."

"Sure, sure. This isn't the first time I've done this, Inspector. Since this is a charitable activity, I expect that we can count on the good officers who will be working the block party will also make a small donation to the ADL."

DI Dennis Bryan frowned fleetingly. He possessed enough of the politician to have made his current rank, but this seemed to him to be overstated. "I am afraid that that will have to be left up to them, Rabbi." He gave the cleric a broad wink. "After all, some of them may be Irish, or even Italian."

Walzman faked a horrified expression. "You mean to say you cannot assure us nice Jewish boys?"

Joe DeCicco

Brian spread his big hands, palms up and gave a big shrug. "What can I say? It depends on who is off that day and shift. The only times our Jewish officers all get the same days off are the High Holy Days. As to the Department ordering the volunteers to give any of the extra money they earn, it's impossible. A matter of policy, and the Union, you understand."

Walzman pulled at his chin, wishing for once that he had grown a beard. "Yes, yes, I know all that. All we can ask is that you take a personal hand, see that as many officers as possible are of our faith."

"And I can accept that. After all, the Anti-Defamation League is an important organization, to your faith and to everyone. I'll see what I can do. Now, is there anything else?"

"There will be refreshments, of course. Some of the officers should be assigned to see that rambunctious youngsters do not finagle a few bits for themselves." Walzman had a merry twinkle in his eyes.

Rambunctious? Finagle? Dennis had not heard those words in years. *Did all Rabbis talk like that?* He thought again of what brought him here to listen to this and vowed again rotten Sergeant Grant. He compelled his face to smile.

"Rest assured, Rabbi, not a gnosch will be purloined."
How's that for fancy talk?

For Mike Romano and the other men of the Three-Two, the weeks sped on into months, which merged into another year before they knew it. Every day on the Job the faces changed, but the complaints and emergencies remained much the same. Except, of course, when Wacko Macko got involved.

CHAPTER THIRTEEN

By the 1st of July, 1977, Inspector Bryan had settled in at his new command, Manhattan South Area. His office was located on 35th Street in the building that housed the Midtown South Precinct. He was not at all happy. Since the incident at his back yard party only a few short weeks before, coupled with having to sleep in the guest room, he remained distant, speaking only when spoken to or in the performance of his official duties. Not a single man in the command mentioned his public shame.

Elizabeth had hardly spoken to him since that fateful evening. About the only conversation she made was to tell him when she received another "gift" from her brother and to caution him, "Toe the mark or I'll have your ass."

Dennis had become increasingly worried about his brother-in-law. Wilkey's zone of enterprise lay within his new command area. The disgusting pervert made his collections right under Bryan's nose. Brian Wilkey oversaw the activities of the gangsters he worked for right in Dennis' back yard.

Bryan grew increasingly nervous. It felt all too close for comfort. He began to sneak a drink in the office.

Back in the Three-Two, Mike and Len, after nearly a year together, had developed their own style. One of their favorite tools was to call for a "bus" when facing a potentially violent person. On this day, they had begun the first tour of a set of four-to-twelves, and had parked alongside the FDR Drive enjoying the river breezes when they received a call from the dispatcher.

"Three-Two Adam, dispute in the lobby of 135 West 135th Street. Please acknowledge, K."

Angel with a Gun

"Adam, 10-4, on the way. Will check and advise, K," stated Len as Mike put the RMP into gear.

They soon arrived at the location, a seven story apartment house occupied by upper middle class professionals and business people.

"Hey, Len, why would people, who can afford better, live in a dangerous area like this?"

Len studied the building and its surroundings. "I guess that they think it is fashionable to remain in the neighborhood to show they had not forgotten where they came from."

"Stupid, you ask me."

Exiting from their car, the team saw two obviously middle-class men attempting to calm down an irate man who seemed intent on turning the well-lighted, tastefully appointed building lobby, into ruins. As the team approached, the man stopped his ravings.

He turned to the cops and asked them, "Are you mother fuckers here to arrest me or what?"

Len took the lead, hoping there would be an ethnic bond. "Sir, will you be so kind to explain why you're so upset. Can you tell us your problem so we can help you?" Len remained calm as usual.

"Yeah, these here niggers won't let me stay in my own apartment. Who the hell do they think they are?" He swung his arm toward the two well-dressed men.

With Len watching the subject, Mike asked, "Will one of you tell us what started this and does he have a right to be here?"

The taller man answered. "I'm Clyde Granger, Officers, and I'm the president of the corporation here." Seeing a question in Mike's face he continued, "This building is a co-operative and I'm the Board President. This man was the boyfriend of one of our resident stockholders. They are no longer an item. She changed the lock on her apartment door a few days ago to keep him out. He still had a lobby door key.

All building residents have the same key. They may only change their individual apartment locks."

Mike and Len got the picture at once. The spurned lover had returned and was denied access to his former girlfriend's apartment. He had entered the building with his own key and later began to take his frustrations out on the lobby. The two men present had attempted to stop him without success and called the police.

The man began to move again, looking for something to damage. Len firmly stated, "Sir, I suggest that you remain calm and still until we sort this out." Keeping his eyes on the irate man, Len asked the spokesman, "Sir, do you want him ejected or arrested?"

His answer came quickly. "Give him one more chance to leave, if he doesn't, lock him up. He did too much damage to get away with it."

Mike slowly approached the man, while he asked, "Hey guy, listen, did you hear the man? Are you going to leave?"

In response to Mike's question, the man picked up an artificial plant and attempted to put it through the glass door. It struck the central pane and bounced to the lobby floor. He hadn't thrown it hard enough.

Len approached the man and said, "Sir I suggest that you stop this foolishness and come along with us quietly."

The unidentified man answered, "Fuck you. Try to take me you Uncle Tom. Do you do the dirty work for all white cops or only this one?" He meaning was clear to Len. If a black officer threw him out, then in his mind, that officer must be working for the white establishment or sucking up to them. It was an all too familiar and increasingly popular theme.

Len calmly answered, "One minute sir. Mike call for a bus please."

Mike quickly called the dispatcher, "Three-Two Adam to Central. Requesting a bus at 135 West 135th Street. We have an injured man here, K."

Len continued with his adversary. "Now Sir, since you refused to cooperate, we notified the dispatcher that we need an ambulance. Shall we proceed?"

His eyes growing large, the man took a backward step. "What do you need an ambulance for? I heard the white guy; he lied. There's nobody hurt here."

Mike answered for his partner. "My partner asked me to call because you're gonna need one, friend. You obviously want to fight. We can do the arrest papers in Harlem Hospital, while they're fixing you up."

Their adversary looked startled. He shifted his gaze first to Len; small, lean and very businesslike. Then he then turned his attention to Mike, six feet tall, who held hand- cuffs in his fist as he replaced the portable radio into its belt holder. His stance radiated combativeness. He started to move toward the suspect.

Hesitantly, the man spoke to Len, "Yo, Brother, there's no need to get heavy. Why you gonna give that white boy a chance to beat a brother? I'll go quietly if YOU put the handcuffs on. Okay?"

At least the slug was learning, Len allowed. "Certainly, sir," came Len's mild reply. "Please turn around and put both hands behind you and stand perfectly still." Then to Mike, "Partner, be ready to use the ambulance."

Once the man had been hooked up, Mike withdrew his radio and canceled the ambulance. The two complainants smiled at the result; then one quietly asked Len, "Does that ploy always work?"

Mike answered the question, "Yes, sir, it always does. Of course there are occasions when there's no time for what we just did, but more often than not we can find the time. If we call in advance, they never fight. Guess we're just lucky."

Exchanging a glance, the board members spoke together. "Amazing."

Then, the Board President responded, "No gentlemen, it's not only luck, you're both professionals. It's nice to see that cops are not all violence prone. Thank you."

After taking the complainants' information, the team brought the arrestee to the station for processing. Len took their collar downtown. The defendant was charged with PL 145.05, Criminal Mischief in the third degree, an E class felony. The New York State Penal Law defined the crime as; 'to intentionally damage property of another person, and having no right to do so, does damage said property in excess of two hundred and fifty dollars' value.'

During the booking process, the defendant cast a dubious eye at Len and asked, "Brother did that white bread really call an am--bu--lance?."

"Count on it." Then Len added, "By calling the ambulance in advance the medical attention that you would have needed for resisting could begin sooner." Len proved very convincing. The man was struck dumb. Throughout the booking and arraignment, he never spoke again.

Summer had reached full swing. The entire Northeast sweltered in a heat wave, even though calendar showed early July. Things happened at a feverish pace in the City, especially in the Three-Two.

Their second night of the set turned out even hotter and more humid then the first. Right before roll call, Mike decided to keep his ear tuned more than usual to the radio dispatcher. He thought that making a good arrest would be a fine way to get out of the patrol car and indoors and into the air conditioning. As he was formulating his game plan, so were several other radio car teams.

Mike quickly learned that the bar on the corner of

W.132nd Street and Eight avenue was the topic of discussion. It was what would be defined as a bad bar, a shit hole. It was called the Amol Bar.

That unsavory establishment was known to every cop in the Three-Two and neighboring commands as a bucket of blood. Whenever a radio call sent a car to the place, at least two additional cars responded as back-up. If men were not available from the Three-Two, the adjacent commands, Two-Eight or the Two-Six would respond. The system was not official, nor was it advised by the bosses. The men and women in blue set the precedent between 1973 and 1977. In the Three-Two alone, no less than half dozen men lost their lives in the line of duty. It was tough out there.

Mike had been in the Amol Bar on several occasions. Dark and cavernous inside, the place stank of stale beer, spilled booze and vomit. Never remodeled, the decor was once Fifties Glitter, now turned dingy. The walls had been painted dark green with white trim. To the left of the front door, an orange wall with birds painted on it pretended to be tropical. To the far left, behind that garish bulwark, the area opened out into a large room. Mike imagined that it had been used for special functions in the past. He surmised that it could hold at least one hundred fifty people. Along the orange wall booths had been installed. The seats had been covered alternately with red and green leather. They looked worn, but comfortable.

Set into the wall opposite the booths were several doorways. One, a double set, obviously led to a kitchen, or the remnants of one. The others, all single, could be anything. The entire floor had been covered with black tiles. Looking around, the entire interior of the "establishment" had an ominous cast as though anything could happen. It usually did.

Mike reviewed all of that while he listened to the men hatching their plans.

"What we do, see, is calling in phony radio runs to the Amol Bar. That way we'll get to go on official business."

"Yeah," Finney observed. "But, I sure wish we could enter the premises without having to notify Radio Central. We'll have to request a supervisor."

"No problem, Finney. For once we're gonna use the system, instead of it using us. Remember that U.S. Supreme Court just ruled that once a dispatcher gave a job and/or description over the air, it is presumed that all officers heard it. That justifies probable cause to stop someone and possibly affecting an arrest. So, whoever's turn it is to go in and cool off don't have to be the guy who calls it in."

Finney thought about that again. "I got a better angle. When one of the teams is ready to enter, they don't use their radio at all. All we gotta do is anonymously call in a gun run to a 911 operator and hang up."

Mike cracked a smile. Clever. The dispatcher would have to put the call out. Two or three teams could respond and enter the bar with their weapons drawn. Someone would yell out to no patron in particular, "You over there, yes, you. Drop the gun."

The theory was that the place had so bad a reputation that several guns would drop to the floor. Roll call interrupted further plans.

At exactly 2230 the radio crackled, "In the Amol Bar, West 132nd Street and Eight Avenue, man with a gun. Three-Two Units to respond. K."

Immediately three Sectors answered the call: Sectors Eddie, John and Adam.

Sector Eddie was manned by two senior cops, John Conners and Paul Brown. Sector John was occupied by none other than Wacko and his partner, Jim Johnson. Mike, wearing a big grin, and Len were in Sector Adam.

It went off as if the three sector cars had rehearsed all day. They arrived at exactly the same moment. Not one driver used lights or sirens. Immediately, the cops poured from their vehicles. With Sector Eddie in the lead, they started for the front door.   In a well-choreographed maneuver, Sector John covered the sidewalk up and down. Sector Adam covered the opposite side of the street.   At a nod from John Conners, the teams started into the saloon.   The occupants of that den of iniquity had no clue as to what was about to happen. By 2231, Mike and Len entered the bar as one of the back-up teams.

John and Paul, followed by Wacko and Jim, spread out. Mike and Len brought up the rear and kept a close eye on the door. It was not unusual for some social misfit to try to shoot a cop from behind. Mike's locker had belonged to an ambushed officer; now dead.

Cautiously, the men of the Three Two shined their flashlights around the room. Their eyes scanned the patrons. In a corner booth on the left of the doorway sat five men. They had their heads down.   Wacko walked up to the table and pounded his fist down hard in the middle. Their drinks spilled. "Show the poooleece some respect boys. Look up and put your hands flat on the table."

While Wacko did his thing, John and Paul faced the bar patrons.   The night remained hot and the place had air conditioning. It was packed. Some points along the bar thronged two people deep. Paul shouted, "Freeze you over there, you know who you are. Drop the gun or you're dead."

Astonished, Mike gaped. He had heard about this, but had never seen it in action. His muscles grew taught. Silently, he vowed that if all hell broke out, both he and Len would survive.

As Paul finished pronouncing the last syllable, Mike heard loud thunks, four times. He swept the floor with his flashlight in the direction of the sounds and saw four handguns on the floor. He couldn't believe it. *So much for the fucking Sullivan Law.* Paul casually asked each man standing in front of a gun to put his hands out. All were summarily handcuffed.

Wacko took over then. "All right, ladies. You are all under arrest for illegal possession of a firearm in the City of New York. You have the right to remain silent. If you give up that right-----"

Pow! Pow!

It came from the direction of a back room, followed by shouts and falling furniture. Every person in the place instantly recognized gunshots. Mike turned his attention and his light toward the direction of the sounds and saw a door fly open. In the doorway, illuminated only by the beam of Mike's flashlight, stood a man wearing a blue suit, holding a silver colored revolver. "Oh shit", shouted the man as he saw the place filled with policemen.

"GUN! DOWN!" screamed Mike as he drew and leveled his weapon. *It's all too fast,* his mind told him. *Here we go again.* Remembering the incident on W.145th Street, Mike shouted, "Freeze you son of a bitch."

Later, in the station house, Mike told fellow cops that he "thought" he saw the man drop the gun as he saw the cops.

"I didn't want to shoot an unarmed man, so I didn't fire." Sergeant Armini nodded approval. "Mike, you were correct in doing that. The guy had dropped his weapon instantly. Blue suit had just robbed the card game in the back room. He had also let go two rounds to assure that he would not be followed as he fled. You got a righteous collar, Mike. We recovered the gun and the money."

After his arrest, the gunman, Albert Washington, made a statement to Mike. "Yo' Sarge be right, man. I fired the two shots into the ceiling in an effort to convince them mofou players that I meant business. That's a big money game in that place. My original idea was, to take off the game and quietly walk out of that shithole." He added that he was leaving New

York that night and was not worried about reprisals.

Albert continued. "One of the dudes at that table was big, man. Six-four tall and wide as a house. He wasn't giving up his money. So I fired the shots as I cleaned the table and ripped the cash from everyone who had it in their hands." He had taken a total of three thousand dollars. "I didn' want to shoot it out with the cops, man, so I dropped the gun. I be a thief, man, not a suicide."

Mike could only charge Albert with possession of a weapon and tell the story to a district attorney because no complainant came forward. All those in the back room, once outside in the bar proper, denied seeing a gun, or even being at the game. *What the hell,* Mike allowed, *it's another gun off the street and he'd pull overtime.*

Mike had worked through the night on his gun collar. He got home shortly before 0800 on the Fourth of July. Tonight would be the fourth tour in the set. Once in the apartment he went straight to bed. Seeing how tired he was, Betty took the children and the dog to her mother's house for the day. Mike's only company was the air conditioner in the bedroom. For all its noise, it didn't seem to want to do the job. In no time, Mike lay bathed in sweat. He slept through most of the day with little time to shower and stop at his mother-in-law's before going to work.

He was angry to be working on a weekend, let alone a National Holiday.

Once at the Three-Two, his anger at having to work began to subside. As the tour began, his sense of right began to take over. The rank air smelled of burned nitrates, the chief ingredient in flash powder. Shredded paper from the wrappings of spent firecrackers littered the streets. Every M-80 and Cherry Bomb that went off caused Mike to instinctively hunch his shoulders in preparation to duck bullets. The muscles in his neck remained tense throughout the tour.

The shift consisted mostly of aided cases. Primarily children in need of medical aid because of injuries caused by fireworks. He wanted to help them all.

"It gon' be aw-raht?" Big, obsidian eyes that welled with unshed tears looked up at Mike while one of the men from the rescue squad applied ointment to a firecracker burn.

This latest call had come from W. 137th Street only two minutes earlier. Mike and Len happened to be only three blocks away. Mike radioed their location and said they would handle the call. They found six black youths, aged from about 8 to 12, clustered around a shirtless boy of ten. The youngsters watched in awed silence while he hopped up and down on bare feet and sucked on three fingers.

Mike called for a bus. In its place, a fire department rescue squad showed up. There was too much business for the ambulances on this festive day. Now, the NYFD medic treated the fingers burned by exploding fireworks.

"Yes, it is," Mike told the lad gently. "You should know better than to hold a firecracker and let it go off."

"I didn', Officer. The fuse done burnt too fast."

Mike tousled his hair and smiled. "Lay them on something before you light them from now on, okay?"

"Yes Sir. I'm sure gonna do that."

In between helping injured kids, Mike and Len responded to several "disputes". Those were usually family arguments, fueled by booze. Every cop in every city in the country knew that domestic violence runs often turned dangerous for the responding officers. Although not necessary, Len constantly reminded Mike of this as they responded to each call.

They received one thoroughly pleasant assignment. Firemen from the local station house had opened a hydrant on the corner of W. 133d and Seventh Avenue. Fully two dozen youngsters cavorted in the pressurized gush of

Angel with a Gun

cooling water. Len and Mike had been sent for traffic control. All in all, they encountered nothing out of the ordinary for the nation's birthday, until near the end of the tour.

It happened four minutes before 2300. Mike and Len had been on the go all night. They had even been denied a meal hour, "due to the contingencies of the job." They both felt the heavy burden of their fatigue.

The radio crackled, "In the Three-Two, units needed to respond to 142nd Street and Seventh Ave. Large fight at that location. Units acknowledge, K."

A bad block, Mike knew from experience. Drugs and more than their share of homicides. Sector cars responded immediately after the dispatcher spoke.

Static crackled and the radio dispatcher urgently announced, "In the Three-Two, units respond forthwith to 142 and Seven. Patrol cars being struck with objects coming from rooftops." Sector Adam was the fifth unit there.

When Len pulled the car near the corner of 142nd Street an object dropped from the corner building and slammed to the ground in front of their car. Mike stared through the windshield at a galvanized steel garbage pail, thirty gallon size.

Around them, the scene resembled uncontrolled mayhem. A mob of teenagers launched fireworks, rockets in particular, in the direction of the cops. Several patrol cars had their windshields broken; some with cobblestones halfway through the glass, sat at skewed angles along the block. Harried police officers attempted to affect arrests with little success. Len and Mike started to exit their auto and wade into the fracas when the cover for the garbage can that missed them seconds it before clattered against their car.

It broke the protective covering of one of their revolving roof lights. A tinkle of plastic shards followed. "So much for 'unbreakable plastic,'" Mike mumbled.

179

Joe DeCicco

From the rooftop on the Southeast corner just to their left came an agonized scream. "Nooo, Pleease, Nooo," the voice pleaded.

At once most of the officers not engaged in adjusting the social mores of the locals beamed flashlights skyward. Mike and his partner couldn't believe what they saw.

CHAPTER FOURTEEN

There, dangling from the roof, hung a young kid; his arms and one leg flailing against the night sky. His immobile leg was held by a police officer.

"If you damn people don't stop throwing shit down on the Pooolice, then I'm gonna throw something down," shouted the cop.

Shrilly, the kid continued to plead. The cop's voice seemed familiar to Mike. He reached into the car and opened the glove compartment. From inside Romano took a hand-held spotlight wired directly to the car's electrical system. Switching the light on, and shinning it on the dangling youth, illuminated the face of Wacko Macko. He held the kid over the edge in a twisted effort to stop the mini-riot.

It worked. Once the crowd looked up and saw the scared boy and the crazed look on the face of the officer, they froze.

Wacko continued, "I'm not gonna let you people hurt your neighbors and the police alone. You seem to like throwing things off the roof so much, it must be fun. So I'm gonna join you and drop something too. That is unless you stop this shit now and clear the corner."

He might have thrown a switch. Instantly, the violence ended. Without a word, Wacko pulled the kid back onto the roof. While the officers below dispersed the crowd, Wacko calmly descended the stairs and walked out of the building entrance. He pointedly ignored the stares of his fellow policemen, and found his partner, Jim. Before complete order had been restored, the team quietly drove off.

Mike thought that he heard Wacko's different drummer again. This time the band had been led by John Philip Sousa himself, complete with a brass section.

"I don't believe it. I don't fucking believe it," said Mike to his partner.

Somewhat in awe, Len agreed that only the continually lucky Wacko could have pulled that one off.

Back at the station house, Len put their radio car out of service to get the roof light repaired, hoping that it would be ready when they returned from their swing in three days. They had one day left in this set to work and as a senior man; Len knew that they would be given a seat (radio car) tomorrow. He and Mike went into the lobby to check out and paused to listen while Mack explained his actions.

"Me an' my partner went up on the rooftop in an attempt to catch anyone throwing things down on us. We also intended to dump anything found over the side in the rear so it couldn't be dropped later. We found three of the punks up there. Two kids jumped over to the next roof. I managed to grab the third and got carried away as usual." His following grin even managed to convey modesty.

Mike and Len signed out and went home, dragging with fatigue.

When he entered the apartment that night, Mike found Betty sitting on the living room sofa. She appeared to be very agitated. He hurried to her side and sat down.

"Bet, Hon, what's wrong". Without waiting for a reply, he continued, "Are the kids okay? I'm here now. Tell me why you're looking so upset."

Betty began to sob heavily as she spoke, her reply almost unintelligible. "Mike. . . he looked at us. . .Anne and me, and smiled. Maybe. . .he looked at Donald, too. I don't know. The smile. . it scared me. Oooh, Mike!" She clung to him tightly.

Joe DeCicco

Softly Mike spoke. "Easy honey.   I'm here nobody's gonna hurt you or the kids. Nobody." As he calmed her, the beat of his heart thrummed like the archangel's wings. Mike Romano felt his avenging spirit rise within him. Now it grew tenfold. His family was possibly in danger.

He tried again. "Betty who smiled at you today? Did anything else happen?"

His words of reassurance had calmed Betty to the point where she could begin answering his questions. "He did Mike, the guy from the diner. The guy that you want to catch. Wilkey!"

Romano felt the complete presence of the archangel now. "Hon, did he speak to you? What did he do?" Mike could hardly contain his rage. This sex pervert, this piece of inhuman shit scared his wife. Had looked at his kids. What was he thinking? Screw his thoughts. He would kill him if he had to, thought Mike as he spoke gently as he could to his wife.

"It's all right, Bet. It's over with. You're here now and I'm with you. Start at the beginning. Tell me everything."

Betty had regained control and began, "Mike, today the children and I went walking on 82nd Street between 37th Avenue and Roosevelt. The children needed some clothes. We just came out of Kid's World and, as I put Donny into the stroller, Anne, who was complaining that she wanted to ride also, pulled my purse strap." She began to become excited again and paused to draw a few breaths before continuing. "When I looked down at her, she, Annie, told me a man waved hello. Looking around I saw Wilkey staring at us and smiling." Betty almost lost it again, and then continued, "It gave me the creeps. Smiling like that at us and me knowing what he is."

"Easy Betty. Smiling like what? Did he speak at all or wave a second time?"

"No, he didn't. He smiled at the children, then me. Sorta twisted, lopsided, like it didn't come from anywhere... inside. It gave me the creeps, Mike. No, he didn't speak."

183

Angel with a Gun

The skin on Mike's neck began to burn. He felt his voice quaver and hoped that it didn't show when he spoke. "Well, listen Honey, he doesn't know who you are. We watched him in the diner that day. He never looked at us. Don't worry; it'll be fine. I'll take care of it. Don't worry." He reached out and pulled his wife into his arms, holding her gently.

"Mike, can we move? Why can't we go looking for a house? The apartment's getting small. And. . .now, Wilkey."

His answer did not comfort Betty. "We can't because we don't have enough money yet. We should be able to move in another year. Two on the outside." He continued to hold her in his arms as he spoke. Mike could feel the tension leave her body. Slowly, she relaxed. Meanwhile, he was shaking with rage inside. Betty offered no comment.

Not wanting to let his wife see the anger inside him, Mike added, "Listen Betty, the kids are sleeping, right? I'm gonna go to the Abbey and see if John is there. Maybe we can do something about Wilkey now. John might have some ideas."

While he spoke, Mike ever so gently pulled away from his wife. He didn't want her to see or feel the fury building inside him toward Wilkey. He had almost forgotten about the man. Now his determination to get the pervert grew even stronger.

Betty suspected something. "Look Mike it's late. Why don't you call there and talk to John over the phone? Please? I want you here."

"It's okay, Honey. Don't be concerned. I'll be back soon. It's two o'clock now; they close at four. That's only two hours away and I'll be back home."

She knew by the look in his eye that he was planning something. She didn't know what, yet she had no choice but to trust him. "Okay, Mike, but hurry back please," she implored him.

After Mike left the sofa, he kissed her and went to look at his sleeping children. Inside his head, Mike felt the archangel's wings throbbing vengefully.

"Mike….." Betty uttered, as he passed her on his way to the apartment door.

"I love you and the kids Betty; it's okay. Please go to sleep. See you soon."

He closed the apartment door behind him. As he took the first step down, he could hear the chain lock being latched inside his apartment.

Once in the street, Mike walked quickly to his car and opened the trunk. Inside lay his old Police Academy duffel bag. Reaching into its depths, Mike extracted a pair of leather gloves and a "Canoe Paddle," a very large slapper, sometimes referred to as a sap. Constructed of black leather and weighted with about six ounces of lead, it could easily cause severe damage or even death. Some police departments used them with abandon. The New York City Police Department frowned on such instruments. He would face department charges if caught with it. Mike left his home determined to adjust Brian Wilkey's personality. He would not even tell him why.

Within minutes, the avenging Romano stood in the hallway of 3545 86th Street. Wilkey had his name listed above the mailboxes inside the lobby. In the fifth floor hallway, Mike put his ear against the door of apartment 5-B. All quiet inside. He now realized that in his haste he didn't look for Wilkey's car. Not having any idea if the social deviate was home, Mike rang the doorbell twice. No sense in causing him alarm. *Gotta get his attention, bullshit him into opening the door and jack the bastard, Mike* reasoned as he pushed the button once more. No immediate answer. While he waited, Mike began to formulate a plan to get the door open. He would tell Wilkey that his brother-in-law sent him. No, thought Mike, his sister needed him. Dennis was with her at home now and acting screwy, Mike elaborated his scheme. An explanation would be given as they drove to Staten Island. It would work. Then, once Wilkey opened the door, he'd beat the shit out of him. The first shot would knock him out so there'd be no noise. Teach the pervert to scare the shit out of his wife and rape kids. His graft taking brother-in-law couldn't protect him here.

Long seconds went by. To Mike it seemed like hours. He quickly grew impatient. He pounded on the door. Mike reasoned that if he could piss the deviate off, Wilkey would open the door to kick the ass of whoever was out there. It didn't work.

From the apartment next door came, "Who the hell's out there. Stop it or I'll call the police." Similar threats erupted from other apartments simultaneously.

Shouting tenants brought Mike back to reality. His quarry was probably not home and the last thing he needed was to be caught by the police. It would be too hard to give a plausible reason for his actions. He went directly home.

Once home, Romano looked at his wristwatch. He had been gone only thirty-five minutes. He had to ring the bell for Betty to come and let him in. After undressing, as he climbed into bed, he spoke. "Yeah, Honey, John wasn't there. You were right. It was too late. You and the kids are fine. This can wait. But listen, don't go around there again until I meet with John and get his opinion on how to handle this. Okay?" He would hide the blackjack again in the morning.

"Sure Mikey." Betty always called him that when she was being sexy or embarrassed. Tonight, she wasn't trying to be sexy. "If you say so. I'm sure I got rattled over nothing. After all, we were out in broad daylight and you know he never will get close to the children. Not while I'm there. And I'm always with them outside this house. Thanks for coming home so fast." She gave him a kiss and snuggled against him.

Betty slept soundly. Mike slumbered fitfully. In his recurring dream, he watched the assault of the little girl on that rooftop. He was two people at once: the little girl and Police Officer Michael Romano. As the little girl, he felt terror and pain. As himself, he watched and saw Wilkey, but could do nothing. He could not move, as though he had been cast in bronze. The pervert continued his dirty deed and smiled at Mike's impotence.

Mike had heard that most caring cops have similar dreams. It was common enough. He wasn't losing his grip, he assured himself. He was just a concerned cop. It was okay.

During the early morning hours, as the sky began to glow right before daybreak, Mike realized that Divine Providence had stepped in when he found Wilkey's apartment empty. Had the man been home, Mike Romano would have ended up in deep shit.

At 9:30 a.m., Betty's mother telephoned. Betty took the call on the kitchen extension. "Yes, Mom. I'm only a little tired is all. Mike had a rough night and it sort of got to all of us."

"He wasn't injured, was he dear? He wasn't shot?"

"No, mother. I. . ." Memory of their argument over Wilkey swept over her. "Oh, Mom, it was really all my fault. I told him about an incident that happened yesterday afternoon. It upset him terribly."

"What was it about?"

"Nothing, Mom. Really, it was nothing serious."

"You're certain of that? In this argument, he didn't hit you, did he?"

Scandalized, Betty gasped and shouted into the handset, "Mother! Mike would never hurt me. Never. I--I. . . honestly I don't want to talk about it."

"All right, I understand you, Dear. The reason I called, are you still coming to dinner on Sunday?"

"Yes, Mother. As far as I know."

"That's nice Dear. I'll let you go now. Bye. I love you."

"I love you, too, Mother. Good-bye."

Around 1 0 : 0 0 a . m . , Betty heard her husband stirring. Thanks to her mother's call, she had rallied her thinking. She now believed she had been an unwarranted alarmist the night before. In an attempt to make amends, she took the time to prepare his favorite breakfast, hash and eggs. Anne had gone to school, and little Donald amused himself in his room.

Mike, came out of the murky grips of Morpheus, sniffed, and then yelled, "Wow, Bet, that's just what I need. Be right there. Love you baby."

He took some time to hide the blackjack. It was like concealing his own guilt.

Munching on a slice of toast smothered with orange marmalade, Betty watched her husband wolf down his breakfast. She was happy to see that he had become himself again. She continued to be embarrassed at her outburst of the night before and decided not to mention it. Hopefully he would not let Wilkey occupy all his conscious thoughts again, as in the past. Mike had hardly mentioned the creep for almost a year.

She had no way to know that the enthusiasm he exhibited came from to his realization that not finding Wilkey home last night had been a blessing. Mike had let his emotions jeopardize his career. The guy wasn't home. His career was safe. The would-be archangel knew that if he remained patient, Brian Wilkey would someday be delivered to him. Justice would be served.

After breakfast, while Betty cleaned up, Mike took a shower. He felt dirty, unclean, because of his actions of the night before. Even though it was summer, he took a scalding shower. The tap water turned his skin lobster red in his effort to wash away his guilt. He knew it was silly, a shower didn't

Joe DeCicco

clean the thoughts in his head, but he felt one hundred times better. Mike spent the next two hours playing with Donald before leaving for work.

Arriving at the Three-Two half an hour early, Mike dressed and went over to the "Hot Sheet". He was determined to make an arrest that night. Any time spent in court would be all overtime; it was his last tour and he would be on a two day swing. The Hot Sheet listed the license plate numbers of all autos stolen in the last twelve hours. Mike learned at the Academy that most cars would be recovered during the first twelve to twenty four hours. If they were recovered at all. He needed to save money in a big time way now. As a result of Betty's incident with Wilkey, buying a house and moving away had become paramount.

Mike busily copied down plate numbers when he heard, "Hi, Mike, anything new and exciting happen since last night? What happened? Betty got another man?" It came from Len. He must have seen the intense expression on his partner's face and decided to attempt some humor.

"No, Len. Just same old me. I'm taking down some plate numbers," Mike stated the obvious. "Gotta save money you know. We want a house soon as possible. Think I'll collar up tonight and then just take it easy at home."

"Fine, partner. You got anything that comes along," replied Jones.

The team began patrol at 1605. The afternoon went by fairly calm, by Three-Two standards. Sector Adam responded to two gun runs, three aided cases (sick or injured), three family disputes and a stabbing.

At the scene of the stabbing, Officer Bert Scales took the collar. He had been assigned the foot post on Lenox Avenue between West 135th Street and West 137th Street. To

189

Bert, three months out of the Academy, this arrest was right out of the movies. It really made his day.

When "Adam" pulled up on the scene, Bert had the perpetrator handcuffed to a banister and was attempting to administer first aid to the male victim. The poor guy had been sliced across the abdomen and stabbed in the left shoulder. Bert looked happily confused when the team arrived.

"Hey, guys, you came fast. The perp's over there, cuffed to the rail." Bert knew that most of the radio car teams carried hospital sheets for emergencies. Strips could be torn off to use as bandages. He asked, "Got any sheets in the trunk?"

"Yeah. We'll give you a hand," offered Len.

Bert continued, "Did you hear my radio call, or did Central dispatch you?" He grimaced at the blood on the man's shirt. His flow of adrenalin had ebbed markedly, now that he had other cops present.

"We got the call from Central. How long ago did this happen?" asked Mike as he began to rip some strips from a sheet he pulled from their patrol car.

Len got on the radio, "Three-Two Adam to Central. We have a man down here, he's cut and stabbed. Is there a bus available? K."

"Negative, Adam," replied the dispatcher. "All ambulances are engaged at this time. Estimated time of arrival is ten to fifteen minutes. Can you transport?"

"Ten-Four Central. We'll transport. We're only two blocks from Harlem Hospital. No problem, K," stated Len as he assisted Mike by holding one end of the sheet.

Len continued as he faced the foot cop, "Bert, request another car to transport you and the prisoner. We're going to take the victim to ER. You did a good job, kid."

"Sure guys. Thanks." Anxious for approval, the rookie asked, "See you later, right?"

"We'll stop off at the arrest room after we take care of this guy," answered Mike. Within seconds, Sector Adam left with the aided, lights and siren blaring.

Joe DeCicco

Later at the station, Bert, after receiving all pertinent information on the victim, gave his account to Len and Mike.

"See, I heard yelling and people shouting, 'Cut the Nigger, cut him', so I ran to the front of 350 West 137th Street. These two guys were arguing about some girl and one of them had a knife." He held up a hunting type knife with about a seven inch blade.

"Some blade," Mike said.

"That's not mine. That's not my knife. I stuck him with a pocket knife," shouted the prisoner in the holding cage.

Bert winked at the other officers, pleased that his ploy had paid off. "Hey guys, you just heard him admit to cutting the victim. Can I put you down on paper as witness to his statements when I get to the ADA?"

Len pulled a face and returned the wink. "Sure Bert, any time."

"Thanks." Bert continued, "The victim calls to me and says, 'Officer, he was sleeping with my girlfriend. I'm gonna kick his ass and he pulls that knife.' That's when I saw the stab wound in his shoulder and pulled my gun. This shithead just looks at me and swings the knife at the guy. It cut across his body. That's when I threatened to kill him and he dropped the knife." Bert pointed at Leroy Karlson, the arrested man in the cage.

Karlson responded with, "That little kiddie cop, the little faggot, is lying. That's not what happened and that's not the knife. He pulls his gun and me with only a pocket knife. If I sneeze', he would of shot me." With a sneer he concluded with, "Biiig, heero. Hero shit."

Mike spoke first, "Listen Karlson, why don't you take this knife," Mike picked it up off the table, "and try to see if I can take it away from you without my gun?" Mike reached for his belt buckle with his free hand. "Maybe you can get it shoved up your ass for your efforts, too."

191

Angel with a Gun

Right then, Romano got a very protective feeling towards Bert. The young cop's integrity was being attacked. Karlson's trash talk had begun to deflate the rookie's elation over a righteous collar.

Karlson looked at Len, a "Black Brother" for some sign, any sign. Len smiled at him and turned his back on the man.

Karlson knew the time had come to own up. "Listen you with the knife. No need to get physical with me. Yeah I cut the guy and the kid here got me fair and square. The guy deserved it. He was screwing my girl. She's my woman, not his like he said." Holding his arms out in a pleading fashion, he continued, "Chill, man. Okay?"

Romano responded with, "Sure man. Now don't give the officer a hard time or when you get out, it's you and me."

"Sure man, sure," came the reply from the holding cage.

Bert sat there, wide-eyed. Even he thought that Mike was really going to give the perp the knife and then kick his ass. "Man-oh-man, Romano I really believe that you were gonna do that spade right here in the holding tank."

Mike laughed, "Ask Len."

The young cop did. Len replied, "Only if necessary Bert, only if necessary. Point is, Karlson believed. He won't give you any trouble."

CHAPTER FIFTEEN

After completing their business with Bert the rookie, Sector Adam took their meal hour. Mike telephoned Betty to ask about the kids while Len called Pat to plan their two day swing.

Every day, the team had made it their standard procedure to check the rear of their patrol car before each tour and after each meal. It was a well-known fact that sometimes prisoners would dispose of contraband in the rear of patrol cars. Len and Mike hadn't transported anyone since turning out. But of course Internal Affairs might run an integrity check. They vowed not to fall victim to one of those. They found nothing. It now bordered on 2200; the men returned to the street.

Mike had written a summons to a Gypsy Cab on Seventh Avenue and W.128th Street when the radio dispatcher spoke. "In the Three-Two, 247 Seventh Avenue, roof landing, female calls for help. Unit to respond?"

Len answered, "Sector Adam is one block away, Central. Will respond. Will check and advise, K."

The voice of Central answered, "Ten-Four Adam."

In fact, Mike and Len were only a hundred yards from the location. They pulled their car over to the curb, locked it, and ran into the housing complex.

Essex complex covered one square block and was run by The New York City Housing Authority. It stretched from Eight Avenue on the west to Seventh Avenue on the south. The northern end faced West 128th Street, with West 127th Street, the southern border. Number 247 was approximately one hundred yards west off Seventh Ave. The development contained seven, fourteen story buildings. As the men entered the building lobby, the portable radio crackled, "Adam, be advised, there has been two more calls on this job. Be further advised that this may be a sexual assault."

Romano's heart began to pound. All he could now hear was a powerful, surf-like roar in his ears. "Come on Len, let's get there." He punched the elevator button.

"Shit," shouted Mike, "it's not working.

Although the wholesale assaults on police officers of the early Seventies were over, Len always did everything by the book, so he cautioned his partner, "Mike, slow down. We have to take the stairs now. We'll each take a stairway. Use the radio if you see anything and for God's sake, note the floor you're on. Please."

Len then radioed the dispatcher to advise any back-up units that the elevator was out and each stairwell contained a police officer.

Mike began his climb in the East stairway. He ran up the steps two at a time. His heart pounded harder. The exertion began to get to him. He dropped back to taking one step at a time. He had vivid thoughts of a little girl in Jackson Heights and his obsession with Brian Wilkey and a possibly crooked cop, Deputy Inspector Dennis Bryan, who covered for him. He wished he really was Saint Michael; then he could fly up the stairs.

His legs felt like lead weights as he approached the fourteenth floor landing. He was barely able to draw a breath. Silently, he pleaded, *"Please God, if there is an assault, let the guy give up; I can't fight him."* Ahead of him, the door to the hallway opened.

Mike reached for his weapon. His chest puffed like a steam locomotive as two women faced him.

They spoke in unison. "Officer, this big guy, he's wearing a long dark coat. It's summer; he's crazy."

Then the older one carried on with their tale. "He has this little woman on the roof. They been drinking wine for a while and he tried to rape her. We called the police and he took her down the stairs."

He could hardly speak. "Wh-where did th-they go? H-how long ago? Wh-wh- what's he look like?"

Across from him, the other stairway door burst opened. "Mike are you here? Are you all right?" It was Len, and in far better shape than his partner. The man played tennis and jogged daily.

"Yeah, Len. I'm ju-just a little winded."

Seeing a second cop there excited the women. "Listen you gotta help her. She's beat to pieces. He must have did her a hundred times by how. You know? I called my friend downstairs and she didn't hear anything. Maybe she's dead."

Puzzled, Mike asked, "Your friend?"

His informant scowled. "No. The woman he have with him."

"Mike, let's go down and listen at each floor. Maybe we'll get lucky. When we reach the bottom, we'll check each floor door to door with back-up." Len lead the way.

Anxiously, the team stopped at each floor. They slowly opened the landing doors, listening for signs of a struggle. Both men now sweated profusely. The climb up and the seriousness of their search took its toll.

After descending all fourteen floors, the men exited the stairwell into the lobby. As back-up teams questioned their findings, they heard the sounds of a scuffle. All eyes turned toward the source. Muted, whimpering cries floated out of the archway that lead to the rear building exit.

They read urgency in the muffled sounds. Mike moved first. The scene in Jackson Heights repeated itself in his mind. Wilkey. *Later,* he sternly told himself. He went through the arch in seconds, followed by Len and two other men.

Once in the corridor, the men heard grunting sounds. It resembled an animal during rutting season. The source of the noise made the men double step in indecision as to the correct course of action.

Angel with a Gun

New York State Penal Law and Police Department Guidelines regarding the use of force were quite clear. Deadly physical force could be used to prevent or terminate several serious crimes. Rape 1st degree was one of them. Rape 1 was defined as to engage in sexual intercourse with a female by forcible compulsion, or with a person who is incapable of giving consent by reason of being physically helpless, or under eleven years old. Rape 1st was a B Felony.

Suddenly they saw a male, approximately six-foot-six, wearing a long dark coat. His penis hung out and dangled past his open fly. His right hand held the neck of a small, frail-looking, Asian female. Her clothes were ripped partially off her body. She bled about the face, head and abdominal region. She wore no panties. The beast before them bit her vaginal area and used his teeth to pull chunks of pubic hair from her body. He had her pinned against the wall with her legs trembling two feet above the floor. The poor woman slowly slipped into unconsciousness.

It seemed that all of the responding officers tried to determine if they could shoot the monster. Mike reacted first. Drawing his weapon, he leaped forward and put his gun barrel against the man's head.

"Freeze, you bastard. One more move and you're dead," shouted Mike. His ferocity startled Len and the other cops, their faces echoed their surprise. As two officers grabbed the assailant, the girl dropped to the ground. She remained still. Mike raised his gun hand. His body shook violently. He made ready to open the man's head with his gun barrel.

Len grabbed his arm. "No Mike," he yelled. "That's not the way." Sensing his partner's emotions, he added, "She's not a little girl. Easy."

Several other officers either didn't hear Len or didn't understand what was going on. They never said a word about Len's comment. As one of them handcuffed the assailant, Romano gave him the Miranda Warnings from memory. It would be his collar and nothing was going to be overlooked.

One of the back-up units had called EMS and an ambulance screamed up to the curb. The victim, a young Korean woman, groggily came to. Mike leaned over her. "Miss, Miss, can you hear me? Can you tell us what happened?"

She answered something in Korean. Mike shook his head. To one of the ambulance crew he asked, "Do you have someone at the ER who speaks Korean or Chinese or something? I think she's been hurt so bad that she forgot her English, if she ever had any."

"We'll find someone," the EMT told him.

She would be transported to Harlem Hospital for medical attention and evaluation.

Len and Mike stuffed the perpetrator into the rear seat of their RMP for transportation to the Three-Two. Mike had his last tour collar.

Once before the desk officer, Lieutenant Fondalar, Mike searched the prisoner. It was there, before the desk, that Mike lost it for a minute.

Because Romano had been the arresting officer, he had the responsibility for removing all the prisoner's property from his person and thoroughly search him. All weapons and other contraband had to be vouchered. Naturally, the prisoner could face additional charges as a result. The guy stank. Mike got increasingly annoyed with this piece of human debris.

On the table before the desk, there now rested a pocket knife and four wallets. Len removed their contents. Lt. Fondalar directed Romano to note what they held and make a memo entry. Something he would have done anyway. Mike had developed good habits under Len's tutelage. Each wallet contained a different set of identification! Not too unusual, especially in the Three-Two, but two of them stated that the owner was white.

Mike asked the prisoner, "Hey guy, what are you doing with white people's ID's? Did you rob somebody?"

His response set Mike off.   "What jou mean, mother fucker?   That shit ain't mine. You want a collar so bad, you flaked me." Mike started to boil; his face flushed red.

Encouraged by that, the prisoner continued, "Hey Lieutenant, your tough white cop flaked me."

Blam! Mike's fist struck the smart-ass prisoner directly, dead center under his chin.   After the first blow landed, the Italian cop slapped him across the face with his left hand. Acting quickly, Len grabbed his partner.

"Romano!" yelled Fondalar as he bolted from his chair, knocking it over. "Just what the hell are you doing?   What's gotten into to you?"

Mike recoiled in embarrassed alarm.   He had never before lost his temper like that. He had yelled and screamed at people in the past, but he always had control. This time he lost it.

Stepping down and around the desk, Fondalar said, "Romano, come over to the side."   He walked toward the Captain's office. Mike knew he was in deep stuff now.

Abruptly, the boss grabbed his subordinate roughly by the arm and said, "Mike, I'm surprised at your behavior. You know better than that. Be thankful that Ruth wasn't sitting at her bullshit receptionist's desk.   You would be going Downtown to answer charges on that little outburst."

Romano began to relax.   There was something in the boss' voice that told him it was OK.

Quietly now, the lieutenant continued, "Mike the next time you want to give a personality adjustment to a prisoner, take him in the back where nobody can see you. Especially the desk officer." Then he raised his voice. "Now take that piece of shit upstairs and charged him with everything you can think of. I'll sign all the paperwork."

"Thank you. Yes, Boss, sorry. Sure thing. Thank you." *Thank you, too, Saint Michael, and your Boss,* he silently prayed.

While Mike walked away, the lieutenant added, "Check out those wallets with stolen property. He can probably be charged with Possession of Stolen Property. Maybe Robbery too. Do it to him, Mike. He deserves it."

Sure, here's one rapist that will see some jail time. Not like Wilkey. Mike's archangel genes kicked into overdrive.

Mike brought the prisoner down to Criminal Court and logged him into the system. He prepared the complaint and settled down in an empty courtroom for the night. It would take all night to process the papers.

Sleeping on court room benches became second nature to most cops at that time. Some claimed to have gotten their most restful nights of sleep there. They maintained that the tomb-like stillness of the closed court rooms was the main reason. The more honest cops told the real reason, the quiet of the temporally abandoned rooms, sure, coupled with the knowledge that while they slept, they were on overtime. Of course, they were on call to confer with an Assistant District Attorney or arraign their prisoner if necessary. But that was highly unlikely.

Mike's sojourn proved an exception. He usually slept like a baby. Not that night. Once again, in his dreams, he was transported to that rooftop in Jackson Heights. In his imagination, he watched that frail young child get assaulted. Again, he stood there, immobile, powerless to do anything. This time, the face of Brain Wilkey melted into the face of his latest prisoner. He awoke several times in a cold sweat. The morning's business could not begin soon enough.

It had come back on him. That damned, insatiable hunger for young flesh. It had gone better than he expected with Tommy and Ashley.   They had been innocent and tractable, although in the end he had been compelled to hurt them both. . .just a little. He'd had to.

"Don't you understand? I had to," Brian Wilkey said aloud as though arguing with someone other than himself. He had thought their cooperation might make it last, keep him from hunting again. But it hadn't.

Perhaps they'd been too cooperative? After this last time he had been very quiet indeed. He had been filled with guilt and fear. Guilt over having to harm either of the twosome he found so precious. Fear over the possibility that they might tell someone that Dennis Bryan might find out. Worse, he had been caught by one of the Costello button men. Not actually in the act, but bad enough.

After he had dried their tears and reassured them, Brian escorted Tommy and Ashley back to the park. They had been sitting on the same bench where he had met them, while he impressed upon the youngsters the importance of telling no one, especially Mommy or Daddy, when Tony DeLucca strolled by. The Wise Guy had been around enough to easily recognize the glow and the scent given off by the trio on the bench. He revealed his knowledge by only a slight hesitation in his step. Brian's world plunged into icy dread.

Later that night, Brian had received the summons. He went to the mid-town apartment of Carlo Banducci, consigliore of the Costello Family. For the longest time, Carlo made him stand alone in the middle of a darkly paneled study, on what must have been a $5000 Isfahan carpet. The counselor stared out the window over the twinkling lights of Manhattan. Then Banducci whirled around and jabbed a long, thin finger at Brian.

"What the fuck were you thinking? It's not so much what you were doing. We know about guys like you. You have this urge, this--this itch. Ya gotta scratch it, right? Thing is you were stupid. You picked the wrong place, and the wrong time. In mid-afternoon, for Christ's sake." He stopped and paced the floor as if searching for the right words.

"You're a crew boss, right? You're supposed to have some smarts. Then you go and parade your kinky pastime out in front of God and everybody. Your boss, Mr. Orlando, is pissed. The Don is pissed. And that makes me pissed. This has got to stop, Wilkey. I mean, absolute cold turkey. It's either that or, to coin an old phrase, 'you'll be sleepin' with the fishes.' Think about it, Brian. You're good. One of the best. Outside a' guys on the pad, we don't think there's anyone knows what you're doin' for us. Keep your nose clean, stay away from the kids, an' you'll go far."

All smiles then, Banducci crossed to Brian and embraced him, gave him a kiss on each cheek. Brian had tried. For a year now, he had tried really hard. And now the itch was back, worse than ever before.

He had to stop. He had to. . .Yet, all he really had to do was find the right time and the right place.

"Okay, gentlemen, time to rise and shine," shouted a court officer.

Mike checked his watch. It was 0730 hours and the cleaning people had to tidy up the room for the day's business. Cracking knees could be heard along with moans as sleeping officers popped up like spring flowers around the large room.

Romano went to use the restroom to tend to nature and wash the sleep from his eyes. God, he felt as grungy as his prisoner looked. Gotta get some breakfast. Within three minutes he walked out the Baxter Street entrance, headed to one of the "cop bars" that served bacon and eggs every morning.

"Hey, Romano, you score a collar, or are you down here to testify?" greeted a sandy-haired cop at the counter. It was Pete Weller, who Mike knew from the Two-Three.

Mike grinned. "Got a collar. A rapist. Best part it came at the end of my set. I'm on swing, and bein' paid OT for it."

"Cool deal," Weller replied. "I wish we could all do it that way."

Mike gave Pete a broad wink. "If we all did, the city would be broke in a month."

"Hell, the City's broke anyway. They just ain't tellin' anyone about it." Pete Weller took a bite of the ubiquitous French fries that accompanied the bacon and eggs in this particular cop hangout, chewed, swallowed and asked, "Rape, eh? Did you catch him in the act?"

"Sort of. He was eating her."

"Cunnilingus? The statutes make that act Sodomy."

Mike laughed. "Naw. This guy was, like really eating her. Bite, chew, and go after some more. She had teeth marks all over her groin." His outrage of the previous night returned and he scowled. "A disgusting bastard."

Weller sipped coffee. "What next?"

"In this town? You tell me."

After breakfast and some more conversation with fellow officers, Mike telephoned home to say good morning to Betty and check on the kids. "You all right, Honey?" he asked the moment she came on the line, his mind on what Fate had dealt the Korean woman.

"Sure, I'm all right. I wouldn't have been," Betty added, "if you had not called last night to tell me you had a collar to process."

"How are the kids?"

"They're fine. Donny tried to climb into the bathtub this morning. He toppled over and bumped his head."

"Oh, my God. Is he hurt?"

Betty's trill of laughter reassured him at once. "Of course not. Only his dignity. I love you, Mikey."

"I love you, too, Bet. I don't know how long this will

take. I should be home by noon. How about we do the beach?"

"Coney Island?" Betty asked expectantly.

"I was thinking Rockaway."

"Okay by me."

"Pack a picnic, right?"

Betty answered absently, her mind already on the delicacies she would buy later that morning to put in their basket. Maybe a bottle of wine? "Sure, that'll be fine."

"Okay, got to run, Sweet. I love you."

"Love you, too. Bye."

Mike returned to the complaint room at 0900. While waiting to be called by an ADA for an interview, he dialed the phone number his complainant/victim had given him the night before. She was home. He had been lucky.

Many times complainants had second thoughts about prosecution a day later. This frail woman had a thick accent coupled with swollen lips that made understanding her near impossible. She said one thing Mike could clearly comprehend.

"I want him punished. I want him in jail, to rot like the animal he is."

Mike answered with more conviction than he felt. "We'll see to that, don't you worry. All we ask is that you show up and testify."

"I will. I am -- how you say? -- a mess. Everywhere my skin shows I have a bruise every four to six centimeters. There are stitches over my right eye. I hope that. . ." She said something in Korean that Mike liked to believe meant, "Son of a bitch…….. gets everything he deserves."

Mike was happy to be of service. He had avenged another injustice. She would be down there in less than an hour.

During their interview with an ADA to draw up an affidavit of formal charges for arraignment, Mike learned what had happened. The victim had immigrated to the States only one year ago. "I live alone," she confided in broken English. "Living on a limited budget and with my limited English, I am having a barrier -- it is called that, yes? -- that has caused many problems." Due to limited finances she resided in the Three-Two. There was a plethora of inexpensive apartments. It was, after all, a ghetto.

She continued, her discomfort slowly melting. "In the twelve months that I reside in that building, I became friendly with---with the man who did this. Only -- how you say? -- buddies. Or at least I think so." She made it clear that there was never anything remotely sexual in their relationship.

A shy smile as she continued. "Yesterday, as we often do, we shared several bottles of wine. Muscatel or Tokay, you understand? As the day progressed, so did our thirst."

It became evident that her drinking partner also had a more lustful craving; for her. Encouraged by their drunkenness, he attacked her on the rooftop. When she resisted, he became violent. Sitting with an Assistant District Attorney was the result.

After reviewing her statement and hearing from Mike, the ADA dismissed them. The complainant accompanied Mike to the courtroom. When the case was called before the judge, she let out a small squeal of delight. As the charges were read, she glowered at the defendant.

"Counselor, based on the charges," asked the Judge, "how does your client plead?"

After a short murmured conversation, "May we approach?" asked defense council.

"Yes?" asked the Judge, looking right into the eyes of the defense attorney.

He began, carelessly from where he stood, "The court is aware, I'm sure that the complainant and the defendant are friends?"

"I don't assault my friends Counselor. Do you?" came the quick retort from the bench.

An embarrassed, "No Judge, but. . .but, they were drinking all day. My client felt that he could--uh--score, so to speak. He claims that she became violent first. She kicked him the crotch."

The jurist looked at the prosecutor, and then turned to the defense attorney again. He commented. "Counselor, just look at that woman, she's literally half the size of your client. He nearly beat the life out of her. He bit her virginal area. Waving the court affidavit, he continued, "It's right here in black and white. He's charged with a set of serious crimes. Don't insult this court."

Hesitantly, the defense Counselor now looked sheepishly at the judge. "Your honor, if it will please the court, we will plead guilty to charges to save time and expense, provided the court will allow us to plea to lesser charges."

"Counselor, these charges are indeed serious. The complainant will possibly never be the same person she was before this attack." He shifted his gaze to the ADA, who gave a curt nod. "However, in the interest of justice, taking in consideration also the complainant's lack of command of the English language and her possible shame during a trial, I will allow a plea to Sexual Abuse, 1st Degree, a D/Felony. I will further recommend a sentence of one to three years."

Shocked, the attorney for the defense turned to look at the smiling prosecutor. The next person he saw as he turned toward the visitors' benches was the complainant. He knew that if the arresting officer had taken photos of the visible wounds on the complainant, he would probably lose a trial. Back of the table in front of the bench stood Police Officer Michael Romano. He looked tall, righteous, and efficient. The attorney knew he would lose. Returning his eyes to the judge, he stated, "As you wish, Your Honor. Thank you."

"You may continue, Counselor" stated the judge.

"If the court pleases, Your Honor, we await any offer by the prosecution."

Quietly, his rising anger tightly reined, the ADA spoke, "The prosecution, in the interest of justice will allow the defendant to plead guilty to Sexual Abuse, First Degree to satisfy all charges in this case."

From the bench came, "How does the defendant plead?"

"Guilty Your Honor," came the response from the defendant's side.

"Does the defendant waive the reading of rights and charges and is he ready to accept sentencing at this time?" asked the Judge.

His response was as expected, "Yes Your Honor."

"Very well then. Mr. Collins," that was the defendant's name, "do you plead guilty to the charge as stated?"

Standing there, the big man responded, "Yes, sir."

Next came, "Are you doing this of your own free will. With the exception of what was discussed with your attorney, have there been any promises or threats made to you in order to obtain this plea?"

"No, sir."

"Is Mr. Collins ready to accept sentencing now?"

The attorney replied, "Yes Your Honor."

The Judge began, "Mr. Collins, let it be known that you have plead guilty to Sexual Abuse, First Degree, Section 130.65 Subdivision 1, a D Felony. The court may impose no more than seven years. At this time the court is sentencing you to one to three years."

Mike received a kiss on the cheek from the complainant as sentence was pronounced. She understood the numbers, right enough. The judge smiled.

Banging his gavel down once on his desk, the judge stated, "Bailiff, remove the prisoner to be lodged. Call the next case, please."

It was over. Once again Romano felt fulfillment. He had again righted a wrong. As he signed out of court and drove home he mused on the outcome. He was not only like an avenging angel; he was another step closer to buying a house for his family. He had spent the last twenty-eight hours on overtime.

Betty and the children were happy to see him. They had eight hours before nightfall. They would make the most of it at the beach.

CHAPTER SIXTEEN

During the week that followed the Korean complainant incident, Mike began again to think about Deputy Inspector Bryan and his brother-in-law, Wilkey. The sexual abuse of the frail victim and her subsequent rape rekindled the burning desire within Romano to punish the child molester and his protector. Not a day passed without them entering his thoughts.

Mike and Len were assigned to the ninth squad within a uniform patrol working chart that included twenty four squads. They presently worked the second set of back-to-back "Four Bys" as the four-to-twelve tour was referred to within the Job.

After completing that set, the team would have three days off. Included in the swing was a full weekend. Monday off was a bonus. Mike added three vacation days to his swing. Betty had reserved a small bungalow in the Pocono Mountains of Pennsylvania about three hours' drive from Jackson Heights. It would be a sort of celebration. The third anniversary of his joining the Force. Saturday would be spent on last minute preparations and shopping for whatever they might need. They planned to leave Sunday morning returning Thursday night.

Returning to work for their second set of four-to-twelve tours, Sector Adam's first tour began typically enough. The team handled their share of calls for service on a summer night in Harlem.

During the first three hours they responded to four violent family disputes, three shots fired scenes, and two auto accidents. In addition, the men took four robbery and three burglary reports. They even vouchered one "found" handgun, handed to them by a concerned citizen within Sector Adam. Somehow they also found the time to write two traffic violations each and make one run up the Harlem River Drive to cool off the interior of their RMP.

All in all it looked to be a normal night in the Three-Two for Mike and Len. Shortly after returning to the streets upon completion of their meal hour it changed.

Mike drove south-bound on Lenox Avenue. They approached West 128th Street at 2010 hours. Suddenly a dark red Chevy crossed their path and stopped on the southeast corner on West 128th. There was nothing unusual about that, except the traffic light was green on Lenox and red for the Chevy.

Mike hit the red dome lights and gave the siren a short burst. The driver was about to receive a Disobey Steady Red summons. There was a passenger in the right front seat; the engine of the red car remained running.

Smoothly, the two officers exited their auto like a well-oiled machine. Mike had the car's high beams on. He focused his three-cell flashlight on the driver before he even stepped around his safety barrier; the open radio car door. Len was in motion on his side too.

Len approached, getting the attention of the car's occupants. Once his partner had the driver and passenger looking his way, Romano left the safety of his open car door. With his right hand holding his service revolver at his side, he used his light to sweep the suspect vehicle interior.

Not more than five seconds had passed since the two stalwart officers exited their RMP. It appeared to be a routine stop in every respect. Len now stood adjacent to the rear fender of the suspect auto. It was team custom and good police work for the recorder, Len in this case, to knock on the car fender before he approached the driver. The two partners knew that approximately half the officers shot in the line of duty were shot while approaching the driver during car stops.

Len knocked on the fender of the stopped Chevy. The passenger turned in his seat and said, "Yo, chill Brother. Don't hurt the car."

By the man's comment, Len knew that these two might be a problem. How right that proved to be.

When Mike began his approach, the street directly under the Chevy's rear wheels erupted with smoke and noise. The driver had the car in gear. They were running. Mike's jaw dropped. For half a heart beat his position remained fixed. He felt as though he had turned to a pillar of concrete. Dimly he saw his partner move into action.

Len brought his handgun up to sight level as the Chevy sped off into the night. He remembered Department guidelines, *"Do not shoot at a moving vehicle unless occupants of said vehicle are using deadly physical force other than the vehicle."* They were fleeing and constituted no threat to himself or Mike. By the end of his thought process, he found himself back at the squad, closing his car door.

Even before Len shut the car door, Mike had put their RMP into gear. The 383 cubic inch, Chrysler engine roared. The four barrel carburetor opened up, pouring gasoline into the eight cylinders. The two officers sped off in pursuit of the suspects adding more smoke from burning rubber to the heavy night air.

The suspects hurtled down W.128th Street and crossed Fifth Avenue. Sector Adam hung only thirty feet behind them as they fishtailed into a right turn. Len broadcast their progress and attempted to note the license plate number of the fleeing red missile.

Mike worked the break and gas at the same time, as he had been taught to do at the Emergency Vehicle Obstacle Course. The police car's flashing dome lights gave grim advance warning to motorists that might cross their path. Yet, the colored beams that bounced off buildings and reflected in glass windows gave a carnival atmosphere to the chase. To Mike it seemed almost surrealistic.

Suddenly the suspects turned against traffic on Fifth Avenue. They headed uptown. At West 139th Street they flew up the entrance ramp in between the buildings of the Delano

Angel with a Gun

Houses and headed north on the FDR Drive.

While Mike took the RMP off up the Drive, other police sirens could heard. Len did a good job of keeping the radio dispatcher and other teams informed of their progress. Mike could only concentrate on his driving. He knew that if he could stay with the fleeing suspects, they would either crash or abandon the Chevy.   Even more than a gunman, radio car officers dreaded a high speed chase. These suspects had put his and Len's life in jeopardy, as well as the lives of innocent bystanders.. Mike had decided that they must be caught.

Len anticipated their next move. He thought that the men intended to head into the Three-Four, and would continue up the FDR to Dykeman Street where the Drive ended. "Sector Adam. Request other units to block off Dykeman Street exit at the FDR, K." He had a good idea, but he was wrong.

Glancing into the rear view mirror, Mike observed what he believed to be two additional RMP's speeding up the Drive behind him. He couldn't be sure. A glance was all he could afford. If he took his eyes off the road for too long it could mean disaster for Sector Adam. They now sped along at 85 miles per hour.

Approaching West 155th Street, the pursued and the pursuer streaked along the center lane of the Drive.   Mike decided to attempt to overtake the red rocket.

He counted off the distance in his mind as the gap closed; *twenty feet. . .still twenty feet. . .all right, fifteen feet, ten, gonna close now.*

About to reach the West 155th Street exit, the crazy driver in the suspect vehicle cut left, entering the exit ramp. The right side of the once good looking Chevy belched a shower of sparks. The fleeing auto repeatedly bounced off the concrete wall that swung around to the left.

Mike tromped down on the brakes. The RMP skidded and began to fishtail.   His knuckles went white against the steering wheel as he slid past the exit. Len hurriedly gave the latest developments to the dispatcher as Mike threw the car into

211

reverse. The force of the backward lurch launched Len forward, causing him to curse as his forehead struck the dashboard.

"Awh, shit!"

A response came quickly. "Units out there, I know that we're all tense from this chase, but careful guys, NO UNAUTHORIZED TRANSMISSIONS."

"Awh, crap," Len panted out. "They heard me. Damn." It embarrassed him. He had lost his cool. He was aware that his partner sometimes referred to him as "Peter Perfect" and knew that the teasing nickname was a sign of respect. He had come to like it.

Mike now followed the exit to the left. The suspect auto had a jump on him, headed down Seventh Avenue.

"Where are they going?" shouted Romano. It was a rhetorical question. Mike knew that his partner had no idea.

Streets flew past. West 148th Street, 139th, 135th. The suspects headed back downtown.

"Call it off in the Three-Two, by authority of the Duty Captain. There's been an RMP accident. The boss doesn't want any more cops hurt. Call it off in the Three-Two", shouted the dispatcher.

"No," shouted Mike to his partner. "We're gonna get them."

A grinning Len rubbed his forehead and shouted his approval. "Stay with them, Partner. They're gonna screw up soon. We can tell them that our radio didn't receive the transmission." Pointing at the fleeing vehicle, Len alerted Mike, "There they go. They're headed back toward the Madison Houses."

It appeared as though they heard Len's statement. The driver struck a fire hydrant just off the corner of Madison Avenue and West 130th Street. The red Chevy bounced on a geyser of water as it abruptly stopped on top of the severed fire plug. Before the car stopped bouncing, both doors flew open, spitting out a suspect each. As the men hit the sidewalk, Mike and Len stopped inches short of hitting the wounded vehicle and jumped out. The foot race was on.

Mike had the portable radio the team shared. He shouted into it, "Central, Sector Adam of the Three-Two is now in foot pursuit of the car chase suspects." He huffed and puffed as he continued, "Both are described as male blacks, short hair, one wearing a brown jacket. We're going into the project at West 130th Street and Madison." More puffs and gasps. "Have back-up cover the Park Avenue side, K."

Their subjects had split up. Len followed the passenger while Romano chased the driver into the project.

Composed of six story buildings, the project loomed over Mike. There were one dozen structures, each containing about sixty families. The once proud grounds of the Fifties had started to show age and neglect. The lawns had gone patchy and the decorative greenery was sparse. Surprisingly, there was still benches scattered through-out the complex. Mike saw that they were in good repair and loaded with people. Most of those residents turned toward the action. They would again have a front row seat.

Some of the loungers became vocal. Shouts of, "Run Brother, run. Don't let the Man get you," rang off the walls. "Stay free. Go, Brother."

Other sentiments Mike heard expressed a different attitude. "Get the niggers officers; its shit like them that messed up this neighborhood. Hope y'all catch the guys."

Sector Adam had become used to the interaction. They each hoped that nobody would attempt to interfere. It would complicate matters.

His man ran like the wind. Mike never got closer than twenty feet behind him. The runner rounded the corner of a building, and Mike lost sight of him for a second. Abruptly stopping, Mike raced to the building wall.

That son of a bitch may try to jump him as he turned the corner, reasoned Mike. He drew his weapon and slowly advanced to the angle of the building. Actually, he felt grateful for the respite. It gave him a chance to catch his breath.

Peering cautiously around the edge of the building, Mike could not see anyone running. He continued to advance slowly. Mike saw the muzzle flash come from two closely set bushes on the lawn in front of him. The sound was thunderous. He fell flat to the ground, raised his weapon, and took aim. *At what?* he thought. *There's people out here beside that asshole. Look around; some of them aren't even aware of the gunshots.* He could hit the wrong person.

Mike remained as still as possible. He reached for his back pocket left-handed. The radio was gone. He didn't know if any other cops were present. Len had chased the other guy and probably heard the shots. He decided to wait it out.

Suddenly, the suspect jumped up and started to run again. It was obvious to Romano that the guy knew a cop would not risk a shot out in a crowded area. Mike came up and began to run, also. He wasn't about to lose the guy now. It had become right personal.

When the suspect passed another building wall, he slammed to a halt, turned and let go two more rounds. Mike dropped to the ground and returned fire. Three rounds lit off in rapid secession. The suspect fell behind a clump of bushes.

Mike remembered his last shootout. The one on West 145th Street. At the time, he wasn't sure if he hit the guy, but he had. The memory brought Mike new worries. Maybe he got this son of a bitch, too. *If this keeps up, somebody's for sure gonna get hit. Maybe not even the right one.* He remained frozen to the ground.

With his concentration riveted on the bushes about fifteen yards in front of him, Mike heard Len shout, "Mike, are you all right? What the hell is going on?"

Romano made quick answer, "Get down damn you. This guy's out there and shooting. I hear you but don't know where you are. Are you okay"

Angel with a Gun

"Fine partner. There's plenty of back-up here. I think they're on the other side and moving in. They're gonna get him." Len crouched behind a bench set up near the expanse of lawn that had been the scene of this explosive confrontation. He couldn't tell his partner his location for fear of alerting the shooter.

"Hey Mike, crawl backwards if you can. You gotta put more distance between him and you", shouted Jones.

Romano began to inch his way rearward, never taking his eyes off the bushes in front of him. He had retreated about one foot when those same bushes were flooded with light. An Emergency Services Truck had silently slid up on the scene. Once in position, they illuminated the gunman's area as though it were daylight.

Mike gave a silent thank you to his patron saint. He knew that he would be able to go home to his family again. His adrenalin level began to return to normal. As his body started to relax, he began to quiver. He shared that reaction with every police officer who had gone through similar ordeals.

Two ESU cops equipped with shotguns and flack vests slowly advanced on the rear of the bushes. From his vantage point flat on the ground, the two armored officers looked to Mike as if they were giant warriors from another world. Silhouetted from the rear by the harsh light, they had the appearance of being at least eight feet tall.

In another three strides, the cops had reached the bushes. With humans standing next to the shrubs, barely three feet tall, Mike now had a size comparison.

The officers next held their weapons high in the air and shouted, "All clear."

Mike's body stopped shaking. Anger had instantly signaled his adrenal glands to flood his body again. His heart bounded. He became flush. Mike turned to Len.

"The bastard got away. Damn. We'll find him through your collar."

Mike added confidently. "You got him for sure. You run like a gazelle."

Sergeant Armini and Len approached the rising Romano. Len flashed a white grin in his mahogany face. "I accept the compliment, misplaced though it is, with gratitude."

"Mike, are you hit?" asked the boss.

"No Sarge, I'm fine." Turning toward his partner, Mike asked, "You did get your guy? We gotta question him. Who's holding him?"

Len tried to temper the effect his answer would have. "Hey Mike, thank God the guy couldn't shoot straight. You would be looking even shittier then you do now. Brush yourself off man."

When Mike looked down at his uniform, Len continued, "No one's got him. My man split, too. The important thing is nobody got hurt."

"Not quite Len, we had two men injured in an RMP accident during the chase." Armini, seeing the look of embarrassment on Len's face, added, "But they're okay. Only cuts and bruises. You guys can see them later."

"Sorry, Sarge," Len said as he advanced to his partner and gave him a quick hug, patting his back in the process.

An ESU officer joined them, "Sarge, there's no blood around the bush and no shell casings. This officer might have missed and we'll assume the perp used a revolver. We're going to search the area now for damages and other possible injuries."

"Thank you. The Duty Captain is on the way. Inform him and any responding detectives. My men and I are going to the station." Turning to Mike, he stated, "Michael, you know that you can go the hospital for trauma. Do you want to? If not we'll go in and begin the paper work. It's gonna be a long night."

Mike's answer could be anticipated. He had refused the option before. "No Sarge. I just need a few minutes to relax and put on a clean shirt when we get in. I'll be okay."

Reaching into his pocket, the now "calm" Romano withdrew the car keys. They tinkled musically in his shaking hand. He extended them to his partner and asked, "Ah--you drive Len, will you? Thanks."

"Yeah, you're relaxed all right," Len drawled.

Back in the Three-Two the partners learned that the red Chevy had been stolen the night before in the Bronx. During a custodial inventory of the vehicle's contents, two semi-automatic handguns and about three ounces of what was believed to be heroin were recovered. It explained why the men took their chances and ran. It worked, they had gotten away.

Mike and Len agreed that they would not telephone their respective wives. They had been together over three years up to that point and the girls were used to their men making arrests and sometimes coming home a few hours late. It had become standard for the men to telephone home if they would be all night. Their wives knew that if their men were hurt, a uniformed officer would knock on the door. The women had been told that notifications of that nature were never done over the phone.

Toward the end of the tedious multitude of forms and notifications, the Duty Captain called the team into the CO's office one at a time. They were interviewed and returned to assist Sergeant Armini. Neither man was questioned as to whether or not they heard the chase being called off. The Captain obviously remembered what it was like being a street cop.

Sergeant Armini had requested a time check from the Central Dispatcher for the incident. It was required information for the Unusual Report. It would also be needed for the write-up in recommending the men for yet another Department Recognition. They, at least Mike, had been under fire again.

Joe DeCicco

Central responded to the sergeant's request. "The first call from Sector Adam was transmitted at 2011 hours, 58 seconds. The foot pursuit began at 2026 hours, four blocks from where the entire incident started. At 2017 hours the RMP accident occurred. By 2030 hours it was determined that the suspects got away. At 2034 hours Three-Two Patrol Sergeant and Sector Adam went 10-62, out of service, to the house. Is that all you need?"

Armini replied, sounding tired. "Yeah. That'll do."

When informed of this, Mike found the time elements incredible. The car chase seemed like only minutes and the foot race and resulting shooting like hours. It had been fourteen and four minutes respectively.

By 0130, one and one half hours past their regular tour, the men of Three-Two Adam left for home.

Arriving home, Mike found Betty asleep. He quietly peeled out of his clothes and slipped into bed, his body exhausted. For once he slept without dreaming that night.

That morning, while her husband slept, Betty found his soiled uniform. She knew that something out of the ordinary must have occurred the night before. Mike slept like a baby. *It couldn't have been too much,* she thought. He'd tell her later if he wanted to.

Not until 11 a.m. did Mike wake up. He padded into the kitchen on bare feet and in his underwear. Betty stood alone at the counter, beginning to prepare lunch for the children. Her back was to him. Donald and Anne were in their room having a tea party with some dolls and their dog, Abigail.

Mike heard Anne talking to the dog as though the animal could respond, "Sip your tea Abby. Let me know what you think." Anne probably had a cup of water on the floor in front of the dog. She then apparently turned to her brother, "Donny, what do you think?"

Angel with a Gun

"Good stuff Annie," replied the three-year-old.

Mike now turned his full attention to Betty. He reached around her shoulders, and cupped her breasts in his hands. "Hi Honey," he said as he kissed her right ear. She squirmed and playfully poked his right hand with a fork. She was mixing tuna salad. "Got anything to tell me?" she asked.

"Sure, I love you," was his answer.

"What else, Michael?" she asked.

"I love you tooooo much and the kids, too." He knew that she must have seen his dirty shirt and was annoyed by it. She would demand an explanation.

She got explicit, "What about last night?"

Ouch, he thought. How to tell her but not worry her?

He enjoyed her warm body against his. Without releasing his hold on his wife, Mike spent the next few minutes filling her in on the entire incident. He made light of the exchange of gunfire, stating only that the perpetrator fired over his shoulder at him while running. He told her he dropped to the ground and returned fire, missing. By design he left out being pinned down in open ground.

"Mike we love you, be careful, please," was all she could think of to say. She pulled herself free of his grasp and continued her work, never turning around. Mike didn't see the streaming tears of fear and concern that silently spilled out of her eyes and added more salt to the tuna.

He returned to the bedroom, pulled on a pair of old pants and shouted, "Here comes Daddy," as he ran to the rear bedroom. The kids giggled and the dog barked. In the kitchen, Betty sighed and wiped away her tears.

The rest of his work week went uneventfully. On Friday, before he left for work, Betty had a reminder for him.

"Don't forget that we are to leave for Pennsylvania on Sunday morning."

"Not likely, Sweetheart.   I'll avoid overtime like the plague. If there are any arrests to be made, Len'll take them."

By 1:30 a.m. Saturday morning, Betty lay coiled around her curly haired Italian husband. Quietly they discussed the up-coming weekend.

"Are you taking your fishing stuff?" Betty asked, envisioning fresh trout broiling for breakfast.

"Naw. It's all surf-casting rods. You've got to have a fly rod for the mountains."

Betty frowned. "I was just thinking of broiled trout for breakfast."

Mike rose on one elbow. "With homemade cornbread?"

"Not with breakfast, silly. You want biscuits."

"Do you make biscuits?" her husband asked. "I thought those last ones were hockey pucks."

Betty punched him, and not lightly. "Rat."

"Pussycat."

"Ummm. I like it when you're mean like that. I wonder if there'll be wild flowers."

Mike shook his head. "Probably too late. They're pretty delicate, I think. Early spring's the time."

Betty surprised Mike. "I want to go hiking. Maybe try rock climbing."

"Not me. I wanna sit in the shade, under a big ol' pine tree and smell the clean air."

"Lazy.   What good's a weekend in a cabin in the mountains if you don't make use of what's around you?"

"Bet, I think I'll be making good use of it. Kick back, drink some beer, listen to the Mets game."

"Men." Betty spat in mock irritation. "Are you all so sedentary?"

"Wow! What's with the two dollar words?"

Betty pinched him. "Don't try to distract me. Don't you want to get out and see the pretty countryside, wade in a stream. . .even just a little bit?"

Mike laughed. "Of course I do. I only wanted to get a little rise out of you."

"There are better ways of doing that," Betty advised him as she took his free hand and cupped it around one of her breasts.

"Put out the light," Mike huskily whispered in her ear.

CHAPTER SEVENTEEN

July 16, 1977 was destined to be etched into the minds of every New Yorker. It would be especially significant to Police Officer Michael Romano and his family.

Completely awake by 10 a.m., the Romano household bustled with activity. Abigail had been out for her walk. Betty, Mike, the children and the family dog scooped up the last stray objects and bundled into their yellow station wagon and on their way to purchase last minute items for their short vacation.

Their day went leisurely enough. The Romanos did some shopping for kids' clothing. They took lunch at the Privateer Diner, a treat for the children. After lunch they did more shopping, with food stuffs being purchased last. By 5 p.m., the Romanos returned home.

Sitting inside their apartment, Mike remembered that as they neared home, he had noticed that all the traffic lights were out along 34th Avenue. He mentioned his observation to Betty.

"Maybe it's only here Mike." Conversationally she added, "Don't worry, they'll be working soon."

Suddenly, the screech of tires wailed up from the street. The sound that followed unmistakable to Mike. Two cars collided on the corner in a violent impact.

Betty looked out and commented, "Well, Mike, looks like I was wrong; the lights are still not working."

Before Mike could reply, the telephone rang. He answered it. It was John Cutbert. "Hello, John, what brings you to call on a Saturday?"

The reply surprised Mike. "Mikey," he sounded sober, so there must be a problem. John continued, "It's not official yet but all leaves are canceled. Turn on the TV news. You'll be getting notification from the Three-Two shortly. There's been an extensive blackout. All New York City is down. Everyone's being ordered in."

"What the hell are you talking about John?" Mike began to rethink his observation that his friend sounded sober.

"Mike, it came over the Teletype. Power lines serving the City are down. They're trying to re-route electric service but it's not working. The Job's gonna declare an emergency. You'll have a choice though. Since you live out of Borough, you get to pick your assigned command or residential command to work in. Naturally, I want you here. It's better for your family too."

"John, you're not joking, are you?"

"No Mike. It's real. Wait for official notice and come on in. Bring a uniform shirt and your shield. Later kid." The line went silent.

When informed of the conversation, Betty more than expressed her disappointment. She threw a bag of tomatoes to the floor. "Damn! Now look what happened." She had been packing groceries for their trip.

"Honey," he began, "don't get so upset. It may work out. The Three-Two didn't call yet. Let's turn on that little portable micro-tv in the kitchen. It runs on batteries and should work." He turned it on, twisted the dial and caught a network news program.

A well-known commentator's face came on. "Con Edison public information sources have released the following information. 'Niagara power lines down. Several towers fell, from as yet undisclosed cause. The incident is being investigated by local and Federal authorities.' " The scene cut to shots taken from a helicopter. They showed a collapsed tower, nothing but a jumble of twisted steel girders. The familiar anchor continued in voice-over to say that efforts to re-route service have not been successful. Then the camera cut back to him and he concluded his report with, "It is projected

Joe DeCicco

that New York City will be without power for at least twelve hours."

Betty mumbled to herself as the newscaster spoke. Mike, upset by knowing that his wife was disappointed, tried to plan ahead. They would have to re-schedule their trip as soon as possible. Betty was about to complain, when the television went dark. The power failed.

A shrill ring from the telephone startled Mike. Behind him, Betty dropped something. He hoped he could make it all up to her soon. He picked up the receiver and asked, "Hello?"

It was the expected reply, "Officer Romano? This is PO Collins, roll call in the Three-Two. The City is in a state of emergency. All active police officers have been ordered into service until further notice. All leaves have been canceled. Authority of the Police Commissioner."

Without waiting for an answer, Collins continued, "You, living out of the Borough of Manhattan, have the option of reporting here or working in your resident command."

Mike's reply came at once, "Here in the One-Ten. Thanks."

Collins answered, "Fine, Romano. Have a working flashlight, uniform shirt, shield and handcuffs if you have a spare set, on your person when you report. Naturally, don't forget your off-duty revolver. If you don't have an Emergency Response Card to record the tour, ask the command. They will issue you one. Good luck." Collins hung up.

Mike looked at Betty, his expression glum. She knew at once that their vacation had disappeared. Mike read her thoughts clearly. Damn, being a cop's wife. If only we could have left sooner. Shit!

Without a word, Mike walked into the bedroom. Reaching to the top shelf of their closet, he brought down his off-duty weapon and a box of cartridges and dumped them onto the bed. He put the loose rounds into his pants pockets. He grabbed a uniform shirt and went to Betty.

Angel with a Gun

"Honey, stay in the house and keep the door locked. If it gets crazy, you know where to find my hunting rifle and the rounds for it. Leave them where they are, for now. Emergency only. In the hall closet are extra flashlights and batteries."

"Where's the portable radio?" Betty asked in a hushed voice.

"I'll get it before I leave."

His children stood behind him as he spoke to Betty. Anne asked, "Daddy, are we still going away?"

"No Sweetie. There's no electric and the city is going to be dark all night. There's no lights or TV. You, Mommy and Donny are safe up here. Daddy has to go out to work and make sure everybody else is safe too." He picked her up and kissed her, then added, "See you tomorrow morning."

Donald looked at his father, smiled and stated, "Daddy goes to work now Anne. We stay with Mommy. See him later."

With his free arm, Mike scooped up his son. "Give Daddy a kiss, Donny."

Betty walked up to the trio and took Anne from him. Holding her daughter against her side, she kissed her husband and stated, "Be careful will you. Keep your head down. Don't get hurt. You owe me a vacation."

Mike handed his son to Betty who could hardly hold them both; boys nearly four years old is heavy as well as wriggly. He kissed her gently and went to a kitchen cabinet, where he retrieved their battery-powered radio. He handed it to Betty, gave her an encouraging wink, and walked to the front door. He had heard blackout stories from older men on the Job. It could be nasty until power was restored. Romano tried to be cheery as he said, "See you guys later."

Mike remained in the outer hallway until he heard the lock snap on his apartment door followed by the chain lock. He then walked down to the street.

When he arrived at the One-Ten, Mike asked for John Cutbert. The desk officer, Lt. Baker, looked up and recognized Romano. "He's out on patrol, Mike." Baker then entered Mike's name, rank and command in the blotter and told him, "just stand fast for now. The next off-duty officer to respond will be assigned along with you to ride in a patrol car accompanied by a uniformed on-duty officer." He smiled warmly at Mike. "It may look like we're playin' this by ear, Mike. But there is a City emergency plan. All we gotta do is stick to it."

Two minutes later another man walked in and introduced himself to Mike. "I'm James Carter. I live here in the One-Ten, but I'm normally assigned to the Seventh Precinct in Manhattan."

Mike wrung his hand firmly. "I live here, too. Work the Three-Two. What a hell of a night we're going to have."

Jim had his doubts. "You really think so? The people around here are really sort of cool."

Mike nodded to the drone of an emergency generator. "That's when the lights are on."

They teamed up with Officer Fred Sweeney of the One-Ten and were given RMP 1411 to use.

"Listen you men, answer jobs as One-Ten, 1411," ordered Lt. Baker. He continued, "You have no sector designation but are expected to patrol the Corona area. Do not respond out of your area unless directed to. Keep the dome lights on. Got that?"

One by one the trio acknowledged the instructions. They then hit the street. With the exception of traffic snarls and arguments at accident scenes between unfortunate motorists, they hadn't much to do, it being still daylight. Darkness would bring looting and the Lord knew what else.

By twilight Mike and his companions had gotten on a "hello" basis with most of the residents within their area. The locals were sitting outside their homes in Corona, where the team patrolled. The area was composed mostly of small private homes, including a poor stretch on Northern Boulevard from Junction Boulevard to 114th Street. The apartment dwellings on that stretch clustered above store front shops. People there sat outside on the sidewalk in a variety of chairs, from the straight-back kitchen type to backyard chaise lounges. The officers observed several other police cars patrolling that strip.

"Looks like a typical summer evening," Mike observed.

Fred Sweeney quickly dampened his optimism. "Yeah. But wait until it gets dark." Subsequently, RMP 1411 and its crew turned their attention to the Italian area of old homes.

Jim Carter asked a question as they rolled down one residential street, blinds and drapes drawn at the barred windows. "D'you think any of the old Mustache Petes in the area are gonna send out their soldiers to take advantage of the blackout?"

Mike Romano answered. "Naw. More likely, they'll have them mob up around their places to keep 'em from being looted."

"In which case, what do we do?" Jim wanted to know.

Mike shrugged. "We 'Protect and Serve,' what else?"

As darkness approached, mayhem broke out. Wherever storefronts filled an area, looting began. Muscular youths ripped down security gates, windows were broken and shops emptied of their goods. The cops tried their best to apprehend those responsible. It quickly proved futile.

Carter, who drove that part of the shift, braked to a sudden halt. "There goes a couple. Over there, with the TV sets."

As the officers exited their patrol car, the thieves dropped their loot and run. Mike started after them, to be called back by officer Sweeney. "Never mind. Hell, man, they get you out there in the dark and ambush you."

For the rest of the shift, Mike and most of the other cops spent their time picking up stolen property and ferrying it to the station. The owners would be called in later to identify their merchandise.

When the men grew tired, they got boisterous in an effort to pump themselves up. Seeing families using barbecues in front of their homes, the men of 1411 began to strike up bargains. They had a car trunk full of recovered loot.

Mike was the first to offer an electric coffee pot in exchange for a couple of hot dogs with mustard for each of them. He and his partners thought it funny. The pot was useless; THERE WAS NO ELECTRICITY. They continued their bartering for about one hour. After all, they reasoned, they were entitled to a meal break.

Cruising past a gas station on Roosevelt Avenue at about 2130 hours. Jim Carter spotted a youth running with a pushcart. It was loaded with plunder. Fred stopped the car giving Mike and Jim a chance to chase the guy on foot. They caught him because he wouldn't abandon his stolen merchandise. The kid fought like a tiger.

"Grab him, get that arm," Sweeney shouted. Mike shouted into Jim's ear, "Hold him down." Squirming in an attempt to escape, the youth lashed out with a kick. "Let go me, lemme go, you mutha-fuckers."

"Watch his legs."

It took all three officers to handcuff the kid. To Mike he appeared to be about sixteen or seventeen years old.

"What you damn cops gonna arrest me for anyway? Everybody is stealin' tonight," pleaded the guy.

Panting from his exertion, Fred answered, "Because we had to work hard to put the cuffs on. That's why."

"Dat ain't fair! You honkey muthuas, it ain't fair."

Jim's face lighted up with an idea. They put the kid into the radio car and the loot into the trunk. "Hey guys, listen. We're having a good time out here playing Santa with people.

Angel with a Gun

Why don't we transport the kid where he can't get into more trouble and give his stuff away too? We don't even know who the complainant is and there's no time to find out."

Fred was the first to answer, "Sure, great idea. We can take him to the swamps near College Point and let him go. Without lights it'll take him a week to find his way back."

Jim was all for the idea. Reluctantly, Mike agreed too. He tried to make himself believe it was a kind of street justice.

Fred told the teenager that they would give him a choice. He could be arrested or driven out of the neighborhood and let go.

That terrified the kid. "What you guys gonna do? Take me out somewhere and shoot me?" his eyes pleaded with them.

Mike took up the response. "No, you little thief. We're going to take you about two miles from here and let you go. We don't have time to play with you. Okay?"

"Sure, man," came his answer.

Mike climbed into the rear seat with the guy. Fred took the wheel and Jim sat next to him, twisting in his seat to tease the young man.

"Listen," Jim said to no one and everyone, "maybe we can shoot the kid. I've never shot anyone. Have either of you two?"

The youth began to cry. Mike attempted to comfort him by saying, "Don't worry kid, I've known my partner for years. He's had lots of chances to shoot people and he doesn't. He's not gonna start tonight." Then, quieter, to Carter. "I have, partner, and believe me it's not something you want to do."

In about five minutes, the car pulled up on the causeway road to College Point. On both sides of the road lay swamps. Fred turned off all the lights. He ordered the boy to get out.

"I ain't goin' nowhere, without you come along," he appealed to Mike.

Mike coaxed him outside. "Listen," he said, "we're going to take the 'cuffs off. You walk away from the car and

229

we leave. Find your own way home. It's better than jail, believe it."

"Yeah, you're okay, but that guy," indicating Jim, "is crazy. I don't trust him. Give me your word you won't let him hurt me; then I'll go."

Mike began to pity the young man. He looked terrified. "Okay, kid, you got my word. Now go."

Uncertainly, the young man began to walk away. Only the faintest orange light hung in the west. To the east it was completely dark. Jim shouted, "Let's shoot him anyway" and drew his revolver.

For a moment Mike thought his team-mate had lost it. Jim pointed his handgun in the air and let four quick rounds go. The kid could hardly be seen at that point, yet they could make out his dark form diving into the cattail rushes. The three of them could hear the kid splashing around in the stagnant water. Weird. To Mike it seemed that all the rules that normally directed them had been suspended.

"He learned his lesson", stated Jim, sounding satisfied. "Let's get back to where we're needed."

They climbed into the car and Fred put the headlights back on. He turned the car around and they returned to Corona. All the way back, Mike grew increasingly ill at ease.

They ran out of toasters, can openers and coffee pots by 2300 hours. Mike felt relieved and wasted no time telling the others about it. Carter gave him a look that questioned Mike's sanity. Sweeney nodded silent agreement. Returning from assisting in the break-up of a fight on Elmhurst Ave. and 81st Street the trio noticed fire blazing from the fourth floor of an apartment building. Fred pulled the car in front, Jim grabbed the radio to report the condition and all three piled out before the car even stopped.

Mike and his partners had to battle their way through the lobby doors. Scores of people tried to get out. One middle-aged man, his short, black hair sprinkled with gray, eyes widened to near-perfect circles, reached out toward Mike, as though to clutch him.

"Git oud th' way. We's got fire in there. We gotta get out."

Mike grabbed the man by one shoulder. "Did anyone call the fire department?"

"I don' know, Officer. Alls I know is we gotta get outta here."

Inside several people attempted to assist evacuation by holding flashlights. Some-one had hooked up a floodlight to a car battery. Mike judged the light ample enough to illuminate the lobby.

In the shadows Mike could see that the lobby must have been something in its heyday. It was about forty feet deep with three elevators on the far wall. On either side of the elevator bank a grandiose stairway flowed magnetically upward, reminiscent of an old movie theater.

Jim headed for the right staircase. Mike and Fred trotted left. As Fred mounted the staircase and began running up, Mike was grabbed from behind. Someone had hold of his shirt. *Not now.* He had work to do and didn't have time to argue or fight.

Mike turned to see a short, dark haired woman, about fifty years old. He saw the pleading look in her eye before she even spoke. "What's wrong?" he asked.

Gripping his hand in desperation, as she answered, "There's people on the roof. I live on the top floor and saw a man and a little girl going up as I ran down. Get them. Help them. Please."

Mike could not believe that anyone would go up during a fire. Flames travel upward. You should get below the flames, not above them.

"Don't worry lady. I'll get them if they're up there. The Fire Department is on their way." He turned and ran up the left stairway.

Joe DeCicco

While he passed the first floor he heard, rather than saw Fred pounding on doors. He shouted, "There's people on the roof. I'm going up to get them. You guys clean out the lower floors."

Mike found the stairway not too smoky. The fire must be on the other side. As he passed the fourth floor, Mike could feel heat and see smoke pouring out from under what must be the fire door separating the two halves of the building. He continued to the roof landing. The roof door was closed.

Back in the Police Academy he had been told to feel any doors for heat before opening them at a fire scene. Mike touched the door. It didn't even feel warm. He kicked it open, flashlight in hand. He saw a light go out. In the darkness he heard the whimper of a small child. He shouted, "Police. It's all right now. I'm gonna get you out of here. Where are you?"

Mike heard the patter of little feet, a flash of lightning and the crack of a gunshot almost simultaneously. Someone had shot at him again. The door swung partially closed. He switched off his light and instinctively fired off two rounds in the direction of the flash. As the sound died Mike again heard a cry of the small child.

CHAPTER EIGHTEEN

One thing flashed through the mind of Mike Romano. *God, please don't let the kid be hurt.* Not from his gunfire especially. He couldn't take that. Cautiously, extending his left arm out and away from his body, he lit his flashlight. No further gunshots. Mike hoped that perhaps he got the shooter. His last encounter, in the Madison Houses; he missed and the guy got away.

Mike swept the roof in front of him. He saw nothing. He pulled the door toward himself. The latch prevented it from closing completely. That was fine with Mike. He could still listen for sounds

From behind him came a ponderous noise. Mike thought of a buffalo trudging up the stairs. He turned, weapon at the ready. In the glow of the flashlight carried by this behemoth, Mike could see the face of John Cutbert.

"John," shouted Mike. "It's me, Mike Romano."

Puffing away, John managed to get out, "Mike we were down on the sixth floor and heard shots. Is anyone hurt?"

"No, Sarge. There's a kid out there and some asshole with a gun. He fired at me. Maybe I got him because it's quiet now. We gotta go and find the kid and the shooter."

"Michael, how do you get yourself into these things? I've been on the force for twenty years and have never been in a gunfight. Remember Mike, you're not bullet proof."

"Maybe I attract bullets?" Mike snapped. He wanted to get out on the roof and do what had to be done. They had a small child out there and a madman. They both had to be found. He would take his chances. He decided to speak to John Cutbert, not Sergeant Cutbert.

"John, are there any more men downstairs? Are they coming up? Last week someone I was after got away. This guy will not. Besides there's a kid out there. I gotta do. . ."

Angel with a Gun

He's not gonna get away like Wilkey. The avenging angel attitude rose aggressively in Officer Romano.

John cut him off abruptly. "Remain here, Mike, and wait for more men."

Mike didn't answer his friend.

Mike only heard the words, "more men". Perhaps that's all he wanted to hear. Fire trucks approached closer now and created quite a dim. Mike crouched low, pushed open the roof door and slid out into the darkness.

Mike squinted in the moonless night. The glow of the fourth floor flames, reflected off the hazy sky, provided the only source of illumination. Again Mike held his flashlight out to throw off the gunman and scanned the roof top in front of him. Mike started, looked again. There, up against the parapet, a small huddled form. To him, it looked like a little girl.

Mike called out, "Police. It's okay. You're okay now." Remembering the gunman, he continued, "Listen little person, crawl toward the light. I'll leave it on. Look I'm a cop."

No comment came from Cutbert.

For one split second Mike took a chance and ran the light up and down his body to show the child that he was really a cop. He braced himself for another gunshot, for the searing impact of a bullet. None came. An audible sigh of relief escaped from deep within Romano. He left his light on and put it down on the roof deck moving to the left of it.

"Jesus glory," mumbled John Cutbert from behind Mike Romano. "The boy's crazy."

Slowly, the child began to move toward Mike. He spoke softly, offered words of encouragement. The small whimpering figure didn't speak. The only sound made was sniffling and sobbing.

It seemed like hours before the child got within arm's reach. It indeed turned out to be a little girl. She appeared to be about six or seven years old. Her clothes were filthy as was

234

her face.

When he reached out for the child, Mike heard his friend behind him. "Damn you Michael, I told you to stand fast. Now pass the child back and stay low."

Romano clutched the girl to his chest and left his flashlight behind, as he crawled five feet to where John crouched in the doorway. John handed the child off to another cop and moved through the opening on his hands and knees to help his friend who still remained on the roof.

Mike made it patently clear that he wanted the shooter. "I'm going after him."

John bit his lower lip. "I'm coming with you."

If circumstances had been different, it would have been a comical sight indeed. John Cutbert, no matter what his position, could never make himself a small target. His shoulders hunched up, moving on bent knees, John reminded Mike of Oliver Hardy in a pink tutu.

Mike and John backed up against the exterior wall of the stairwell. The structure sat on the rooftop like a square wart. Slowly they each slid around the wall. Each man went in a different direction. Around the far side, Mike could see two more square brick structures on the roof: the other stairwell and the elevator machine room.

Mike saw that the elevator machine room had a metal stairway in front of the door. It lay cast in heavy shadow. Smoke from the fire below now hung over the roof.

Mike and John took turns crossing over to the stairwell housing. Mike reached out and grasped the knob. The door was locked, and a quick check revealed it to be warm. It became clear that if the gunman remained on the roof, he was either in or on top of the elevator machine room. The two friends were alone. There would be no assistance. Everyone had plenty to do elsewhere.

Mike's vivid imagination kicked into high gear. *Maybe whoever it is went down the fire escape. Damn. He can't get away.* He had visions of a skulking creature in a crab-like scuttle disappearing down an alley.

He called to Cutbert, "Sarge, the machine room. He's in there." Of course, that had only been a guess.

Again the two of them leap-frogged across the open space. Each in turn covered the entrance of the cubical with his service revolver. They were more than fellow officers. They were friends, too. Each had silently vowed that nothing must happen to either one of them.

Plastered against the exterior wall of the machine room, Mike and John turned their lights on and allowed the beams to crawl along the roof verge of the structure. No visible sign of anyone. They heard nothing.

They knew that they had to check inside. That would be tricky. It would be pitch black there. Even the low level of light on the rooftop would silhouette anyone in the doorway.

Mike spoke first. "Listen John, I'm the smaller target, if there's somebody inside let me go first. We can't both fit in there anyway. You cover the roof. Make sure I'm not shot from above."

Cutbert agreed. Michael was quick thinking, quick moving, and a good cop. He knew that his friend would be fine. He would cover the roof. "How's your pucker factor?" he asked Mike in a friendly tone.

"I could slice washers off it. Well, here goes."

John remained in place. He had a clear view of the doorway, the stairs leading up to it, and the edge of the roof over the door. If a gunman reached over the top, John would get him first. It was pure Hollywood, John knew. But, sometimes life emulated the movies.

Mike moved under the steel stairway that led to the machine room doorway. He shined his light on the door above him. No reaction. Quick as a cat, he glided around to the bottom step. Extending his body, he began a snake-like climb, trusting his safety to his partner at his rear.

Arriving at the landing, Mike glanced down at John and gave a thumbs up sign. John returned it.

Mike took a deep breath, and then turned his flashlight on.   He used the same hand to grip the handle as he slowly opened the door. He had his revolver in his right hand at the ready. Again, no reaction. He let go of the door and crouched down.   Still no counteraction.   He slowly pulled the door partially open. This time he slid his right foot against the door jamb. His right leg could be extended to push the door wide enough to allow him to enter. His breath rasped in his ears. He waited.

When he received no response from again opening the door, Mike decided that he'd reached the time to enter.   He extended his right leg.   His accelerated pulse made high tide surf roar in his head.   The door opened about thirty inches. Reaching across his own body, he brought his light into the doorway.   Peering into the room, he held his light above his head and swept the interior. Mike could see the machinery that now stood useless. Three squat motors filled the interior, each big enough to hide a man.   Mike knew he had to enter the room. His gut cramped as he made ready.

Down below, John surmised that his friend was about to enter the room. With no other action on the roof he decided to climb the stairs and be more readily available to assist Mike.

John slid to the base of the steel staircase. Above him, Mike stood in a crouch and steadied his left hand against the door jamb.   His   flashlight   illuminated   one   of   the elevator machine configurations.

Without warning, just outside the beam, came the flash of a gunshot. Mike jumped back as he felt a stinging in his left hand and arm.   He heard the bullet ricochet.   *Just paint or concrete chips.* But his hand stung viciously. His right hand extended into the doorway.

His gun barked twice, lighting up the room for a split second.   The would-be archangel saw what looked like the prone figure of a man bounce at the impacts.

Romano lurched rearward. The door slammed shut.

"Mike," John shouted. "Are you all right?" Cutbert tripped on a riser as he launched himself up the stairs. He cursed as his shin struck one of the steps.

Mike's mind raced. *We gotta get inside and get him. How the hell are we going to do it?*

As John reached the top step, Mike removed his uniform shirt.

"Mike, what the hell are you doing?" asked the puzzled Cutbert.

Mike's grin appeared a bit forced. "I'm gonna make a scarecrow. What I do is, I hold up my shirt. In the doorway. If he's gonna shoot again, I'm not going to be inside the shirt. Maybe he'll empty his gun and we can rush him."

Hesitantly, John suggested, "Mike maybe we can contain him and wait for Emergency Service? What do you say Buddy?"

While Mike readied his shirt, he saw blood on it. With his light, he found the source. His left hand bled in a slow trickle. "Fuck ESU John. The bastard shot me. He's mine."

Before John could react, Romano had the door open, his shirt in the doorway and his light beam inside the room. Nothing happened. Mike's heart spoke to him in a timpani roll. He jumped into the room, firing a shot in the process to keep the assailant down. At that instant, he saw a redheaded male. His arm outstretched. Near the extended hand lay a revolver.

"Move you son of a bitch and you're dead," Mike shouted as he focused the beam on the man's head. Romano reasoned, should the guy move to take action, the head must move too. If it did, he would put a hole in it.

"John, get in here. He's down."

John brought his bulk into the room beside Mike. "Mike, watch the hand," he cautioned as he kicked the gun further from the downed man. He reached down and attempted to pull the arm to the small of the man's back. The gunman moaned.

While John pulled the shooter's arms together at the small of his back and cuffed him, Mike attempted to look at his face.

"Holy shit, John. Turn him over. This is hot. I'm not sure, but. . ." Mike had grown so excited that he couldn't get his mouth to catch up with his brain.

Roughly, the Sergeant pulled the man toward him. He went belly up in a fusillade of soft curses, moans and gurgles.

Mike's eyes widened in surprised recognition. "You dirty bastard, I finally got you!" he shouted. "John, its Wilkey." He had been shot to the left of the heart. Twice.

"Are you sure Mike?" asked Cutbert, wanting it to be him. His friend's obsession could finally end.

"Yes. I'm sure. He's about to receive justice." Mike gave fleeting thought to arresting the man, should he survive.

John thought Mike's comment meant something else. "No ,Mike. Don't do it. It isn't worth it. Let me call an ambulance or firemen to help him survive."

"Fine John. I just want to talk to him first." Mike put the child molester's head against his leg.

Leaning over the man who had obsessed him for almost four years gave Mike a feeling of power. He had him now. He had the power of life and death over the disgusting pervert. The stinging in his hand had vanished. John, there beside him, could be a witness. He would get a confession, a dying declaration. He would not finish him off. Let the courts, or God, do that.

Mike asked gently, "Brian, can you hear me?"

Wilkey nodded and coughed. "P-please, I want a priest."

Mike ignored his request. "Why were you on the roof?"

After coughing again, pink spittle ran out of his mouth. He answered, "To show the little girl, Jennifer, how pretty the sky was. . . There's no electric you know." As an afterthought he added, "How did you know my name?"

Icy steel grated in Mike's voice. "Because you raped a little girl four years ago. You got away with it. Until tonight. I've been looking for you." Mike's voice began to rise. He heard John behind him shouting for medical assistance. "You were gonna do it again weren't you? You're sick, did you know?"

Light and breathy, Wilkey's words came after a pause. "Yeah. You shot me."

"No, I mean for chasing little girls and hurting them. Why did you shoot at me?"

John cut in, "Help is on the way Mike." He then leaned in closer to the conversation.

Wilkey answered, "Because I was going to make love to her and I know that the cops would catch me some day. I didn't want to get caught." He continued much softer, a note of sadness in his voice. "After all those kids, I knew that I had to be punished. I couldn't help myself. Get me. . .get me a priest."

He was fading quickly. Mike looked up at John and asked, "Did you hear it? Everything?"

"Yes, Michael. You did good."

"Brian," continued Mike, "did you rape a little girl on a roof top on 90th Street four years ago?"

Wilkey gave a week smile, a hesitant nod. "So many years. . .so--so many little girls. Little boys, too." From deep within his throat rolled out a rattle. He gave a shudder and a final breath. His body fluids released as he died. The man lay dead at Mike's feet. Unceremoniously, Mike backed up and let Wilkey's head strike the cement floor.

Mike stood up. He stared at his left hand. It throbbed now. "John, we can call George Cali now. Maybe he can close the case. Exceptional clearance. They can't prosecute because the perp's dead." Romano's tone made it clear he was not entirely happy with that. He would rather have had Wilkey suffer in jail. The inmates don't like child molesters. The skinny little bastard would have become someone's woman. That would have been real justice.

"Yeah Mike. We'll call him. Let me see that hand," said John while he reached for it. "Saint Michael protected you again, Mike. And he got your Wilkey."

Mike gave that some thought. "Yeah, he sure did," commented Mike. "He sure did."

Within five minutes, John had the crime scene secured as best he could. Detectives would respond and do their thing. The firemen would handle the fire. John drove his friend to Elmhurst Hospital for treatment.

While Mike had his hand in a disinfectant bath, the Duty Captain arrived. "Being a cowboy, Romano?" Lt. Baker asked to mask his deep, genuine concern. He inspected Mike's wound. "I'm happy to see that the wound is only a graze. The bullet broke the skin on the fleshy outside part of the palm." It would require only a dressing.

Lieutenant Baker went on, speaking earnestly. "I want you to listen to me closely on this, Mike. You hear me? I'm advising you to go sick in the line of duty. While you're here have that treated. It may take a couple of stitches. And I am going to personally put you in for the Combat Cross."

It took several hours to do the follow up paper work. Fred and Jim, his partners of that night slapped him on the back for a job well done. "Hey, guy, you done good," brayed Fred.

"Yeah, Mike," put in Jim Carter. "We're sorry we missed all the action. Who was that guy?"

Mike restrained the welling emotion within him. "A Class A pervert. In his dying declaration, he admitted he had done lots of little girls, some boys, too. Raped them all."

Fred slapped Mike on the shoulder. "He deserved what he got."

"It was you who shot him?" Carter asked.

"Yeah. He was shootin' at me. Two rounds right beside his heart." At that, Mike noted, Jim turned a little green around his mouth.

Daylight stroked Manhattan before Mike returned home. Betty saw the bandage and immediately became worried. She rushed to him and snatched up the hand, none too gently.

"Hey, Honey, there's nothing wrong," he assured her. Then in a burst of tired, macabre humor said, "But, Honey, you should see the other guy."

She cried with tears of joy. Betty led him to his favorite chair and sat him down. "Tell me about it. Every last word." After telling her the entire story, her only comment was, "I'm glad."

He fell asleep in her arms.

CHAPTER NINETEEN

Electric power returned to New York City by 5 p.m. on the July 17th, on the same day that the sister of Brian Wilkey had him brought to a small mortuary on Staten Island. Later that day, back at the Bryan household, Liz busily made arraignments for her brother's funeral. It would be a private affair.

Dennis slouched in an oversized chair pensively thought of his past visit to Queens Sex Crimes. If anyone remembered his veiled threats, he could be implicated in a cover up.

Her voice as acid and disparaging as her inner thoughts, Liz asked, "You will be coming to the funeral, Dennis?"

Dennis sighed. "No Liz, I'm not going to the damn funeral. Hell, not even to the wake. Your perverted, shy locking, brother was caught on a roof top with a little girl. He had most of her clothes off and had already violated her with his hand. He shot it out with a cop. Some kid named Mike Romano." Dennis could not let his wife know that he knew the cop's name well.

He continued, "He got shot in the hand, Romano that is. You saw the cop's photo on television last night. He's a hero for Christ's sake. Contrary to the belief of some, I'm a cop too. I'm not showing respect to that piece of shit. The cop works in the Three-Two in Manhattan. That's part of my Borough Command. My career will be flushed down the crapper if someone puts it all together. So, screw your brother. Good riddance." Dennis hovered on the verge of crapping in his pants. There might be an investigation.

In a furor, Liz crossed to him in three rapid strides. She bent low, got right in his face. "De mortuis nihil nisi bonum, remember? Of the dead, nothing unless good."

243

Dennis fortified himself with another shot of scotch. "Not this time. The sorry son of a bitch got what he deserved. And, for the final time, no, I am not going to the funeral."

Liz countered him icily, her voice taunting, as she put her foot down.. "Don't worry. There's no choice. The funeral parlor is obscure and only family will be there. If you don't go, I'll guarantee your career is gone. And. . .I'll file for divorce."

Dennis still slept in the guest room with occasional requested conjugal visits to his wife's bed. She had not forgiven his former affairs.

Reluctantly he acquiesced, "Ok, Liz. You win."

Mike Romano had been busy. He telephoned George Cali, knowing that detectives kept tabs on the funerals of criminals. George gave him the time and date of the funeral.

"Got it right here, Mike. It'll take place on July 19th at noon. Hell of an hour for a funeral, don't you think?" George added parenthetically. "Wilkey is laid out at the Brunswick Funeral Home in Mariner's Harbor on Staten Island. He will be interred locally."

"Thanks, George. I appreciate this."

Humor rang in the voice on the far end of the wire. "Gonna piss on his grave, Mike?"

For a moment, the idea appealed. . .in a kinky sort of way. "No. But, I'll think of something. Bye, George."

Romano had secured a pass from the Department Surgeon to allow him out of his home for four hours daily. He planned his sojourn well.

On the morning of July 19th, Betty stopped him at the front door to their apartment. Mike was dressed in civvies and she knew his destination. "Mike, I don't think you should be doing this. You're taking an unnecessary risk. Wilkey's dead.

Why can't you just let it lie?"

"Because." That, a quick kiss, and a one-armed hug was Mike's only answer. Over the objections of his wife, Mike left the apartment and traveled to Staten Island. It took some time to find the Brunswick Funeral Parlor. Posting himself outside, he rehearsed in his mind what he would say to Deputy Inspector Dennis Bryan, should he show up. The words rang in his mind as though spoken aloud. *Yeah and I'm gonna get you, too, you thieving crook. Or is it that you're also perverted? You protected him. Was the money worth it?* Then, as he turned away, *Oh, still cheating on your wife?*

When Bryan finally showed up Mike said nothing. He just leaned against the rails alongside the entrance steps and smiled at the dishonored Inspector. The nickname Mike had given him, The Great Pumpkin, took on new meaning now that he once more saw Bryan close up. The bright red hair, round face, and large protruding ears seemed even more prominent. He made sure that his bandaged hand was visible. The Great Pumpkin looked at him with interest.

Inside the parlor, Bryan sweated while a lay brother delivered the eulogy. At least Liz had the decency not to have arranged a Requiem Mass. He kept running the young man's face through his mind. He strained to identify this familiar stranger at the rail. Suddenly it hit him. *That's who it is. It's the cop who shot Wilkey. That kid from the Academy, Mike Romano. He's the guy always asking about the bastard. Shit. What the hell is he doing outside? Why was he smiling at me? He's the kid that killed Brian. What does he know? Did he make the connection between them? How did he find out about the funeral?*

Those questions continued to torment him until, mercifully, the service ended. Dennis and his wife, along with the small group of relatives filed out of the parlor. There at the curb stood that damned cop again. He looked right at him and smiled. Dennis couldn't control himself. He had to know what Romano was about. He advanced to the smiling cop.

He knew that he had to be careful. "Young man, I'm a member of the deceased's family. I don't recognize you. Are you a friend?"

Mike Romano heard the thrumming of what sounded like the wings of a large bird. He took a long time answering, while he flashed a lopsided smile at Dennis Bryan. When he answered, his tone lilted with mockery. "No Inspector, I'm not." He smiled into the face of the shocked man once again and turned to walk away.

Sweat beaded his forehead, his eyes and throat burned with a foretaste of Hell, and Deputy Inspector Dennis Bryan swallowed hard.

Patrolman Michael Romano laughed uproariously all the way home. By God, being a policeman had to be the best job any man could ever have. In his inside jacket pocket nestled the letter that notified him that his request for a transfer to Manhattan South had been approved. He would be in the same station house with Dennis Bryan and he would be on his ass every second. And, one day, he'd have the corrupt son of a bitch. Have him good.

www.ingramcontent.com/pod-product-compliance
Lightning Source LLC
Chambersburg PA
CBHW031151270326
41931CB00006B/221